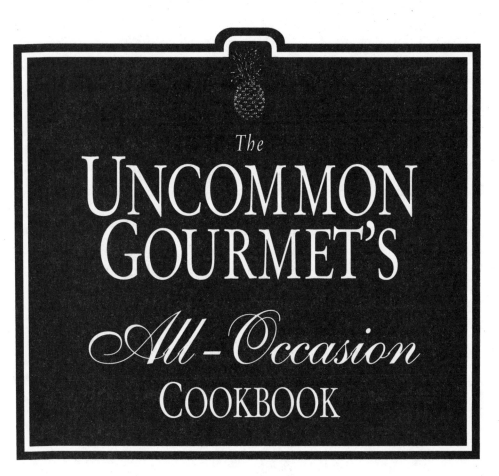

The

UNCOMMON GOURMET'S

All-Occasion

COOKBOOK

To Susan, David, and Andrew —
Wonderful neighbors and
dear friends!
Enjoy!   Ellen

ELLEN HELMAN

Published by
Font & Center Press
P.O. Box 95
Weston, MA 02193

Library of Congress Cataloging in-Publication Data

Helman, Ellen.
The uncommon gourmet's all-occasion cookbook / Ellen Helman.
p.   cm.
Includes Index.
ISBN: 1-883280-08-7
1. Cookery.   I. Title
TX714.H443   1996

641.5--dc20   96-28569
                                                                              CIP

First Printing 1996
Published in the United States of America
1 2 3 4 5 6 7 8 9 10

My very special thanks to

Bobby, Lee, Jen
Sam, Amy, and Cleo
for their love and enthusiastic support throughout this project

Bucky and Bubsy
Vivian and Jookie
for their ideas and critiques

Ilene and Sam
for their friendship and guidance

my friend, Ellen
for giving so generously of her time testing recipes.

TABLE OF

CONTENTS

PREFACE

The Uncommon Gourmet's All-Occasion Cookbook focuses on the foods and flavors of the 90s. It presents a kaleidoscope of exciting ingredients that will turn ordinary meals into culinary events with relative ease and practicality. It is with an abiding passion that I have created these recipes. I have lived with them, worked with them, played with them, slept with them, dreamt of them, and most importantly, savored them.

The fusing of ethnic cuisines is the hottest trend in cooking, offering a wealth of intriguing and seductive flavors from around the globe. To capitalize on this new culinary wave, I have included a plethora of grilled foods, beans and grains, and regional American favorites. There is a variety of ethnic foods (especially Asian, Latin American, and Mediterranean), a blending of cultural seasonings, and foods with bold and assertive flavors that are zesty and spicy, but not searingly hot. Also featured are tropical relishes and salsas, various chutneys, and such American icons as barbecued ribs and mashed potatoes.

With flavors and ingredients being diverse and exciting, putting together a well-balanced, tasty meal is still a culinary challenge. For your convenience, I have provided menu suggestions throughout the book to assist you in meal planning. Recipes found in my previous cookbook, *The Uncommon Gourmet*, are denoted by ❖.

When preparing a meal for family or friends, create a visual experience that's irresistible. Eye appeal is of utmost importance; it's what dresses up the food and shows it off. Consider the color as well as the texture of the foods presented. It only takes a few minutes to make the food look tantalizing, whether arranging it in a fabulous container or platter, or garnishing it with fruits, herbs, or flowers. I use complimentary colors when putting together a menu, such as green beans set against red tomatoes. I accent a bland-looking meal, such as roast chicken, with a sprig of fresh herbs, grilled meats with fresh berries, or poached shrimp with a spray of edible flowers, such as pansies.

I have streamlined the preparation of these recipes to accommodate all lifestyles and have used ingredients that are readily available. The great tastes of the various dishes in this book will add interest and flair to your meal times and entertaining. Do not limit your cooking experiences. Take risks and try new flavors. The more you experiment, the more adventurous you'll become, expanding your palate to new levels of culinary awareness. What you cook and create is sharing a part of yourself with others. Whether planning for family meals, casual get-togethers, formal dinner parties, or special celebrations, these recipes are tailored for all such occasions. These family favorites and exciting new combinations will help to make your meal times memorable.

The preparation and enjoyment of good food is one of my greatest pleasures in life. Therefore, I hope you enjoy the recipes in *The Uncommon Gourmet's All-Occasion Cookbook* as much as I've enjoyed creating them for you. Wishing you glorious meals and happy times!

Ellen Helman

THE PINEAPPLE

The pineapple, the symbol of hospitality, has long been revered as a fruit of excellence. Native to Central and South America, this tropical beauty was first discovered by the Spaniards in the 15th century on the islands of the Carribean. It had been cultivated by American Indians long before the Europeans first came upon it. Early symbolic representations of the fruit have been found on ancient Peruvian pottery. The Carrib Indians hung pineapples at the entrance to their abodes as a sign of welcome and refreshment to all visitors.

The first Europeans who saw the fruit thought it looked like a large pine cone, thus, the fruit came to be known as a pineapple. These explorers were responsible for introducing the pineapple around the world. The discovery of this delightful fruit was received with immediate approval. The whaling ships that returned to New England were laden with the tropical pineapple. It quickly came to be used as a symbol of hospitality and as a popular decorative motif in Colonial times. Evidences of the design can be found in carved wood, stone sculpture, and the like.

As a member of the bromelia family, the pineapple does not grow from seed, but from the crown of another pineapple. A ripe pineapple boasts exceedingly juicy flesh and a sweet-tart flavor. To date, the Hawaiian pineapple dominates the world crop, even though it was not planted on the islands until the late 18th century. Of all the fruits that were introduced to the world from the tropics, the pineapple continues to hold the greatest success story. It has secured a place of importance in European markets and is enjoyed throughout the world as a king of fruits.

TABLE OF RECIPES

MUFFINS AND TEA BREADS

THE SOUP KETTLE

COLD WEATHER COMFORTS

HOT WEATHER COOLERS

PASTA FARE

MAIN ATTRACTIONS

SAVORY MEATS

POULTRY PLEASERS

GARDEN VEGETABLES

SUPER SALADS

GARDEN VARIETIES

GRAIN AND LEGUME SALADS

BASICS

Here are some guidelines and basic ingredients that help to make cooking easier and more enjoyable. In addition, this section contains some specific bits of information that will be useful in preparing the recipes in this book:

1. A well-stocked pantry is essential. I've provided a list of suggested ingredients that you may want to add to your cupboard.

2. For those who are health-conscious and are trying to cut down on their intake of fat and cholesterol, I have included a list of acceptable low-fat or lite version substitutions for certain products.

3. Margarine may be substituted for butter in any recipe.

4. Always use extra-large eggs in baking or cooking unless otherwise specified.

5. Whenever possible, use fresh herbs instead of dried. 1 teaspoon of dried herbs is equivalent to 1 tablespoon of fresh.

6. If you do not have a grill accessible, broiling the food is the next best alternative. You compromise the barbecued flavor, but you'll still have a delicious meal.

7. When planning a meal, make every effort to balance it. Include a protein, a starch, and a fruit or vegetable. Do not double up in one area and eliminate or exclude another. Try not to duplicate ingredients.

8. Always check ahead to make sure you have all of the ingredients on hand before commencing to prepare a dish. Do not wait until you're deep into it, only to discover that you've run out of a specific supply—that can spell disaster.

9. Flustered and short of time? Don't fret. All sauces can be prepared a day ahead and stored in the refrigerator. Whether cooking for family, friends, or company, I always try to do as much advance preparation as possible. I make all of my marinades, salad dressings, and sauces ahead which really streamlines cooking, taking the burden out of last minute preparation.

10. The sauces and relishes in this section are sublime. I have listed several uses for them; however, don't limit yourself to these suggestions. Be creative!

11. Remember, the end product is only as good as its components. Start with the freshest ingredients to ensure flavor-packed results.

Find pleasure in cooking and comfort in the food you prepare. Enliven mealtime with appetizing, well-balanced, delicious recipes. Enjoy!

THE PANTRY

Stocking the pantry with the proper selection of goods is essential. Basic items should always be readily available, facilitating preparation time. Once you are well-stocked, replenishing used items is easy. For those of you who are familiar with my first cookbook, *The Uncommon Gourmet*, you will see that I have extended my signature pantry to be more complete. I hope this will help to make cooking more pleasurable.

Basic Pantry Items:
Anchovies
Apple butter
Artichoke hearts
Baking powder
Baking soda
Beans
    canned: cannelli, chick peas, black beans
    dried: black, Great Northern, lentils, navy, split peas, red kidney
Broth: beef, chicken
Butter
Buttermilk
Capers
Caraway seeds
Chocolate: semi-sweet, unsweetened, chocolate chips
Cocoa, unsweetened
Coconut, sweetened, shredded
Coffee, instant
Cornstarch
Corn syrup: light, dark
Dried fruits: apricots, cherries, currants, dates, figs, raisins, prunes
Eggs, extra-large
Extracts: almond, coconut, vanilla
Flour, all-purpose
Garlic, whole heads
Gingerroot
Goat cheese
Grains: bulgur, cornmeal, couscous, oats, wheat germ
Herbs
    dried: basil, bay leaves, dill, marjoram, mint, oregano, rosemary, sage, savory, tarragon, thyme
    fresh: basil, cilantro, parsley

Hearts of palm
Hoisin sauce
Honey
Horseradish
Liquid smoke
Liqueurs and liquors: Amaretto, Grand Marnier, rum, Triple Sec,
    Tequila, sweet vermouth
Maple syrup, pure
Mayonnaise
Molasses
Mustard: Dijon, Pommeroy
Nuts: almonds, hazelnuts, peanuts, pecans, pine nuts,
    pistachios, walnuts
Oils: olive oil—extra-virgin and pure, Oriental sesame,
    vegetable, walnut
Olives: Greek black, ripe black, pimiento-stuffed green
Oyster sauce
Parmesan cheese
Pasta
Peanut butter
Pesto
Preserves: apricot, blueberry, ginger, raspberry, strawberry
Puff pastry, frozen
Rice: Arborio, long-grain, wild
Roasted red peppers
Sesame seeds
Sour cream
Soy sauce
Spices: cayenne pepper, chili powder, cinnamon, ground cloves,
    ground cumin, curry powder, garlic powder, ground ginger,
    nutmeg, onion powder, dried orange peel, sweet paprika,
    peppercorns, pickling spices, crushed red pepper flakes,
    salt—table and coarse, turmeric
Sugars: confectioners', granulated, light brown, dark brown
Sun-dried tomatoes
Tabasco sauce
Tomatoes, canned Italian plum
Tuna, canned
Vinegars: balsamic, cider, red wine, rice wine, tarragon, white,
    white wine
Wasabi
Wines: cream sherry, mirin, Port, dry red, dry white
Wonton wrappers
Worcestershire sauce

SUBSTITUTIONS

If you're on a restricted diet, there are certain products that are acceptable substitutions to reduce the fat and cholesterol in the recipes in this book. Whenever possible I use the low-fat, low-cholesterol foods with equal success.

Eggs: use egg-beaters or egg whites; ¼ cup egg-beaters or egg whites = 1 egg

Whole milk: use low-fat or skim milk

Heavy cream: use light cream

Sour cream: use low-fat or fat-free sour cream

Yogurt: use low-fat or nonfat yogurt

Cream cheese: use fat-free cream cheese for dips and spreads; use low-fat cream cheese when baking

Cottage cheese: use low-fat or fat-free cottage cheese

Mozzarella or cheddar cheeses: use reduced fat or light varieties

Ricotta cheese: use low-fat ricotta cheese

Butter: for cooking and baking, use margarine. To make a fat-free baked product (cakes, muffins, and quick breads), use an equal amount of unsweetened applesauce

Pork sausages: use chicken sausages

Peanuts: use dry-roasted varieties

Salt: use reduced sodium salt

Soy sauce: use light soy sauce

Enriched egg pasta: use enriched pasta

Chocolate: for 1 ounce unsweetened chocolate, use 3 tablespoons cocoa and 1 tablespoon margarine

OLIVE OIL

The olive tree, native to the Mediterranean area, bears a small, oily fruit Americans have come to adore. Olive oil is the flavorful, much-prized oil from olives.

The big question is . . . which olive oil is the right one for cooking? There is no simple answer. Olive oils differ dramatically depending on the variety of the olive used, the climate of the grove, and the process used to extract the oil. Colors range from deep green to light yellow and flavors vary from rich and full-bodied to light and rather bland.

The best grades of olive oils are the extra-virgin and virgin oils. These are the first oils extracted from the olives by a "cold pressed" process. They are fruity, green, rich, and intensely flavored and are best suited for salad dressings, marinades, and as a condiment.

The pure or simply "olive oils" are an inferior grade. These oils are extracted from the fruit by a further pressing which uses heat and chemicals. They are not nearly as prized as the first grade of oils and are milder in flavor. These are best used for sautéing.

You really need more than one variety of olive oil. When choosing an oil, select one that is the most suitable for the job on hand. I like to keep both an extra-virgin and pure olive oil in my pantry. I use the extra-virgin in salad dressings, the pure strictly for sautéing. Sometimes in marinades and sauces, I'll mix the two together to balance the strong flavor of the extra-virgin so it doesn't overpower the dish.

BAKING SODA VS. BAKING POWDER

Unraveling the Mystery

Baking soda and baking powder are both leavening agents that help to make baked goods rise. The big question that stymies most cooks is why do some recipes call for baking soda, some for baking powder, and some for both? The choice depends on whether the recipe contains an acid ingredient as well as the characteristic texture of the cookie, cake, muffin, or tea bread.

When a batter contains an acid ingredient—buttermilk, citrus juice, vinegar, chocolate, fruit, ginger, or molasses—baking soda is used. Baking soda is an akaline; when it comes in contact with a wet acid, as in the batter, it neutralizes it quickly, giving rise to carbon dioxide which causes the batter to expand or rise. It creates a relatively coarse texture. When a finer texture is desired, baking powder is frequently used in conjunction with the baking soda.

Baking powder contains both akaline and acid components. It is used in recipes that do not host acid ingredients. Most baking powder is double-acting, meaning it contains two kinds of acids. The first type is activated by contact with moisture, neutralizing the alkaline base; the second is activated by the heat from the oven, forming tiny bubbles in the batter which produces a fine texture.

EDIBLE FLOWERS

Certain garden flowers are not only beautiful, colorful, and fragrant, but are also edible, provided you do not spray them with pesticides. Bring the vibrancy of the garden indoors and garnish your appetizers, salads, entrees, and desserts with any one of the following blossoms:

Bachelor's Buttons
Calendulas
Chrysanthemums
Daylilies
Fuchias
Geraniums—I do not recommend using these flowers as they
    have a very strong, pungent smell.
Impatiens
Lavender
Lilacs
Nasturtiums
Pansies, Violas, and Jonny-Jump-Ups—my favorites
Primrose
Roses
Tulips
Violets
Chive Blossoms

CHUTNEYS

Chutneys are those tantalizing, gustatory relishes that enliven foods with their characteristically hot, piquant, sweet, and spicy nature. Native to Indian cuisine, they contain fruits, vegetables, vinegar, sugar, and spices. These condiments range in texture from smooth to chunky and can be mildly spicy or quite hot. Big and bold in flavor, chutneys are healthful, easy to prepare, and absolutely delicious. They're best served at room temperature, being paired with grilled or roasted poultry, fish, pork, or steak, or atop omelets. They embellish foods, adding new dimensions to a simple dish.

Cranberry-Orange Chutney:
12-ounce package fresh cranberries
1 yellow pepper, diced
1/2 cup raisins
3 large shallots, diced
1/4 teaspoon cayenne pepper
1/2 cup orange marmalade
1/4 cup minced crystallized candied ginger
1/2 cup packed dark brown sugar
1/3 cup orange juice
1/4 cup red wine vinegar

1. Put all of the ingredients in a large saucepan. Bring the mixture to a boil, lower the heat, and simmer for 15 to 20 minutes until thick, stirring occasionally.

2. Pack into sterile jars and store in the pantry until needed. Refrigerate after opening. The chutney will keep for 3 weeks once opened.

About 3¼ cups of chutney

Rhubarb Chutney:
3 cups rhubarb pieces, cut 3/4-inch thick
1 medium-size red pepper, diced
1/2 cup diced red onion
1/2 cup dried cherries
1 large clove garlic, minced
1/2 teaspoon crushed red pepper flakes
salt and pepper to taste
3/4 cup pure maple syrup
1/4 cup cider vinegar

(continued on next page)

1. Combine all of the ingredients in a large saucepan. Bring the mixture to a boil, lower the heat, and simmer for 1¹/₂ hours until thick, stirring occasionally.

2. Pack into sterile jars. Refrigerate after opening. The chutney will keep for 3 weeks once opened.

2 cups of chutney

Tomato Chutney:
4 large, ripe tomatoes, chopped
1 large yellow onion, chopped
¹/₂ cup golden raisins
3 large cloves garlic, minced
1 large jalapeño pepper, seeded and finely diced
¹/₂ cup ginger preserves
¹/₃ cup light brown sugar
¹/₄ cup cider vinegar
4 whole cloves
1 cinnamon stick
¹/₂ teaspoon salt
freshly ground pepper to taste

1. Combine all of the ingredients in a non-aluminum saucepan. Bring the mixture to a boil, lower the heat, and simmer for 2 or more hours until thick, stirring occasionally.

2. Pack into sterile jars. Refrigerate after opening. The chutney will keep for 3 weeks once opened.

3 cups of chutney

Apple-Pear Chutney:
2 large Granny Smith apples, peeled, cored, and diced
2 large ripe pears, peeled, cored, and diced
1 medium-size yellow onion, chopped
1 medium-size red pepper, chopped
1 jalapeño pepper, seeded and finely diced
1 tablespoon grated gingerroot
¹/₄ cup white vinegar
³/₄ cup packed light brown sugar
salt and pepper to taste

GIFTS FROM THE HEARTH

Olivada
· · ·
Pecan Bread
· · ·
Tomato Chutney
· · ·
Vanilla Extract
· · ·
Pistachio Shortbreads
· · ·
Composed Butters

PICNIC FARE

Strawberries Balsamic

· · ·

Smoked Chicken
Salad with
Apricot-Date Chutney

· · ·

Mixed Green Salad

· · ·

Orange Muffins

1. In a large saucepan, combine all of the chutney ingredients. Bring to a boil, lower the heat, and simmer for 1 hour, stirring occasionally until thick.

2. Pack into a sterilized jar and store in the refrigerator until needed. (It will keep for 1 month once opened.)

3 cups of chutney

Ginger-Peach Chutney:
$2/3$ *cup ginger preserve*
2 large peaches, skinned and coarsely chopped
(If not in season, use 1 pound canned peaches,
drained and chopped.)
2 tablespoons thinly sliced scallions
2 large cloves garlic, minced
1 tablespoon soy sauce
2 tablespoons lemon juice
$1/4$ *teaspoon cayenne pepper*

Combine all of the chutney ingredients and set aside. (This may be prepared 2 to 3 days in advance and stored in the refrigerator.)

Apricot-Date Chutney:
1 cup coarsely chopped dried apricots
1 cup coarsely chopped dates
$1/4$ *cup chopped pecans*
$1/2$ *cup apricot preserves*
$1/4$ *cup diced red onion*
2 large cloves garlic, minced
$1/4$ *teaspoon cayenne pepper*
1 teaspoon mustard seeds
$1/4$ *cup red wine vinegar*

1. Put all of the ingredients in a saucepan. Bring the mixture to a boil, reduce the heat, and simmer for 10 minutes until thick.

2. Let cool, then pack into a sterilized jar and refrigerate until needed.

About 2 cups of chutney

See also Curried Chicken with Mango Chutney, page 211, Ginger-Peach Chutney, page 216, and Apple-Pear Chutney, page 340.

SALSA REDEFINED

Americans' love affair with salsa has altered this exciting condiment. It is no longer limited to the basic tomato and chilies theme; we have expanded the idea to include interesting fruit and vegetable combinations that are fat-free, savory, and refreshing. Fruits add dimension to these relishes and pair extremely well with meats, fish, and poultry, adding a sweet, sparkling lift to the food.

Use the following salsas with grilled or roasted meats, chicken, or fish—whatever your preference.

Tomato-Corn-Avocado Salsa:
1 medium-size ripe tomato, chopped
1 ripe Haas avocado, peeled and diced
1/2 cup fresh or frozen corn kernels, blanched
1/4 cup diced red onion
2 tablespoons finely chopped fresh cilantro
1 jalapeño pepper, seeded and diced
salt to taste
1/4 teaspoon black pepper
1 tablespoon lime juice

Combine all of the ingredients and mix well. Serve at room temperature.

About 21/2 cups of salsa

Watermelon Salsa:
2 cups diced watermelon
3/4 cup diced cucumber
2 tablespoons chopped scallion
1 teaspoon dried mint
1/4 teaspoon freshly ground black pepper
1 teaspoon finely grated lime zest
1 tablespoon lime juice

Combine all of the ingredients and mix well. Serve at room temperature.

About 3 cups of salsa

SUNDAY BARBECUE

White Bean Dip with Crudités
· · ·
Grilled Steak with Tomato-Corn-Avocado Salsa
· · ·
Cornbread Salad
· · ·
Watermelon
· · ·
Cookies

SUMMER FEST

Grilled Swordfish with
Nectarine Salsa
· · ·
Oven-Roasted
Asparagus
· · ·
Vegetable Rice Pilaf
· · ·
Coconut Cake

Nectarine Salsa:
2 large, ripe nectarines, diced
1/2 cup diced red pepper
2 tablespoons snipped chives
1 tablespoon grated gingerroot
1 tablespoon honey
1 tablespoon lemon juice

Combine all of the ingredients and mix well. Serve at room temperature.

About 2¹/₂ cups of salsa

OLIVADA

Olivada is a black olive paste. It's good on sandwiches, added to mayonnaise as a dip for vegetables or a sauce for fish, spread over cold, roasted meat, chicken, or pasta, added to salad dressing, or as a topping for pizza.

1 cup pitted ripe black olives
1 medium-size clove garlic, crushed
freshly ground pepper to taste
¼ cup extra-virgin olive oil

1. Put the olives, garlic, pepper, and olive oil in the bowl of a food processor and purée.

2. Transfer the Olivada to a container and chill until needed. Return to room temperature before using. This will keep for 4 to 5 days in the refrigerator.

About ¾ cup of Olivada

ITALIAN FARE

Pita with Olivada
· · ·
Pumpkin Lasagne
· · ·
Autumn Salad
· · ·
Chocolate-Almond Biscotti

**ITALIAN-INSPIRED
MEAL**

Salad Asiago
. . .
Chicken Marsala
. . .
Pasta with Pesto
. . .
Romano-Crusted
Eggplant
. . .
Melon Wedges

PESTO

Pesto, the Italian basil sauce, continues to enchant Americans. Its versatility is limited only by one's imagination, so experiment, create, and play with this beloved sauce.

1 cup firmly packed fresh basil
1/2 cup pine nuts, toasted
2 medium-size cloves garlic, crushed
6 tablespoons Parmesan cheese
1/2 cup extra-virgin olive oil

1. Put the basil, pine nuts, garlic, and Parmesan in the bowl of a food processor. Grind to a fine paste.

2. With the motor running, add the olive oil in a slow, steady stream until it is completely incorporated. Transfer the Pesto to a container and store in the refrigerator for up to 1 week. You may also choose to freeze the Pesto.

1 cup of Pesto

RANCH DRESSING

This ever-popular dressing is ideal over a simple iceberg lettuce, tomato, cucumber, and red onion salad. I love to serve it as a dip for crudités or spooned over baked potatoes.

1/2 *cup sour cream*
1/4 *cup mayonnaise*
1/4 *cup buttermilk*
1/2 *teaspoon sugar*
1/2 *teaspoon salt*
1/2 *teaspoon garlic powder*
1/2 *teaspoon onion powder*
2 1/2 *tablespoons red wine vinegar*
2 *tablespoons vegetable oil*

1. Whisk together the sour cream, mayonnaise, buttermilk, sugar, salt, garlic powder, onion powder, vinegar, and oil.

2. Refrigerate until needed. The dressing will keep for 3 to 4 days. Stir thoroughly before using.

1 1/4 cups of dressing

**SUPER BOWL
SUNDAY BASH**

Jen's Salsa with Chips
· · ·
Snake Bikes
· · ·
Turkey Chili
· · ·
French Bread
· · ·
Green Salad with
Ranch Dressing
· · ·
Hermits

SUN-DRIED PEPPERS

The rich, intense flavor of slow-roasted peppers shines in this easy to prepare specialty item. They make a marvelous addition to salads, pasta dishes, pizzas, and sauces, as well as a delicious snack for eating out of hand. Once sampled, once savored! To add more vibrancy, use an assortment of peppers: red, green, yellow, and orange.

3 red peppers, cut into eighths
3 green peppers, cut into eighths
coarse salt

1. Preheat the oven to 200°F. Line a baking sheet with a wire rack.

2. Place the pepper slices on the rack, cut side up. Sprinkle gingerly with coarse salt.

3. Roast in the middle of the oven for 6 to 7 hours until dry and leathery. Let cool, then pack in a tightly sealed container and store in the refrigerator. (You may choose to pack them in olive oil and refrigerate.) These will keep up to 1 month—if they last that long!

VINEGAR PEPPERS

Vinegar peppers are a typically Italian condiment that add sparkle to antipastos, pork chops, chicken, and fish. Also try them as an accent in your favorite sandwich.

2 large red peppers, cored, seeded, and cut into 1-inch wide strips
2 large yellow peppers, cored, seeded, and cut into 1-inch wide strips
1¹/₂ cups white vinegar
2 cups water
¹/₂ teaspoon salt

1. Put the peppers, vinegar, water, and salt in a 2-quart saucepan. Bring the mixture to a boil, lower the heat, and simmer for 5 to 10 minutes until the peppers are tender-crisp.

2. Pack the peppers into a sterile jar with the poaching liquid. Cool completely and refrigerate. These will keep for 3 to 4 weeks.

AN ITALIAN AFFAIR

Bruschetta with
Artichoke Pesto
· · ·
Chicken with
Vinegar Peppers
· · ·
Roasted Potatoes
· · ·
Romano-Crusted
Eggplant
· · ·
Citrus Angel Food
Cake with Berries

HERBED YOGURT CHEESE

This low-fat alternative to the triple-cream herbed cheese is infused with Provençal flavors—garlic, basil, thyme, savory, and marjoram. It makes a tasty stuffing for chicken breasts and is enchanting atop bruschetta.

1 pound plain low-fat or non-fat yogurt
cheesecloth
1 large clove garlic, minced
salt to taste
¹/₄ teaspoon freshly ground black pepper
1 teaspoon dried basil
¹/₂ teaspoon dried thyme
¹/₂ teaspoon dried savory
¹/₂ teaspoon dried marjoram

1. Line a colander with a double thickness of cheesecloth. Pour the yogurt into the cloth and tie the corners together. Place the strainer over a bowl and refrigerate for 24 hours. Drain the liquid from the bowl occasionally. Transfer the fresh cheese to a bowl.

2. Add the garlic, salt, pepper, basil, thyme, savory, and marjoram and mix well. Serve the cheese spread on endive leaves or crackers. Any extra cheese may be stored in the refrigerator for 1 week.

About ²/₃ cup of cheese

COMPOSED BUTTERS

Sweet, composed fruit and nut butters add distinction to breakfast muffins, toast, waffles, pancakes, quick breads, and English muffins. They can also be served atop grilled fish, chicken, or meat, or to enhance steamed vegetables. They're easy to prepare, flavorful, and sure to become family favorites.

Apricot-Almond Butter:
6 tablespoons butter, softened
1 tablespoon confectioners' sugar
1/4 cup apricot preserves
1 tablespoon Amaretto

1. Cream the butter and sugar. Add the apricot preserves and Amaretto and mix well.

2. Pack the butter into a crock and store in the refrigerator. It will keep for 2 to 3 weeks.

2/3 cup of butter

Maple-Walnut Butter:
1/2 cup butter, softened
1 tablespoon dark brown sugar
2 tablespoons pure maple syrup
1/2 cup ground walnuts

1. Cream the butter and brown sugar. Add the maple syrup and ground nuts and mix well.

2. Pack the butter into a crock and store in the refrigerator. It will keep for 2 to 3 weeks.

1 cup of butter

GIFTS FROM THE HEARTH

Olivada
. . .
Pecan Bread
. . .
Tomato Chutney
. . .
Vanilla Extract
. . .
Pistachio Shortbreads
. . .
Composed Butters

SUNDAY BRUNCH

French Toast with
Cranberry-Orange
Butter
· · ·
Bacon
· · ·
Coconut Muffins
· · ·
Strawberries
and Cream
· · ·
Mugs of Coffee

Cranberry-Orange Butter:
6 tablespoons butter, softened
1 tablespoon confectioners' sugar
$1/4$ cup whole berry cranberry sauce
1 tablespoon Triple Sec
1 teaspoon dried orange peel

1. Cream the butter and sugar. Add the cranberry sauce, Triple Sec, and orange peel and mix well.

2. Pack the butter into a crock and store in the refrigerator. It will keep for 2 weeks.

$2/3$ cup of butter

VANILLA EXTRACT

Vanilla is the stuff of which dreams are made, adding a magical taste to confections and desserts. It is the seductive, aromatic flavor of the vanilla bean, native to tropical America. The pod is actually the fruit of a variety of orchid.

The true essence of the vanilla bean is embracing in this easy to fix recipe for vanilla extract. Once you sample this homemade version you'll never use store-bought again. I always have a batch on hand and one in the making.

2 cups brandy
2 vanilla beans, cut into quarters

1. Place the brandy and vanilla beans in a jar and seal tightly.
2. Let sit for 2 months at room temperature in a dark area for the flavor to develop.* Remove the pieces of vanilla beans before using. This will keep indefinitely in the well-sealed jar.

About 2 cups of extract

*If the alcohol smell is still potent, pour the extract into a shallow baking pan and let it aerate at room temperature for about 8 hours. Then return the extract to the jar.

**GIFTS FROM
THE HEARTH**

Olivada
. . .
Pecan Bread
. . .
Tomato Chutney
. . .
Vanilla Extract
. . .
Pistachio Shortbreads
. . .
Composed Butters

FOR STARTERS

Appetizers and hors d'oeuvres should titillate the palate and stimulate the appetite, awakening the taste buds for the meal that follows. They set the stage for the festivities, welcoming your guests. They should be sparkling, colorful, and flavorful, have style and panache, and serve as a form of entertainment for the hostess.

Meal openers should embrace the flavors and should not be a repeat of the ingredients of the main course or dessert. For example, do not serve a cheese-laden appetizer if you're serving a cheesecake for dessert, just as you shouldn't serve a shrimp hors d'oeuvre and a shrimp entree in the same meal.

Variety is just as important as taste. If you're offering several appetizers, balance the food groups—a fish, a cheese, and a vegetable. Combine flavors that are compatible with each other. Make them unusual, enticing, and savory!

DIPS AND SPREADS

FETA-SPINACH DIP

This Greek-influenced dip offers the flavors of spanakopita—
a spinach base enhanced with dill, scallions, and the marvelous
taste of feta cheese. Serve the dip with raw vegetables or wedges
of pita bread; also try it as a stuffing for hollowed-out tomatoes or
potato skins.

MIDDLE EASTERN MENU

Feta-Spinach Dip
. . .
Grilled Shrimp
. . .
Middle Eastern Chick
Peas and Tomatoes
. . .
Mediterranean
Couscous
. . .
Apricot Bon Bons

10-ounce package frozen chopped spinach, thawed and squeezed of
*   excess water*
1 pint sour cream
1/2 pound feta cheese, crumbled
1 1/2 teaspoons dried dill
freshly ground pepper to taste
1/4 cup thinly sliced scallions

1. Combine the spinach, sour cream, feta, dill, pepper, and
scallions in a bowl. Stir until evenly mixed.

2. Let marinate for 1 to 2 hours for flavors to mellow. (This may
be made up to 24 hours in advance and refrigerated; return to room
temperature to serve.)

About 3 1/2 cups of dip

GUACAMOLE

This is a chunky, snappy version of the classic Mexican dip that features the illustrious avocado.

> 2 ripe Haas avocados, peeled, pitted, and mashed with a fork
> 2 ripe plum tomatoes, diced
> 1/4 cup thinly sliced scallions
> 1/2 cup sour cream
> 2 tablespoons lemon juice
> 2 large cloves garlic, crushed
> 1/2 teaspoon Tabasco sauce
> salt and pepper to taste

1. In a bowl, combine the avocados, tomatoes, scallions, sour cream, lemon juice, garlic, Tabasco, salt, and pepper.

2. Cover and refrigerate for 1 to 2 hours for flavors to mellow. Serve at room temperature with tortilla chips.

6 portions

MEXICAN-INSPIRED PICNIC

Guacamole
· · ·
South-of-the-Border Chicken
· · ·
Southwestern Corn Salad
· · ·
Red Cabbage Slaw

Chocolate-Chocolate Chip Wafers

JEN'S SALSA

Salsa actually means sauce—it's the catsup of the 90s. In its simplest form, tomatoes, onions, lime juice, and cilantro are combined with hot chili peppers for a blast of flavor. This is a zesty and chunky rendition of the infamous Mexican sauce, redolent with garlic and jalapeño pepper. Serve it with tortilla chips or raw vegetables, atop bruschetta, or with grilled burgers or chicken.

28-ounce can Italian tomatoes, chopped and drained in a colander
1/2 to 1 jalapeño pepper, finely diced (with its seeds if you like it fiery)
1 large clove garlic, minced
2 tablespoons finely diced onion
3 tablespoons finely diced green pepper
3 tablespoons finely diced red pepper
1 tablespoon finely chopped fresh cilantro
1 tablespoon cider vinegar
salt and freshly ground pepper to taste

1. Combine all of the ingredients and mix well.

2. Let marinate for 1 to 2 hours for flavors to mellow. Stir well and serve. (This may be made 24 hours in advance and refrigerated; return to room temperature to serve.)

About 2 cups of salsa

WHITE BEAN DIP

Legumes have become a most fashionable food. In this dish, cannelli beans are paired with assertive seasonings, giving this creamy spread a tantalizing kick! Serve it with bruschetta or crudités. It also makes an unusual topping for pasta and grilled seafood.

19-ounce can cannelli beans, rinsed and drained
1 large clove garlic, minced
salt to taste
1/4 teaspoon black pepper
1/2 teaspoon cayenne pepper
4 to 5 drops Tabasco sauce
3 tablespoons lime juice
1/2 cup virgin olive oil

1. Put the beans, garlic, salt, pepper, cayenne pepper, Tabasco, lime juice, and olive oil in the bowl of a food processor. Purée until smooth and creamy.

2. Serve at room temperature. (This may be made 24 hours in advance and chilled; return to room temperature to serve.)

2 cups

COCKTAIL PARTY FOR THE CHRISTMAS SEASON

Chili-Spiced Pecans
. . .
Sweet Potato Pancakes
. . .
Dates Marais
. . .
White Bean Dip with Crudités
. . .
Cured Beef Tenderloin au Poivre
. . .
Grilled Chicken with Curried Apple Butter
. . .
Marinated Shrimp and Artichoke Hearts◆

CRANBERRY-GLAZED BRIE

The elegant, triple-cream, French cheese is baked with a fruity cranberry-apricot glaze and served with wedges of pears and apples. In the fall when fresh cranberries are in season, I buy several extra bags and freeze them so that I can make this dish year-round.

1¹/₂ cups fresh or frozen cranberries
¹/₄ cup sugar
¹/₄ cup water
¹/₄ cup apricot preserves
1¹/₂ pounds Brie cheese, top white rind removed, at room temperature

1. Put the cranberries, sugar, and water in a medium-size saucepan. Bring to a rapid boil and cook until the berries pop and are soft, about 5 minutes. Stir in the apricot preserves and remove the pan from the heat. Let cool. Transfer to a container, cover, and chill until needed. (This may be made up to 1 week in advance and stored in the refrigerator.)

2. Preheat the oven to 350°F.

3. Place the wedges of Brie in a small baking dish. Cover with the cranberry sauce.

4. Bake for 15 minutes until warm and glazed. Serve at once with apple and pear wedges and ginger snaps.

8 to 10 portions

MIDDLE EASTERN EGGPLANT SPREAD

Akin to the classic baba ghanoush, this tahini-eggplant spread is redefined with a slight smoky flavor. Try it with wedges of pita bread.

1 large eggplant (1¹/2 pounds)
2 large cloves garlic, crushed
¹/2 teaspoon salt
¹/2 teaspoon liquid smoke
¹/4 cup tahini
¹/4 cup lemon juice
1 tablespoon virgin olive oil

1. Preheat the oven to 400°F.

2. Pierce the eggplant with a fork on all sides. Bake for 40 minutes. When cool, peel off the skin and let drain in a colander.

3. Place the cooked eggplant, garlic, salt, liquid smoke, tahini, lemon juice, and olive oil in the bowl of a food processor. Purée until smooth and creamy.

4. Serve at room temperature.

4 to 6 portions

MIDDLE EASTERN DINNER

Middle Eastern
Eggplant Spread
· · ·
Roast Lamb with
Mint Pesto
· · ·
Cracked Wheat and
Olive Salad
· · ·
Baklava

MUSHROOM PÂTÉ

This recipe was shared by my dear friend, Ellen Forst, who is a creative cook in her own right! I've taken the liberty of making minor changes to an already glorious ground walnut-mushroom pâté. It can be served with crackers or vegetables, as a stuffing for chicken breasts, or as a topping for bruschetta. The ground nuts give the pâté body and lend a rich, nutty flavor.

2 tablespoons butter
3 large shallots, minced
1 pound fresh cultivated mushrooms, finely chopped
1 teaspoon lemon juice
3/4 cup ground toasted walnuts
3 splashes of Worcestershire sauce
lots of freshly ground black pepper

1. Heat the butter in a large skillet. Add the shallots and mushrooms and cook over low heat for 30 to 35 minutes, stirring occasionally, until all the liquid from the mushrooms is absorbed. Transfer the mixture to a bowl.

2. Add the lemon juice, walnuts, Worcestershire, and pepper and mix well.

3. Pack the pâté into a crock and refrigerate for several hours until firm. Return to room temperature to serve.

6 portions

FINGER
FOODS

BRUSCHETTA WITH ROASTED GARLIC

Bruschetta is thickly sliced bread that's grilled and then rubbed with garlic. It can be further embellished with tomatoes, fresh basil, pesto, Parmesan, buffalo mozzarella, olivada, or pâté. The combinations are limited only by one's imagination. This presentation is mellow, nutty, and divine—a garlic lover's *pièce de résistance*. When whole heads of garlic are baked they take on a different personality that's irresistible.

> 3 heads garlic, top points cut off
> 1 tablespoon olive oil
> salt and pepper to taste
> 1 large loaf French or sourdough bread, cut into 3/4-inch thick slices
>   and toasted or lightly grilled

1. Preheat the oven to 400°F.

2. Place the garlic heads sitting upright in a baking dish. Brush each head with 1 teaspoon olive oil. Season with salt and pepper.

3. Roast for 30 minutes. Cover and bake for 30 minutes more.

4. To serve, squeeze the roasted cloves from their skin, spreading the garlic paste on each slice of bruschetta.

6 to 8 portions

BRUSCHETTA PROVENÇAL

Slices of sourdough bread are covered with a fresh tomato topping, fragrant with basil. I find that toasting the bread gives better results than grilling it—the bread browns more evenly; grilled bread burns very easily!

2 tablespoons olive oil
1 medium-size yellow onion, diced
1 large clove garlic, minced
4 ripe plum tomatoes, quartered
2 tablespoons all-purpose flour
1/3 cup coarsely chopped fresh basil
salt and pepper to taste
1 round sourdough bread, cut into 3/4-inch thick slices
    and toasted until golden

1. Heat the olive oil in a medium-size saucepan. Add the onion and garlic and cook for 5 minutes over medium heat until the onion is translucent.

2. Add the tomatoes. Sprinkle with the flour and stir well. Add the basil and season with salt and pepper.

3. Cook over low heat for 15 minutes, stirring occasionally. Spoon over slices of bruschetta and serve at once.

4 to 6 portions

BRUSCHETTA WITH ARTICHOKE PESTO

Toasted slices of French bread are covered in a creamy artichoke heart purée highlighted by garlic and Parmesan.

Artichoke Pesto:
14-ounce can artichoke hearts, drained
salt and pepper to taste
1 medium-size clove garlic, crushed
2 tablespoons Parmesan cheese
1 tablespoon lemon juice
3 tablespoons extra-virgin olive oil

1 loaf French bread, cut into 1-inch thick slices and lightly toasted

1. Put the artichoke hearts, salt, pepper, garlic, Parmesan, lemon juice, and olive oil in the bowl of a food processor. Purée until smooth and creamy. Cover and chill until needed; return to room temperature before proceeding. (This may be made 2 to 3 days in advance.)

2. Preheat the oven to 400°F.

3. Spread 1 tablespoon of pesto atop each slice of bread. Place on a cookie sheet and bake for 10 minutes. Serve hot.

20 bruschettas

ONION CROSTINI

Sautéed red onion relish, fragrant with rosemary, is spread on rounds of French bread. Sprinkled with Parmesan cheese and baked until golden, these crostini are indeed savory.

¹/₄ cup olive oil
4 cups thinly sliced red onions
1 teaspoon sugar
1 teaspoon dried rosemary
salt and pepper to taste
1 large French bread, cut into ³/₄-inch thick slices (you'll need 16 slices)
¹/₄ cup Parmesan cheese

1. Preheat the oven to 400°F.

2. Heat the olive oil in a large skillet. Add the onions and sprinkle with the sugar, rosemary, salt, and pepper. Sauté over medium-high heat until lightly browned, about 10 to 15 minutes, stirring occasionally.

3. Spread equal amounts of the onion relish, along with any pan juices, atop the bread rounds.

4. Arrange the crostini on a baking sheet. Sprinkle with the Parmesan.

5. Bake for 10 minutes until golden. Serve hot.

16 crostini; 8 portions

ITALIAN-INSPIRED MENU

Pasta Marinara
· · ·
Antipasto◆
· · ·
Onion Crostini
· · ·
Cannoli

CROSTINI GIACOMO

Toasted slices of French bread are spread with mascarpone, the sweet Italian dessert cheese, topped with sliced peaches, and dusted with crushed pistachio nuts.

1 large loaf French bread, cut into ³/₄-inch thick slices on the diagonal (about 24 slices) and lightly toasted

8 ounces mascarpone cheese
3 peaches or nectarines, each sliced into 8 wedges
¹/₃ cup finely chopped pistachio nuts

1. Preheat the oven to 400°F.

2. Spread 1 scant tablespoon of mascarpone on each slice of bread.

3. Top each crostini with a wedge of fruit. Sprinkle with a dusting of chopped nuts.

4. Heat in the oven for 5 minutes until the cheese is warm. Serve at once.

6 to 8 portions

CHILI-CHEESE PUFFS

Southwestern flavors—green chilies, black olives, and cheddar cheese—prevail in these pop-in-the-mouth puffs. I always have a batch in the freezer for unexpected guests!

4-ounce can chopped green chilies, drained
2/3 cup finely chopped ripe black olives
1/2 pound sharp cheddar cheese, grated
1/2 cup mayonnaise
6 English muffins, split in half

1. In a bowl, combine the chilies, olives, cheddar, and mayonnaise and mix well.

2. Spread equal amounts of the mixture on each muffin half.

3. Cut each muffin into 6 wedges. Spread out pieces on a cookie sheet and place in the freezer for 1 hour. When frozen, store in a plastic bag in the freezer.

4. When ready to serve, remove the puffs directly from the freezer to a baking sheet. Broil 4 inches from the heat source for 3 to 5 minutes until browned and bubbly. (Keep a watchful eye on them so they don't burn.) Serve at once.

72 pieces; allow 3 to 4 pieces per person

MEXICAN MENU

Chili-Cheese Puffs
· · ·
Mexican Caesar Salad
· · ·
Mexican-Flavored
Shrimp
· · ·
White Rice
· · ·
Orange Freeze◆

PITA WITH OLIVADA

Akin to pizzettas, rounds of pita bread are lavishly spread with Olivada, the rich, robust-flavored, black olive paste, and baked to perfection.

4 medium-size pita rounds (about 6 inches in diameter)
Olivada (see page 14)

1. Preheat the oven to 400°F.

2. Place the bread on a cookie sheet. Spread each pita round with 2 to 3 tablespoons of Olivada.

3. Bake for 10 minutes. Cut each piece of pita into 6 wedges and serve.

24 wedges; allow 3 pieces per person

MEDITERRANEAN PITA WEDGES

Rounds of pita bread are lush with pesto, goat cheese, and sun-dried tomatoes and baked to a turn.

4 medium-size pita rounds (about 6 inches in diameter)
³/4 cup Pesto (see page 15)
1 cup coarsely chopped sun-dried tomatoes
8 ounces goat cheese, crumbled

1. Preheat the oven to 400°F.

2. Place the bread on two cookie sheets. Spread each round with 3 tablespoons of pesto. Sprinkle each pita with ¼ cup sun-dried tomatoes and 2 ounces of goat cheese.

3. Bake for 10 minutes. Cut each round of pita into 6 wedges and serve.

24 wedges; allow 2 to 3 pieces per person

HORS D'OEUVRE PARTY FOR 12

Mediterranean
Pita Wedges
· · ·
Baked Stuffed Oysters
· · ·
Butternut Squash
Pillows
· · ·
Hickory-Glazed
Scallops
· · ·
Grilled Fruits

CURED BEEF TENDERLOIN AU POIVRE

Beef tenderloin is coated with a dry-rub spice mix and left to cure for an extended period of time. This flavorful, peppery dish brings out the best in the beef. It's served with French bread and mustard mayonnaise.

*2-pound beef tenderloin roast
1 tablespoon garlic powder
1 tablespoon coarse or Kosher salt
1/4 cup coarsely ground black pepper
2 tablespoons dried rosemary
1 tablespoon mustard seeds
Mustard Mayonnaise (recipe follows)*

1. Place the beef on a large piece of silver foil.

2. In a bowl, combine the garlic powder, salt, black pepper, rosemary, and mustard seeds and mix well.

3. Rub the roast with the spice mix, pressing the spices into the meat. Wrap the meat up tightly in the foil and refrigerate for 10 to 12 days. (If you wish the meat more well done, let it sit for as much as 15 days—I prefer my roast rare to medium-rare.)

4. When ready to serve, brush off the excess pepper and slice the meat thinly. Serve with the Mustard Mayonnaise and slices of French or sourdough bread.

8 to 10 appetizer portions; 14 or more hors d'oeuvre portions

*Mustard Mayonnaise:
1 cup mayonnaise
2 tablespoons Dijon mustard
1 tablespoon prepared white horseradish*

Mix the mayonnaise, mustard, and horseradish together. Store in the refrigerator until needed.

About 1 cup of sauce

BLUE CHEESE NUGGETS

Glorious Saga Blue cheese is coupled with cream cheese and rolled in chopped walnuts, making the perfect cocktail bites. They're absolutely divine.

6 ounces Saga Blue cheese, white rind removed
3 ounces cream cheese, at room temperature
1/2 cup finely chopped walnuts

1. In a bowl, mix together the blue cheese and cream cheese. Using a teaspoon measure, form the mixture into balls, 3/4-inch in diameter.

2. Roll the balls in the chopped walnuts to coat generously. Chill for 2 to 3 hours before serving.

30 nuggets

LUNCH BOX TREATS

Blue Cheese Nuggets
· · ·
Sun-Dried Peppers
· · ·
Peach Muffins
· · ·
Nectarines and Tomatoes
· · ·
Honey-Nut Granola Bars

CHERRY TOMATOES AND MOZZARELLA

The popular tomato and cheese theme is further embellished with pesto. This typically Italian combination is colorful, easy to prepare, and can also double as a salad or as a topping for freshly cooked pasta.

2 pints ripe cherry tomatoes, halved
1 pound mozzarella cheese, cut into 1/2-inch cubes (You may choose to use fresh mozzarella for a real treat!)
3/4 cup pesto (see page 15)

1. Heap the tomatoes and cheese in a large bowl.

2. Spoon the pesto over the mixture and toss gently until evenly distributed. Serve at room temperature. (This may be made 24 hours in advance and refrigerated; return to room temperature to present.)

10 to 12 portions

GRILLED CHICKEN WITH CURRIED APPLE BUTTER

The sweet taste of apple butter is spiked with the assertive flavors of ginger, curry, and cayenne pepper in this slightly sweet, slightly spicy, somewhat fruity sauce. The sauce perks up grilled chicken, does justice to grilled sausages, and adds pizzaz to grilled tuna. This dish is always a big hit at cocktail parties.

> *4 boneless, skinless chicken breasts, split in half*
> *3 tablespoons olive oil*
> *salt and pepper to taste*
> *Curried Apple Butter (recipe follows)*

1. Brush the chicken with the olive oil. Season with salt and pepper.

2. Grill the chicken over hot coals, 4 inches from the heat source, about 4 to 5 minutes per side. Cut the chicken into bite-size chunks and serve at room temperature with the Curried Apple Butter.

10 to 12 portions

> *Curried Apple Butter:*
> *3/4 cup apple butter*
> *1/4 cup boiling water*
> *1 tablespoon grated onion*
> *1 tablespoon soy sauce*
> *1 teaspoon curry powder*
> *1 teaspoon ground ginger*
> *1/8 teaspoon black pepper*
> *1/8 teaspoon cayenne pepper*

1. Beat the boiling water into the apple butter until it is completely incorporated.

2. Add the onion, soy sauce, curry, ginger, black pepper, and cayenne pepper and mix well. (The sauce may be made up to 1 week in advance and kept refrigerated; return to room temperature before using.)

About 1 cup of sauce

MOROCCAN-INSPIRED MENU

Spice-Roasted
Chick Peas
. . .
Curried Chicken
Tenders with
Mango Chutney
. . .
Couscous
. . .
Moroccan Grilled
Vegetables
. . .
Fresh Fruit

SPICE-ROASTED CHICK PEAS

Roasting chick peas gives them a somewhat nutty, crunchy texture. They're more nutritious than peanuts, being low in fat and high in fiber. They make for addictive munching. Pack them into lunch boxes for a snack or use them as a garnish for salads.

19-ounce can chick peas, rinsed and drained
1½ tablespoons olive oil
½ teaspoon chili powder
¼ teaspoon garlic powder
½ teaspoon curry powder
¼ teaspoon ground ginger
¼ teaspoon cayenne pepper

1. Preheat the oven to 400°F.

2. In a bowl, toss the chick peas with the olive oil.

3. In a separate small bowl, combine the chili powder, garlic powder, curry, ginger, and cayenne pepper, stirring until evenly mixed.

4. Sprinkle the spice blend over the legumes and mix well. Spread the chick peas out in a single layer on a baking sheet.

5. Bake for 50 minutes, shaking the pan after 30 minutes to stir up the chick peas. Let cool and store in an airtight container.

About 1⅓ cups

CUCUMBERS AND CAVIAR

Thick rounds of cucumber sport a heavenly topping of sour cream and caviar. This elegant, delicious, and vibrant finger food is definite party fare.

3 medium-size cucumbers, ends trimmed off
³/₄ cup sour cream
3 tablespoons snipped chives
2-ounce jar red lumpfish caviar

1. Cut each cucumber into eight ³/₄-inch thick rounds.

2. Mix the sour cream and chives together. Spoon a dollop of the mixture on each slice of cucumber.

3. Top each round with about ¹/₂ teaspoon of caviar. Serve at once.

24 rounds; 6 to 8 portions

**BUFFET PARTY
FOR 12**

Cucumbers
and Caviar
· · ·
Crab Rangoon
· · ·
Poached Salmon◆
· · ·
Orange Wild
Rice Salad
· · ·
Springtime
Asparagus Salad◆
· · ·
Maple-Pecan
Pound Cake

DATES MARAIS

Dates are wrapped in bacon and then baked to a turn. These tasty morsels are rich, moist, and fruity. No one can eat just one!

¹/₂ pound pitted dates
¹/₂ pound bacon, each slice cut into thirds

1. Preheat the oven to 375°F.
2. Wrap each date in a piece of bacon and secure with a toothpick.
3. Bake for 10 minutes. Turn the dates over and bake for 5 to 10 minutes more until golden brown. Drain on paper towels and serve.

Approximately 30 tidbits

PICKLED GRAPES

This refreshing finger food stars red grapes marinated in an orange-balsamic dressing spiked with pickling spices.

4 cups seedless red or green grapes (or a combination)
1/3 cup balsamic vinegar
1/4 cup orange juice
1 large clove garlic, crushed
1 teaspoon pickling spices

1. Put the grapes in a glass bowl.
2. In a separate bowl, combine the vinegar, orange juice, garlic, and pickling spices. Pour the dressing over the grapes. Let marinate for 1 to 2 hours or as much as overnight.

8 portions

HOT WEATHER FARE

Pickled Grapes
. . .
Grilled Shrimp and Artichoke Hearts with Cumin Mayonnaise
. . .
Spinach, Smoked Salmon, and Goat Cheese Salad
. . .
Focaccia
. . .
Ginger-White Chocolate Chunk Cookies
. . .
Strawberries

STUFFED GRAPE LEAVES

MIDDLE EASTERN DINNER

Stuffed Grape Leaves
. . .
Grilled Lamb Chops
. . .
Couscous with
Tomato-Mint Sauce
. . .
Green Beans
. . .
Dates Almondine

Grape leaves are a Middle Eastern finger food. This vegetarian version features a seasoned rice with a medley of complementary, yet complex flavors—the sweetness of raisins, the nutty flavor of pine nuts, the lushness of tomatoes, and the fragrant taste of mint. To ease the work load, make the filling a day in advance. Handle the grape leaves gently and be sure not to over stuff them!

16-ounce jar grape leaves, rinsed well under cold water
$1/2$ cup extra-virgin olive oil
1 large yellow onion, diced
1 medium-size clove garlic, minced
1 cup chopped fresh parsley
$3/4$ cup raisins
$1/3$ cup pine nuts, toasted
1 cup canned plum tomatoes, drained and chopped
1 tablespoon dried mint
$1/4$ cup lemon juice
$13/4$ cups water
salt and pepper to taste
1 cup raw long-grain rice

1. Blanch the grape leaves in boiling water for 2 to 3 minutes. Drain in a colander.

2. Heat $1/4$ cup olive oil in a medium-size saucepan. Add the onion and garlic and sauté over medium heat until the onion is soft.

3. Add the parsley, raisins, pine nuts, tomatoes, mint, lemon juice, water, salt, and pepper. Bring the mixture to a boil. Stir in the rice, cover, lower the heat, and simmer for 20 minutes undisturbed. (The mixture will be somewhat wet.) Let cool.

4. Preheat the oven to 350°F. Grease a large baking pan.

5. Spread the leaves out on a flat surface. Place a heaping table-spoonful of the stuffing in the middle of each leaf. Fold the sides in and roll up tightly, cigar-fashion.

6. Place the rolled leaves in the prepared pan, seam side down. Pack the leaves tightly in the pan. Drizzle with the remaining $1/4$ cup olive oil. Cover and bake for 30 to 35 minutes. Let cool and serve at room temperature. (These may be made 1 to 2 days in advance and refrigerated; return to room temperature to serve.)

Approximately 50 stuffed leaves; allow 3 to 4 per person

SNAKE BITES

Jalapeño peppers are stuffed with a delicate garlic and herb cheese filling, coated with crumbs, and baked until crisp. For those who like it hot, these are sure to set your taste buds dancing!

12 large jalapeño peppers
4-ounce package garlic and herb Rondelé cheese
3 tablespoons vegetable oil
1/3 cup cornflake crumbs

1. Preheat the oven to 450°F. Grease a baking sheet.

2. Wearing gloves, cut the jalapeño peppers partially in half lengthwise, leaving the halves attached at the stem end. Remove the seeds from the peppers.

3. Fill each pepper with 2 teaspoons of the cheese and press the halves firmly together.

4. Dip each pepper in the oil and roll in the crumbs to coat completely. Arrange the peppers on the prepared baking sheet.

5. Bake for 10 to 12 minutes until golden. Serve at once.

4 portions

**SUPER BOWL
SUNDAY BASH**

Jen's Salsa with Chips
. . .
Snake Bites
. . .
Turkey Chili
. . .
French Bread
. . .
Green Salad with
Ranch Dressing
. . .
Hermits

MARINATED SHIITAKE MUSHROOMS

This is a new slant on the traditional marinated fungi. The wonderful, woodsy flavor of these gourmet mushrooms shines in this Oriental composition.

1 pound shiitake mushrooms, tough stem ends removed
2 tablespoons soy sauce
1/8 teaspoon black pepper
1 teaspoon Dijon mustard
2 teaspoons finely grated gingerroot
1/4 cup balsamic vinegar
1/4 cup vegetable oil

1. Heap the mushrooms in a large bowl.

2. In a separate bowl, whisk together the soy sauce, pepper, Dijon, gingerroot, vinegar, and oil.

3. Pour the vinaigrette over the mushrooms, toss well, and let marinate for 1 to 2 hours. (These may be made up to 24 hours in advance and refrigerated; return to room temperature to serve.)

6 to 8 portions

STUFFED SHIITAKE MUSHROOMS

The earthy, gourmet, Oriental mushroom is complemented by the distinct salty taste of prosciutto, the Italian-cured ham, and Romano cheese, giving rise to an unusual marriage of flavors.

¹/₂ pound shiitake mushroom caps, each about 2-inches in diameter
¹/₄ pound sliced prosciutto, coarsely chopped
²/₃ cup shredded Romano cheese
¹/₂ cup mayonnaise
2 scallions, chopped

1. Preheat the oven to 400°F.

2. Arrange the mushroom caps on a baking sheet.

3. Combine the prosciutto, Romano, mayonnaise, and scallions.

4. Fill each mushroom cap with a heaping spoonful of the filling, pressing the stuffing into place.

5. Bake for 10 minutes, then run under a hot broiler until browned and bubbly. Serve at once.

6 portions

DINNER MENU

Stuffed Shiitake
Mushrooms
· · ·
Sautéed Scallops
Niçoise
· · ·
Rice Pilaf◆
· · ·
Green Beans Olivada
· · ·
Pot de Crème◆

GRAZING PARTY

Bruschetta with
Herbed Yogurt Cheese
. . .
Martini Splash
. . .
Tortellini with
Jalapeño Pesto
. . .
Smoked Trout Pâté
. . .
Peanut Butter-Bacon
Roll-Ups
. . .
Assorted Cheeses
and Fruits

MARTINI SPLASH

Martini ingredients—onions, olives, and vermouth—team up in a light, tasty finger food. They're perfect for nibbling with cocktails.

1¹/₃ cups boiled pearl onions
1¹/₄ cups small pimiento-stuffed green olives
²/₃ cup sweet vermouth
freshly ground black pepper to taste

1. Combine the onions, olives, vermouth, and pepper in a container. Mix well, cover, and refrigerate for at least 3 days and up to 1 week for flavors to blend. The longer these steep, the better they taste!

2. When ready to serve, drain the marinade and present. (If desired, the marinade can be consumed.)

8 or more portions

SPICED MEDITERRANEAN OLIVES

Greek or Calamata olives are purple-black, almond-shaped, and of the highest quality. They're tossed with a top-grade olive oil and are fragrant with garlic, fennel, crushed red pepper, and the essence of orange.

2 cups imported Greek black olives, drained
1 large clove garlic, coarsely chopped
1 teaspoon fennel seeds
1/4 teaspoon crushed red pepper flakes
1/4 teaspoon dried orange peel
freshly ground pepper to taste
2 tablespoons extra-virgin olive oil

1. Place the olives in a bowl or container.

2. In a separate bowl, combine the garlic, fennel, red pepper flakes, orange peel, pepper, and olive oil.

3. Pour the seasoned oil over the olives. Toss to mix and let marinate overnight in the refrigerator. Return to room temperature to serve.

6 to 8 portions

ANTIPASTO
PARTY FOR 24

Spiced Mediterranean
Olives
. . .
Cherry Tomatoes
and Mozzarella
. . .
Oranges and
Red Onion
. . .
Green Beans Olivada
. . .
Bruschetta with
Artichoke Pesto
. . .
Marinated
Mushrooms◆
. . .
Roasted Pepper Salad
. . .
Melon Wrapped
with Prosciutto
. . .
White Bean Salad
. . .
Italian Pasta Salad◆
. . .
Focaccia and
Bread Sticks

CHILI-SPICED PECANS

Whole pecans are encrusted with gutsy Southwestern flavors, tempered by sugar. These make for addictive munching.

2 cups whole pecans
2 tablespoons butter, melted
2 tablespoons sugar
1 teaspoon coarse salt
1 teaspoon ground cumin
1 teaspoon chili powder
1/4 teaspoon cayenne pepper

1. Preheat the oven to 300°F.

2. Put the nuts in a bowl. In a separate bowl, combine the butter, sugar, salt, cumin, chili powder, and cayenne pepper.

3. Pour the spice mixture over the nuts and toss until evenly coated. Spread the nuts out in a single layer on a baking sheet.

4. Bake for 20 minutes, stirring the nuts after 10 minutes.

About 2¹/₄ cups of nuts

STRAWBERRIES BALSAMIC

Plump, whole berries are sprinkled with sugar and splashed with balsamic vinegar for a slightly sweet-tart flavor, providing a refreshing meal opener. Always let your nose be your guide when purchasing strawberries. Strawberries are a member of the rose family and should smell sweet and fragrant. Do not buy any that have a woody aroma.

1 quart ripe strawberries, hulled
1 tablespoon sugar
2 tablespoons balsamic vinegar

1. Heap the berries in a glass bowl. Sprinkle with the sugar. Drizzle the vinegar over the berries and toss well.

2. Let marinate for at least 30 minutes and as much as 6 hours. Serve at room temperature.

6 to 8 portions

PICNIC FARE

Strawberries Balsamic
. . .
Smoked Chicken
Salad with
Apricot-Date Chutney

Mixed Green Salad
. . .
Orange Muffins

SWEET POTATO PANCAKES

The nutritious value of the sweet potato has long been overlooked; it's high in vitamins C and A. Grated sweet potato and apple star in this version of the ever-popular potato pancake. They're rich with the sweet flavor of the orange-fleshed vegetable and laced with a whisper of nutmeg. They also make a savory accompaniment to roasted pork or chicken.

1 large sweet potato, peeled and coarsely grated
1 large Granny Smith apple, peeled and coarsely grated
1/2 small yellow onion, coarsely grated
3 eggs, beaten
1 teaspoon salt
pepper to taste
1/4 teaspoon nutmeg
1/4 cup all-purpose flour
6 tablespoons vegetable oil

1. Combine the sweet potato, apple, onion, eggs, salt, pepper, and nutmeg in a large bowl. Stir in the flour until evenly coated.

2. Heat 3 tablespoons oil in a large skillet. Drop large spoonfuls of the potato batter into the pan. Fry over medium heat until brown and crisp on both sides. Repeat, adding the remaining oil to the pan for the second batch. Keep the first batch warm in a low oven while cooking the second batch. Serve at once with the Apple-Sour Cream Sauce.

14 pancakes

Apple-Sour Cream Sauce:
1/3 cup sour cream
1/3 cup applesauce

In a small bowl, combine the sour cream and applesauce and refrigerate until needed.

2/3 cup of sauce

GRILLED CHICKEN SAUSAGES WITH HOT PEPPER JELLY

This dish was designed with sausage lovers in mind. The marvelous grilled taste of sweet sausages is heightened by a sweet and spicy pepper jelly-dipping sauce that bursts with flavor. The pepper jelly is also marvelous on grilled and roasted pork, chicken, and steak, and as a garnish for omelets.

2 pounds sweet chicken sausages
olive oil
Hot Pepper Jelly (recipe follows)

1. Rub the sausages lightly with olive oil. Grill (or broil) the sausages over hot coals, 4 inches from the heat source, for 10 to 12 minutes, turning every 3 to 4 minutes to brown evenly.

2. Slice the sausages into ½-inch thick rounds and arrange them on a serving dish. Serve at room temperature accompanied by a small bowl of the Hot Pepper Jelly.

10 to 12 portions

Hot Pepper Jelly:
1½ cups chopped green peppers
½ cup chopped jalapeño peppers (You may choose to use some of the seeds with discretion, depending on how fiery you want the jelly.)
2 cups white vinegar
6 cups sugar
3-ounce package liquid fruit pectin

1. Put the green and jalapeño peppers and 1 cup vinegar in the bowl of a food processor and purée.

2. Transfer the pepper purée to a very large pot. Add the remaining 1 cup vinegar and sugar. Bring to a full rolling boil, then boil for 5 minutes. Remove the pot from the heat.

3. Stir in the liquid pectin. Return the pot to the heat and boil for 1 minute more. Pack into sterilized jars, leaving ¼-inch head space. Seal at once. Cool completely and store in the refrigerator. The jelly will keep refrigerated for 3 months.

3 pints

HORS D'OEUVRE
PARTY FOR 20

Spiced Walnuts◆
. . .
Crostini Giacomo
. . .
Grilled Chicken
Sausages with
Hot Pepper Jelly

Poached Shrimp with
Curry-Garlic Dip◆
. . .
Grilled Chicken with
Peanut Sauce◆
. . .
Stuffed Shiitake
Mushrooms

TORTELLINI WITH JALAPEÑO PESTO

Roasted green and jalapeño peppers form the base of this pesto that's spiked with garlic, cilantro, and toasted sunflower seeds. It's served up as a dipping sauce for cooked tortellini. Also try it as a sauce atop grilled chicken or fish.

1 pound cheese tortellini
1 tablespoon olive oil

Jalapeño Pesto:
3 large green peppers, roasted
2 to 3 jalapeño peppers, roasted and seeds removed
2 large cloves garlic, minced
1/4 cup dry roasted, shelled sunflower seeds, toasted
1/2 cup loosely packed fresh cilantro
salt and pepper to taste
1/2 cup extra-virgin olive oil

1. Cook the tortellini according to the package directions. Drain well and transfer to a bowl. Drizzle with 1 tablespoon olive oil and toss well.

2. Prepare the pesto. Put the roasted green and jalapeño peppers, garlic, sunflower seeds, cilantro, salt, and pepper in the bowl of a food processor. Purée to a fine paste. With the motor running, add the olive oil in a slow, steady stream until all the oil is incorporated. Transfer the pesto to a bowl. (This may be made 3 to 4 days in advance and refrigerated until needed; return to room temperature to serve.)

3. Serve the tortellini at room temperature with the pesto accompaniment.

6 to 8 portions

FOODS UNDER WRAPS

ARTICHOKE HEART ROLL-UPS

These tasty tidbits strut a chopped artichoke heart filling spiked with curry, Worcestershire, and dry mustard, lending a piquant flavor.

8 slices white bread, crusts removed
14-ounce can artichoke hearts, drained and chopped
1/2 cup mayonnaise
2 scallions, chopped
1 teaspoon curry powder
1/2 teaspoon Worcestershire sauce
1/2 teaspoon dry mustard
salt and pepper to taste
6 tablespoons butter, melted

1. Preheat the oven to 350°F. Grease a baking sheet.

2. Flatten the bread slices with a rolling pin.

3. Combine the artichoke hearts, mayonnaise, scallions, curry, Worcestershire, mustard, salt, and pepper and mix well.

4. Spread equal amounts of the artichoke mixture on the bread slices. Roll up jelly-roll fashion. Dip each roll in the melted butter. Place seam side down on the prepared baking sheet.

5. Bake for 25 to 30 minutes until golden. Using a sharp knife, cut each roll-up in half and serve.

16 pieces; 6 to 8 portions

PEANUT BUTTER-BACON ROLL-UPS

The all-time favorite combination of peanut butter and bacon stars in this mouth-watering finger food. The roll-ups are glazed with brown sugar and baked to a turn.

1-pound loaf white Pepperidge Farm sandwich bread, crusts removed
  (16 slices)
1 cup chunky peanut butter
16 slices bacon, cut into thirds
dark brown sugar

1. Preheat the oven to 425°F.

2. Flatten each slice of bread with a rolling pin. Spread 1 tablespoon of peanut butter on each slice of bread. Roll up jelly-roll fashion and cut into thirds.

3. Wrap a piece of bacon around each roll-up and secure with a toothpick. Repeat with the remaining slices of bread.

4. Coat the roll-ups generously with the brown sugar. Place on a baking sheet.

5. Bake for 15 minutes, turning the tidbits over after 10 minutes. Serve at once.

48 roll-ups

GRAZING PARTY

Bruschetts with
Herbed Yogurt Cheese
· · ·
Martini Splash
· · ·
Tortellini with
Jalapeño Pesto
· · ·
Smoked Trout Pâté
· · ·
Peanut Butter-Bacon
Roll-Ups
· · ·
Assorted Cheeses
and Fruits

BUTTERNUT SQUASH PILLOWS

A ginger and garlic-flavored butternut squash purée makes a savory filling for wonton skins that are baked until golden.

1¹/₂ pound butternut squash, peeled and cut into 1-inch chunks
2 tablespoons butter, melted
1 large clove garlic, crushed
1 tablespoon finely grated gingerroot
salt and pepper to taste
1 package wonton wraps
2 tablespoons vegetable oil

1. Boil the squash for 10 to 15 minutes until tender. Remove to a colander and drain well. Place the squash in the bowl of a food processor and purée. Transfer the purée to a bowl.

2. Add the butter, garlic, gingerroot, salt and pepper and mix well. Chill for 2 to 3 hours until firm or as much as overnight.

3. Preheat the oven to 350°F. Grease two large baking sheets.

4. Place ¹/₂ tablespoon of the filling in the middle of a wonton skin. Fold over to form a triangle; slightly dampen the outer edges with cold water. Press the edges together to seal. Place on the prepared baking sheet. Repeat with the remaining wonton skins until all the squash has been used.

5. Brush the top of the pillows with the vegetable oil. Bake for 12 to 14 minutes until golden. Serve at once with duck sauce.

45 pillows; allow 3 to 4 per person

CHÈVRE TURNOVERS

Wonton wrappers are stuffed with the heady taste of goat cheese, baked, and topped with an intensely flavored Sun-Dried Tomato Relish.

6 ounces chèvre
12 wonton wraps
1 tablespoon olive oil
Sun-Dried Tomato Relish (recipe follows)

1. Preheat the oven to 350°F. Grease a baking sheet.

2. Place 1 tablespoon of goat cheese in the middle of a wonton wrapper. Fold over to form a triangle; slightly dampen the outer edges with cold water. Press the edges to seal. Place the turnover on the prepared baking sheet. Repeat with the remaining wonton skins and cheese.

3. Brush the top of the turnovers with the olive oil. Bake for 12 to 15 minutes until golden. Serve at once with a dollop of the relish atop each turnover.

12 turnovers; allow 2 to 3 per person

Sun-Dried Tomato Relish:
²/₃ cup sun-dried tomatoes
1 large clove garlic, minced
salt and pepper to taste
4 teaspoons balsamic vinegar
3 tablespoons extra-virgin olive oil

1. Place the sun-dried tomatoes in the bowl of a food processor and pulse until chopped.

2. Add the garlic, salt, pepper, vinegar, and olive oil and purée. Refrigerate up to 3 days until needed; return to room temperture to serve.

Enough relish for 12 turnovers

**DINNER PARTY
FOR 6**

Chèvre Turnovers
· · ·
Salmon Olivada
· · ·
Asparagus with
Balsamic Butter
· · ·
Pilaf with
Popped Wild Rice
· · ·
Fruit Tart

CRAB RANGOON

**BUFFET PARTY
FOR 12**

Cucumbers
and Caviar
· · ·
Crab Rangoon
· · ·
Poached Salmon♦
· · ·
Orange Wild
Rice Salad
· · ·
Springtime
Asparagus Salad♦
· · ·
Maple-Pecan
Pound Cake

Wonton wrappers are filled with a delectable crab and herb and garlic cheese mixture, then baked until puffed and golden. These pillows sport a fusion of ingredients with heavenly results.

1 cup crabmeat
4-ounce package Boursin cheese
3 tablespoons thinly sliced scallions
freshly ground pepper to taste
1 package wonton wraps
1 tablespoon vegetable oil

1. Preheat the oven to 350°F. Grease two baking sheets.

2. Combine the crabmeat, cheese, scallions, and pepper and mix well.

3. Place ½ tablespoon of the filling in the middle of a wonton skin. Fold over to form a triangle; slightly dampen the outer edges with cold water. Press the edges together to seal. Place on the prepared baking sheet. Repeat with the remaining wonton skins until all the filling has been used.

4. Brush the top of the wontons with the vegetable oil. Bake for 12 to 15 minutes until puffed and golden. Serve at once.

About 25 crab pillows; allow 3 to 4 per person

POTSTICKERS

This is a baked version of the classic Oriental pan-fried dumpling about which Americans are passionate. The vegetarian filling will appeal to all, whether on a restricted diet or just in love with these plump dumplings. Watch them disappear!

1 tablespoon soy sauce
pepper to taste
¹/₂ teaspoon sugar
1 teaspoon Oriental sesame oil
2 tablespoons vegetable oil
1 cup chopped Chinese cabbage
2 scallions, thinly sliced
1 medium-size carrot, coarsely grated
¹/₄ cup chopped water chestnuts
1¹/₂ teaspoons finely grated gingerroot
1 package wonton wraps

1. In a small bowl, combine the soy sauce, pepper, sugar, and sesame oil and mix well. Set aside.

2. Heat 1 tablespoon vegetable oil over high heat in a wok or large skillet. Add the cabbage, scallions, carrot, water chestnuts, and gingerroot and stir-fry for 2 minutes.

3. Add the soy mixture and stir-fry for 1 minute more. Remove the wok from the heat.

4. Preheat the oven to 400°F. Grease a large baking sheet.

5. Place 1 tablespoon of the filling in the middle of a wonton skin. Fold over to form a triangle; slightly dampen the outer edges with water. Press the edges to seal. Place the potsticker on the prepared baking sheet. Repeat with the remaining wonton skins until all the filling has been used. (Any extra wonton wraps may be frozen for later use.)

6. Brush the top of the potstickers with 1 tablespoon vegetable oil. Bake for 8 to 10 minutes until browned and crisp around the edges. Serve at once.

15 potstickers; allow 3 per person

CHINESE MENU

Potstickers
. . .
Honey-Glazed
Walnut Chicken
. . .
White Rice
. . .
Fortune Cookies
. . .
Ginger Ice Cream

CHEDDAR-CHUTNEY WONTON CUPS

Wonton wrappers are first baked in mini-muffin tins, forming tartlet shells. The cups house a delectable cream cheese, cheddar, and chutney filling that's baked until bubbly. The filling combinations for these tartlet shells are endless, so be adventurous!

27 wonton skins
vegetable oil
1¹/₂ cups grated sharp cheddar cheese
8 ounces cream cheese, at room temperature
¹/₄ cup Mango Chutney (see page 211)

1. Preheat the oven to 350°F. Grease mini-muffin tins.

2. Place a wonton wrapper in each muffin cup, molding it to the sides of the cup. Brush each with oil. Bake for 7 to 8 minutes until lightly golden. (You may prepare these 2 days in advance; store them in an airtight container in the refrigerator. If longer storage is required, freeze the cups for later use. Defrost before filling.)

3. Combine the cheddar, cream cheese, and chutney and mix well. Using a tablespoon of the cheese mixture, fill each tartlet shell. (This may be done several hours in advance and refrigerated; return to room temperature before baking.)

4. Bake for 5 to 7 minutes until the filling is hot. Serve at once.

27 wonton cups; allow 3 or 4 per person

IDEAS FOR WONTON CUPS

For an interesting and flavorful finger food, try any one of the following filling ideas for baked wonton cups; then heat in a 350°F oven for 5 to 7 minutes.

- Chopped prosciutto and grated Swiss cheese.
- Spinach, feta cheese, and dill.
- Smoked mussels, garlic, and grated mozzarella cheese.
- Chopped shrimp, diced avocado, and salsa.
- Mashed sweet or white potato with butter and nutmeg.
- Pâté.
- Chunky peanut butter and cooked, crumbled bacon.
- Crabmeat, cream cheese, and scallions.
- Boursin cheese and chopped sun-dried tomatoes.
- Sautéed onion, rosemary, and goat cheese.
- Brie cheese, diced red onion, and chopped apple.
- Sliced banana, chopped prosciutto, and brown sugar.
- Hoomis or white bean dip.
- Chopped, seeded tomato, diced green pepper, diced red onion, and Parmesan cheese.
- Chopped smoked salmon, goat cheese, and chives.
- Cooked crumbled sausage and grated Romano cheese.
- Guacamole, chopped tomato, and black olives.
- Shredded, cooked chicken, mayonnaise, curry, and chutney.

MUFFULETTA

Muffuletta, or more commonly known as "muffy," is a favorite sandwich native to New Orleans. Modeled after the Italian antipasto, this new wave version of the crowd-pleasing loaf combines an olive salad, Italian meats, and cheese.

SUMMER SUPPER

Cream of
Tomato Soup
. . .
Muffuletta
. . .
Shredded
Romaine Salad◆
. . .
Sliced Melons

1 cup chopped pimiento-stuffed green olives
3/4 cup chopped ripe black olives
1 large red pepper, roasted and chopped
2 tablespoons capers, rinsed and drained
2 large cloves garlic, minced
1 teaspoon dried oregano
1/4 cup minced fresh parsley
1/4 teaspoon freshly ground black pepper
1/4 cup virgin olive oil
1 pound puff pastry, thawed
1/4 pound thinly sliced Genoa salami
1/4 pound thinly sliced prosciutto
1/2 pound thinly sliced provolone cheese
1 egg, beaten

1. Combine the green olives, black olives, roasted pepper, and capers in a bowl.

2. In a separate bowl, whisk together the garlic, oregano, parsley, pepper, and olive oil. Pour the dressing over the olive mixture and let marinate in the refrigerator for 2 to 3 hours or as much as overnight.

3. Roll out the puff pastry on a floured board to form a rectangle 12 x 20 inches. Place it on a large cookie sheet and chill for 30 minutes.

4. Preheat the oven to 350°F.

5. Overlap slices of salami down the center of the dough to within 1 inch of each end. Spread half of the olive mixture over the meat and cover with layers of half of the provolone. Place even layers of the prosciutto over the cheese. Spoon the remaining olive mixture over the ham and cover all with layers of the remaining cheese.

6. Fold the dough over like a turnover, overlapping the sides. Crimp the ends together firmly to seal.

7. Brush the pastry with the beaten egg. This will give the loaf a golden glaze when baked.

8. Bake for 25 minutes. Transfer the loaf to a platter, slice into 1½-inch wide pieces and serve.

6 portions

SPINACH AND SMOKED SALMON EN CROÛTE

This stellar dish features a pastry turnover encasing a delectable filling of spinach, Rondelé cheese, sun-dried tomatoes, and smoked salmon, fragrant with dill. This also makes a spectacular statement for brunch.

SUMMER DINING

Beet Gazpacho
. . .
Spinach and Smoked
Salmon en Croûte
. . .
Salad Aromatica
. . .
Berries and Cream

> 1 pound frozen puff pastry, thawed
> · 10-ounce package frozen, chopped spinach, thawed and squeezed
>   of all its liquid
> 8 ounces Rondelé cheese
> 1/3 cup coarsely chopped sun-dried tomatoes
> 1/4 cup chopped fresh dill
> pepper to taste
> 6 ounces Nova Scotia lox, sliced
> 1 egg, beaten

1. Roll out the puff pastry on a floured board to form a rectangle 12 x 20 inches. Place it on a large cookie sheet and chill for 30 minutes.

2. Preheat the oven to 350°F.

3. In a bowl, combine the spinach, Rondelé, sun-dried tomatoes, dill, and pepper and mix well.

4. Spread the spinach mixture down the center of the length of the dough forming a layer 4 inches wide and extending to within 1 inch of each end.

5. Cover the spinach with even layers of the smoked salmon.

6. Fold the dough over like a turnover, overlapping the sides. Crimp the ends together firmly to seal.

7. Brush the pastry with the beaten egg. This will give the loaf a golden glaze when baked.

8. Bake for 30 minutes. Transfer the loaf to a platter, cut into 1½-inch wide slices, and serve at once.

6 portions

JEWELS OF
THE SEA

BLUEFISH GRAVLAX

Gravlax is classically prepared with salmon filets and seasoned with dill. Extending this theme, I have utilized the distinct, strong-flavored bluefish, curing it with Oriental flavors, and serving it with a Ginger Mayonnaise. This makes a grand buffet dish.

2 pound bluefish filet, cut in half across the center
1/2 cup coarsely grated gingerroot
1/4 cup coarse or Kosher salt
3 tablespoons dark brown sugar
1 tablespoon coarsely ground black pepper
1 tablespoon mustard seeds
Ginger Mayonnaise (recipe follows)

1. Place both pieces of the bluefish on a plate.

2. Combine the gingerroot, salt, sugar, pepper, and mustard seeds and mix well. Spread the seasoning mixture evenly over the top of the pieces of fish. Flip the second piece of bluefish over on top of the first piece of fish, forming a fish sandwich with the spices in the middle.

3. Place the fish sandwich in a plastic bag and seal it tightly. Put the bag in a glass dish and cover it with a 5-pound weight. (I use a brick.) Refrigerate for 3 to 4 days, turning the bluefish over every day.

4. When the bluefish is cured, remove the filets from the marinade. Scrape away the excess seasonings. Thinly slice the bluefish on the diagonal.

5. Serve with crusty bread and the Ginger Mayonnaise.

8 portions

Ginger Mayonnaise:
1 cup mayonnaise
2 tablespoons soy sauce
1 tablespoon honey
1 medium-size clove garlic, crushed
1 teaspoon ground ginger

Mix the mayonnaise, soy sauce, honey, garlic, and ginger together. Store in the refrigerator until needed.

About 1 cup of sauce

MUSSELS ORIENTAL

This is an East meets West rendition of the illustrious, steamed mussel. The shellfish is poached in an Oriental oyster-based sauce that's punctuated with plum tomatoes, scallions, and ginger.

2 pounds mussels, scrubbed and debearded
2 ripe plum tomatoes, chopped
¹/₂ cup chopped scallions
1 large clove garlic, minced
1 tablespoon grated gingerroot
2 tablespoons oyster sauce
1 teaspoon Oriental sesame oil
¹/₂ cup dry white wine

**ORIENTAL
DINNER**

Mussels Oriental
. . .
Peking Chicken
. . .
Rice
. . .
Kai Seki Asparagus
. . .
Ginger Ice Cream✦

1. Rinse the mussels under cold running water to make sure they are free of sand. Heap them into a large saucepan.

2. Add the tomatoes and scallions.

3. Combine the garlic, gingerroot, oyster sauce, sesame oil, and white wine. Pour the sauce over the mussels.

4. Cover, bring to a boil, and simmer gently just until the mussels open, about 5 minutes.

5. Transfer the mussels to a large bowl, discarding any unopened ones. Spoon the Oriental sauce over the shellfish and serve at once.

4 appetizer portions; 2 main-course portions

BAKED-STUFFED OYSTERS

Oysters, the quintessential shellfish, bask under a topping of shredded Italian radicchio and mascarpone, the sweet, creamy dessert cheese. Baked to bubbly perfection, these are absolutely heavenly!

24 raw oysters in their shells
1 cup shredded radicchio
1 cup mascarpone cheese
1 tablespoon lemon juice
salt and pepper to taste

1. Preheat the oven to 475°F.

2. Shell the oysters. Insert the tip of a knife near the hinge of the oyster shell. Run the knife between the shells, cutting through the muscle. Remove the flat shell, and cut through the muscle where the oyster is attached to the deeper shell. Rinse the oyster under cold water, pat dry, and replace it in the deeper shell. Repeat with the remaining oysters.

3. Set the oysters on their half shells on a large baking pan.

4. Combine the radicchio, mascarpone, lemon juice, salt, and pepper and mix well.

5. Place a heaping tablespoonful of the radicchio mixture atop each oyster.

6. Bake for 3 minutes, then run under a hot broiler, 4 inches from the heat source, for 1 to 2 minutes until lightly browned. Serve at once.

4 to 6 portions

SALMON PÂTÉ

This is a smooth and creamy salmon, roasted red pepper, and caper purée with hints of orange and raspberry. Serve this appetizer with toasted French bread slices or raw vegetables.

> *½ pound poached salmon*
> *1 large red pepper, roasted*
> *1 tablespoon capers*
> *1 tablespoon Dijon mustard*
> *freshly ground pepper to taste*
> *1 teaspoon dried orange peel*
> *¼ cup chopped fresh parsley*
> *2 tablespoons raspberry vinegar*
> *⅔ cup virgin olive oil*

1. Place the salmon, roasted pepper, capers, Dijon, pepper, orange peel, parsley, and vinegar in the bowl of a food processor. Purée until smooth.

2. With the motor running, add the olive oil in a slow, steady stream and continue to process until the oil is completely incorporated and the sauce is creamy. Serve at room temperature. (This may be prepared 24 hours in advance and refrigerated; return to room temperature to serve.)

6 to 8 portions

SEAFOOD FARE

Salmon Pâté
with French Bread
· · ·
Fettuccine with
Shellfish in
Tomato-Cream Sauce
· · ·
Green Salad
· · ·
Heavenly Strawberries
Adorned◆

AVOCADO AND SMOKED SALMON WITH WASABI VINAIGRETTE

Fashioned in the style of sushi, avocado wedges are covered with strips of smoked salmon and drizzled with a light wasabi-soy vinaigrette. This is a grand meal opener, and also makes a tasty salad or light luncheon dish.

3 ripe Haas avocados, peeled, pitted, and sliced into wedges
3 ounces sliced Nova Scotia lox, cut into bite-size strips

Wasabi Vinaigrette:
1¹/2 tablespoons rice vinegar
2 tablespoons soy sauce
1 tablespoon vegetable oil
1 tablespoon wasabi powder mixed with ¹/2 tablespoon water
    to make a paste

1. Fan slices of avocado wedges on six plates, allowing ¹/2 avocado per person. Adorn the avocado with pieces of the smoked salmon.

2. In a small bowl, whisk together the vinegar, soy sauce, oil, and wasabi paste. Drizzle the vinaigrette over each portion and serve.

6 portions

GRILLED SHRIMP AND ARTICHOKE HEARTS WITH CUMIN MAYONNAISE

Grilling the shrimp and the artichoke hearts adds a distinctive barbecued flavor that's further enhanced by a light cumin-flavored mayonnaise dipping sauce. Try the sauce on grilled fish or atop cooked vegetables for a change of pace.

> 1 pound raw extra-large shrimp, peeled
> 14-ounce can artichoke hearts, drained and cut in half
> 2 tablespoons vegetable oil
> salt and pepper to taste
> dash Worcestershire sauce
> Cumin Mayonnaise (recipe follows)

1. Skewer the shrimp and artichoke hearts. Brush with the oil and season with salt, pepper, and Worcestershire sauce.

2. Grill over hot coals, 4 inches from the heat source, for about 2 minutes per side until cooked and lightly charred. Remove from the skewers and serve with the Cumin Mayonnaise.

6 to 8 portions

> *Cumin Mayonnaise:*
> ³/₄ cup mayonnaise
> 1 tablespoon ground cumin

Combine the mayonnaise and cumin and mix well. Store in the refrigerator until needed. (Any unused sauce will keep up to 2 weeks.)

³/₄ cup of sauce

HOT WEATHER FARE

Pickled Grapes
. . .
Grilled Shrimp and Artichoke Hearts with Cumin Mayonnaise
. . .
Spinach, Smoked-Salmon, and Goat Cheese Salad
. . .
Focaccia
. . .
Ginger-White Chocolate Chunk Cookies
. . .
Strawberries

SHELLFISH REMOULADE

Fruits of the sea—shrimp, scallops, and mussels—are set against a glorious, piquant, tarragon and caper sauce. This presents itself well as an elegant appetizer for formal dinners, and also makes a tantalizing hors d'oeuvre for cocktail parties.

1 pound medium-size shrimp, poached and shelled
1 pound scallops, poached
48 mussels, steamed and shelled

Remoulade Sauce:
1 cup mayonnaise
1 tablespoon Dijon mustard
2 tablespoons capers
2 tablespoons finely chopped celery
2 tablespoons finely chopped onion
1 tablespoon chopped fresh parsley
1 teaspoon dried tarragon
1/4 teaspoon salt
1/2 teaspoon black pepper
1 teaspoon Worcestershire sauce
1 tablespoon red wine vinegar

1. Arrange the shellfish on a platter.

2. In a bowl, combine the mayonnaise, Dijon, capers, celery, onion, parsley, tarragon, salt, pepper, Worcestershire, and vinegar. Stir until well blended. (This may be prepared 2 to 3 days in advance and refrigerated until needed.)

3. Serve the shellfish accompanied by the remoulade dipping sauce.

10 to 12 portions

SMOKED TROUT PÂTÉ

This creamy spread is elegant, delicate, and delightful. The smoky flavor is effected without having to use a smoker, simply by adding liquid smoke to the cooked trout.

1 pound trout filets, boned
salt and pepper to taste
1/2 pound cream cheese
1 tablespoon lemon juice
1 1/2 teaspoons liquid smoke
1 1/2 tablespoons minced onion
1/2 teaspoon prepared white horseradish

1. Preheat the oven to 350°F.

2. Place the trout in a baking pan. Season with salt and pepper and cover with foil. Bake for 15 to 20 minutes until cooked. Remove the skin and transfer the fish to the bowl of a food processor.

3. Add the cream cheese, lemon juice, liquid smoke, onion, and horseradish. Purée until smooth. Cover and chill several hours until firm. Serve with rounds of French bread.

6 to 8 portions

GRAZING PARTY

Bruschetta with
Herbed Yogurt Cheese
· · ·
Martini Splash
· · ·
Tortellini with
Jalapeño Pesto
· · ·
Smoked Trout Pâté
· · ·
Peanut Butter-Bacon
Roll-Ups
· · ·
Assorted Cheeses
and Fruits

MUFFINS AND TEA BREADS

Breakfast or brunch needn't be a formal affair, but should be something magical. It's the perfect opportunity for the resourceful cook to highlight a basic breakfast of oatmeal, pancakes, or eggs with quick breads and muffins, fresh fruits, cheeses, composed butters, juices, and flavored coffees.

Whether you're entertaining or just getting the day underway, start with some sparkle and shine. Serve morning tea loaves and muffins, fragrant with spices, laden with fruits, and textured with nuts.

Note—Always use extra-large eggs when preparing the muffins and quick breads. Do not overmix the batter as it results in tough breads.

COCONUT MUFFINS

A taste of the tropics dominates these coconut-infused muffins.

1/2 cup butter, melted
1 cup sugar
2 eggs, lightly beaten
1 cup milk
1 teaspoon coconut extract
2 cups all-purpose flour
2 teaspoons baking powder
pinch salt
1 cup sweetened, shredded coconut

1. Preheat the oven to 375°F. Line a 12-cup muffin tin with paper baking cups.

2. In a large mixing bowl, stir together the butter, sugar, eggs, milk, and coconut extract until well blended.

3. Sift together the flour, baking powder, and salt.

4. Add the dry ingredients to the batter, stirring only until the mixture is combined. Fold in the coconut.

5. Spoon the batter evenly into the muffin tins. Bake for 20 minutes. Remove the muffins to racks to cool completely.

12 muffins

GLORIOUS MORNING MUFFINS

These muffins brighten up the breakfast table. They're chock full of fruits and nuts—carrots, zucchini, walnuts, raisins, and coconut— and perfumed with aromatic spices.

¹/₂ cup butter
³/₄ cup granulated sugar
¹/₄ cup packed dark brown sugar
2 eggs
1 cup all-purpose flour
2 teaspoons baking soda
¹/₄ teaspoon salt
1¹/₂ teaspoons cinnamon
pinch cloves
pinch nutmeg
¹/₂ cup sweetened, shredded coconut
¹/₂ cup chopped walnuts
³/₄ cup coarsely grated carrot
³/₄ cup coarsely grated, unpeeled zucchini
¹/₃ cup raisins

1. Preheat the oven to 350°F. Line a 12-cup muffin tin with paper baking cups.

2. In a large mixing bowl, cream the butter and sugars until fluffy. Add the eggs and mix well.

3. Sift together the flour, baking soda, salt, and spices.

4. Add the dry ingredients to the batter, stirring until combined.

5. Gently stir in the coconut, nuts, carrot, zucchini, and raisins.

6. Spoon the batter into the muffin pans, filling each cup ³/₄ full. Bake for 20 minutes. Remove the muffins to racks to cool completely.

12 muffins

BREAKFAST BUFFET

Assorted Yogurts
· · ·
Granola
· · ·
Glorious Morning
Muffins
· · ·
Pear Bread with
Ginger Cream Cheese
· · ·
Fresh Melon Slices
· · ·
Orange, Cranberry,
and Mango Juices
· · ·
Mugs of Coffee

ORANGE MUFFINS

These citrus-scented morning muffins are defined by fresh orange peel and orange marmalade.

PICNIC FARE

Strawberries Balsamic
· · ·
Smoked
Chicken Salad with
Apricot-Date Chutney
· · ·
Mixed Green Salad
· · ·
Orange Muffins

3/4 cup butter
1 cup sugar
2 eggs
1 tablespoon grated orange peel
1 teaspoon vanilla
1/4 cup orange marmalade
2 cups all-purpose flour
1 tablespoon baking powder
1/2 teaspoon salt
1/2 cup milk
1/2 cup orange juice
1 tablespoon sugar for topping

1. Preheat the oven to 375°F. Line a 12-cup muffin tin with paper baking cups.

2. In a large mixing bowl, cream the butter and sugar until fluffy. Add the eggs, orange peel, vanilla, and marmalade and mix well.

3. Sift together the flour, baking powder, and salt.

4. Combine the milk and orange juice.

5. Add the dry ingredients alternately with the milk mixture to the batter, until all is blended.

6. Spoon the batter into the muffin pans, filling each cup 3/4 full. Sprinkle 1 tablespoon sugar over the tops of the muffins.

7. Bake for 20 minutes. Remove the muffins to racks to cool.

12 muffins

PEACH MUFFINS

Sweet, fragrant, and chock full of peach chunks, these almond-encrusted muffins top the list for summertime breakfast and brunch.

¹/₂ cup butter
1 cup sugar
2 eggs
1 teaspoon almond extract
2 cups all-purpose flour
2 teaspoons baking powder
1 teaspoon baking soda
pinch salt
2 cups peaches, skinned and cut into ¹/₂-inch chunks
  (place in a bowl for juices to accumulate)

Topping:
¹/₂ cup sliced almonds
2 tablespoons sugar
¹/₂ teaspoon cinnamon

1. Preheat the oven to 350°F. Line a 12-cup muffin tin with paper baking cups.

2. In a large mixing bowl, cream the butter and sugar until fluffy. Add the eggs and almond extract and mix until well blended.

3. Sift together the flour, baking powder, baking soda, and salt. Add the dry ingredients to the batter.

4. Gently fold in the peaches and any acculumated juice.

5. Pile the batter high in each muffin cup. Mix the topping ingredients together and sprinkle over the tops of the muffins.

6. Bake for 25 minutes. Remove the muffins to racks to cool completely.

12 plump muffins

LUNCH BOX TREATS

Blue Cheese Nuggets
. . .
Sun-Dried Peppers
. . .
Peach Muffins
. . .
Nectarines and Tomatoes
. . .
Honey-Nut Granola Bars

PERSIMMON MUFFINS

TEA AND . . .

Persimmon Muffins
. . .
Vanilla Tea Cookies
. . .
Chocolate Meringues
. . .
Strawberries with
Sour Cream and
Brown Sugar

I had my first fruitful encounter with this bright, orange beauty very recently, and immediately became an enamored fan! These muffins are lush and fragrant with the magical essence of persimmon.

1/2 cup butter
1 cup sugar
2 eggs
1 teaspoon vanilla
2 cups all-purpose flour
1 tablespoon baking powder
1/2 teaspoon baking soda
1/4 teaspoon salt
2 large, ripe persimmons, peeled and mashed
2 tablespoons sugar for topping

1. Preheat the oven to 375°F. Line large muffin pans with paper baking cups.

2. In a large mixing bowl, cream the butter and sugar until fluffy. Add the eggs and vanilla and mix until well blended.

3. Sift together the flour, baking powder, baking soda, and salt. Add the dry ingredients to the batter.

4. Gently fold in the mashed persimmons.

5. Spoon the batter into the muffin pans. Sprinkle 2 tablespoons sugar over the tops of the muffins.

6. Bake for 20 to 25 minutes, until a cake tester inserted in the center of a muffin comes out clean. Remove the muffins to racks to cool completely.

14 large muffins

RASPBERRY MUFFINS

The raspberry, the queen of berries, debuts in these moist breakfast muffins that are laced with raspberry preserves.

1/2 cup butter
1 cup sugar
2 eggs
1 tablespoon vanilla
1/4 cup raspberry preserves
2 cups all-purpose flour
2 teaspoons baking powder
1/2 teaspoon salt
1/2 cup buttermilk
2 cups raspberries
2 tablespoons sugar for topping

1. Preheat the oven to 375°F. Line a 12-cup muffin pan with paper baking cups.

2. In a large mixing bowl, cream the butter and sugar until fluffy. Add the eggs, vanilla, and raspberry preserves, and mix until the batter is smooth.

3. Sift together the flour, baking powder, and salt. Add the dry ingredients alternately with the buttermilk to the batter.

4. Gently fold in the raspberries, being careful not to break up the fruit.

5. Spoon the batter into the muffin tins. Sprinkle 2 tablespoons sugar over the tops of the muffins.

6. Bake for 25 to 30 minutes, until a cake tester inserted in the center of a muffin comes out clean. Remove the muffins to racks to cool completely.

12 muffins

AFTERNOON TEA FOR 12

Lemon Tea Bread
. . .
Raspberry Muffins
. . .
Cream Cheese
. . .
Chocolate-Almond Biscotti
. . .
Peter's Sugar Plums
. . .
Heavenly Strawberries Adorned◆
. . .
Assorted Teas

CINNAMON-RAISIN LOAF

Whether for breakfast or brunch, this tea loaf is the best of both worlds. The quick bread is plump with raisins and rippled with a cinnamon-infused cheesecake swirl.

2/3 cup raisins
1/2 cup butter
1 cup sugar
2 eggs
1 teaspoon vanilla
2 cups plus 1 tablespoon all-purpose flour
1 teaspoon baking powder
1 teaspoon baking soda
1/2 teaspoon salt

Cheesecake swirl:
4 ounces cream cheese, at room temperature
1/4 cup sugar
1 egg, beaten
2 teaspoons cinnamon

1. Preheat the oven to 350°F. Grease a 9 x 5-inch loaf pan.

2. Plump the raisins in a bowl of boiling water to cover for 5 minutes. Drain well and dust with 1 tablespoon flour.

3. In a large mixing bowl, cream the butter and sugar until fluffy. Add the eggs and vanilla and mix well.

4. Sift together the 2 cups flour, baking powder, baking soda, and salt. Add the dry ingredients to the batter, stirring until well blended.

5. Gently fold in the raisins.

6. Turn the batter into the prepared pan.

7. In a separate small bowl, mix the cream cheese, sugar, egg, and cinnamon until well blended. Spread dollops of the cream cheese mixture over the batter and swirl with a knife to get a rippling effect.

8. Bake for 1 hour. Remove to a rack to cool in the pan for 20 minutes, then remove the bread from the pan to a rack to cool completely.

1 loaf

LEMON TEA BREAD

This cake-like tea bread has a delicate lemon flavor that's highlighted with a lemon crunch topping.

Topping:
2 tablespoons sugar
1 teaspoon finely grated lemon zest

¹/₂ cup butter
1 cup sugar
2 eggs
1 tablespoon finely grated lemon zest
¹/₄ cup lemon juice
2 cups all-purpose flour
1 tablespoon baking powder
¹/₂ teaspoon salt
¹/₂ cup sour cream

1. Preheat the oven to 350°F. Grease and flour a 9 x 5-inch loaf pan.

2. Combine the topping mix in a small bowl and set aside for 20 minutes.

3. In a large mixing bowl, cream the butter and sugar until fluffy. Add the eggs, lemon zest, and lemon juice and mix well.

4. Sift together the flour, baking powder, and salt. Add the dry ingredients alternately with the sour cream to the batter, stirring until evenly blended.

5. Turn the batter into the prepared pan. Sprinkle the topping mix over the bread.

6. Bake for 45 to 50 minutes, or until a cake tester inserted in the center comes out clean. Remove to a rack to cool in the pan for 10 minutes, then remove the bread from the pan to a rack to cool completely.

1 loaf

AFTERNOON TEA FOR 12

Lemon Tea Bread
. . .
Raspberry Muffins
. . .
Cream Cheese
. . .
Chocolate-Almond Biscotti
. . .
Peter's Sugar Plums
. . .
Heavenly Strawberries Adorned◆
. . .
Assorted Teas

PEAR BREAD WITH GINGER CREAM CHEESE

This fragrantly sweet, autumn tea bread is dappled with the buttery taste of pears, and served up with a ginger-pecan cream cheese.

1/2 cup butter
1 cup sugar
2 eggs
2 teaspoons vanilla
2 cups all-purpose flour
1 1/4 teaspoons baking powder
1 teaspoon baking soda
1/4 teaspoon salt
1/4 cup milk
2 cups peeled, diced pears
Ginger Cream Cheese (recipe follows)

1. Preheat the oven to 350°F. Grease two 8 x 4-inch loaf pans.

2. In a large mixing bowl, cream the butter and sugar until fluffy. Add the eggs and vanilla and mix well.

3. Sift together the flour, baking powder, baking soda, and salt.

4. Add the dry ingredients alternately with the milk to the batter, stirring until well blended. Fold in the diced pears.

5. Turn the batter into the prepared pans. Bake for 45 to 50 minutes, or until a cake tester inserted in the center comes out clean. Remove to a rack to cool in the pans for 15 minutes, then remove the breads from the pans to a rack to cool completely.

6. To serve, spread slices with the Ginger Cream Cheese.

2 mini loaves

Ginger Cream Cheese:
8 ounces cream cheese, at room temperature
1 tablespoon milk
1 tablespoon minced crystallized candied ginger
2 tablespoons chopped pecans

Mix the ingredients together until well blended. Refrigerate until ready to serve. This may be prepared 4 to 5 days in advance.

Enough to embellish 2 mini loaves

PECAN BREAD

The taste of the famous congo bar, bespeckled with pecans, is packed into this tea bread. It's especially tasty served with cream cheese, yet it's most glorious unadorned.

1/2 cup butter
1/2 cup granulated sugar
1/2 cup packed light brown sugar
3 eggs
2 teaspoons vanilla
2 cups all-purpose flour
1 teaspoon baking powder
1 teaspoon baking soda
1/4 teaspoon salt
1 cup milk
1 cup coarsely chopped pecans

1. Preheat the oven to 350°F. Grease two 8 x 4-inch loaf pans.

2. In a large mixing bowl, cream the butter and sugars until fluffy. Add the eggs and vanilla and mix well.

3. Sift together the flour, baking powder, baking soda, and salt.

4. Add the dry ingredients alternately with the milk to the batter, stirring until blended.

5. Fold in the pecans.

6. Turn the batter into the prepared pans. Bake for 40 minutes, or until a cake tester inserted in the center comes out clean. Remove to a rack to cool in the pans for 30 minutes, then remove the breads from the pans to racks to cool completely.

2 mini loaves

**GIFTS FROM
THE HEARTH**

Olivada
. . .
Pecan Bread
. . .
Tomato Chutney
. . .
Vanilla Extract
. . .
Pistachio Shortbreads
. . .
Composed Butters

SPICE BREAD

Reminiscent of the taste of gingerbread, this breakfast bread is enhanced with the richness of prunes.

¹/₂ cup butter
1 cup sugar
2 eggs
2 cups all-purpose flour
1¹/₂ teaspoons baking powder
1 teaspoon baking soda
¹/₄ teaspoon salt
1 teaspoon cinnamon
¹/₂ teaspoon nutmeg
¹/₂ teaspoon ground cloves
1 cup sour cream
2 cups prunes, plumped in boiling water for 5 minutes,
*   drained, and chopped*

1. Preheat the oven to 350°F. Grease two 8 x 4-inch loaf pans.

2. In a large mixing bowl, cream the butter and sugar until fluffy. Add the eggs and mix well.

3. Sift together the flour, baking powder, baking soda, salt, and spices. Add the dry ingredients alternately with the sour cream to the batter, mixing until well blended.

4. Fold in the prunes.

5. Turn the batter into the prepared pans. Bake for 45 to 50 minutes, or until a cake tester inserted in the center comes out clean. Remove to a rack to cool in the pans for 20 minutes, then remove the breads from the pans to a rack to cool completely.

2 mini loaves

SUMMER LUNCH

Smoked Salmon Soup
· · ·
Spice Bread with
Cream Cheese
· · ·
Watermelon,
Cantaloupe, and
Honeydew Slices

STRAWBERRY BREAD

A taste of summertime abounds in this tea bread, fragrant with the succulence of strawberries and textured with pecans. The loaf makes a grand statement embellished with cream cheese for brunch, snack, or dessert.

3/4 cup butter
1 cup sugar
2 eggs
1 1/2 teaspoons vanilla
1/3 cup strawberry preserves
2 cups all-purpose flour
1 teaspoon baking powder
1 teaspoon baking soda
1/4 teaspoon salt
1 cup mashed strawberries
1/2 cup chopped pecans

LUNCHEON MENU

Bacon and
Orange Salad
· · ·
Country Bread
· · ·
Scallop Chowder
· · ·
Strawberry Bread

1. Preheat the oven to 350°F. Grease two 8 x 4-inch loaf pans.

2. In a large mixing bowl, cream the butter and sugar until fluffy. Add the eggs, vanilla, and preserves and mix well.

3. Sift together the flour, baking powder, baking soda, and salt. Add the dry ingredients to the batter.

4. Fold in the mashed fruit and nuts, stirring until evenly blended.

5. Turn the batter into the prepared pans. Bake for 45 minutes. Remove to a rack to cool in the pan for 20 minutes, then remove the breads from the pans to racks to cool completely.

2 mini loaves

CORNBREAD

**WINTER SUNDAY
SUPPER**

Slow-Roasted
Texas Brisket
. . .
Cornbread
. . .
Carrots and
Turnips Gilbert
. . .
Assorted Cookies

Cornbread is as indigenous to Southern cooking as is barbecued ribs. This bread is a double-corn and cheese medley, chunky with corn kernels and green chili peppers that elevate it to new heights.

1 cup all-purpose flour
1 cup cornmeal
3 tablespoons sugar
2 teaspoons baking powder
1 teaspoon baking soda
1 teaspoon salt
2 eggs, beaten
³/4 cup buttermilk
5 tablespoons vegetable oil
1 cup corn kernels (either fresh or frozen)
1 cup grated mild cheddar cheese
4-ounce can mild green chilies, chopped

1. Preheat the oven to 375°F. Grease a 9-inch square pan.

2. In a large bowl, combine all of the dry ingredients.

3. In a separate small bowl, mix together the eggs, buttermilk, oil, corn, cheese, and chilies. Add this to the dry ingredients and stir only until evenly combined. Do not over mix.

4. Pour the batter into the prepared pan and bake for 25 minutes until golden. Serve hot out of the oven or let cool.

12 pieces

GRANOLA

Start the day off with this stellar multi-grain, dried fruit, and nut medley that's scented with cinnamon, maple syrup, and brown sugar. As well as a cereal, try it for snacking out of hand, atop fruit or yogurt, mixed into cookie dough, or sprinkled on ice cream.

4 cups old-fashioned oats
1 cup grapenuts cereal
1$^1/_4$ cups wheat germ
1 cup slivered almonds
$^1/_2$ cup coarsely chopped pecans
1 tablespoon cinnamon
$^1/_2$ cup firmly packed dark brown sugar
$^3/_4$ cup pure maple syrup
$^1/_3$ cup vegetable oil
2$^1/_2$ cups mixed dried fruits—chopped apricots, dates, prunes,
　　and dried cherries

1. Preheat the oven to 350°F.

2. Combine the cereals, nuts, cinnamon, sugar, maple syrup, and oil in a large bowl and mix well.

3. Divide the mixture between two 9 x 13-inch pans, spreading it into an even layer.

4. Bake for 15 minutes. Stir the granola well and bake for 5 minutes more. Remove the pans to a rack to cool.

5. When cooled completely, stir in the dried fruits. Store in an airtight container.

11 cups

BREAKFAST BUFFET

Assorted Yogurts
· · ·
Granola
· · ·
Glorious Morning Muffins
· · ·
Pear Bread with Ginger Cream Cheese
· · ·
Fresh Melon Slices
· · ·
Orange, Cranberry, and Mango Juices
· · ·
Mugs of Coffee

THE SOUP KETTLE

Soup, wonderful soup! I have an abiding passion for soup. It's a most glorious food, offering comfort, nutrition, and marvelous taste, making us feel warm and secure. Nourishing and satisfying, soup provides basic sustenance. A bowl of hot soup teeming with vegetables, beans, grains, and fishes soothes the soul and takes the chill out of a cold, wintry day. Cold soup can be refreshing and sublime on a hot, sultry day. Both serve as gala meal openers.

Soup gives the cook creative license, providing the setting for intriguing combinations to develop—embracing liquids, interesting textures, and exciting flavors. Soup is sublime, be it a bubbling broth, chunky chowder, or creamy purée. The category of soups is large and extensive, ranging from vegetable and fruit potages to more substantial pasta and bean soups, as well as hearty poultry, seafood, and beef stews.

Soups are actually better if made in advance, allowing the flavors to mellow. Simply return the soup to room temperature for a cold soup presentation, or reheat until piping hot.

COLD WEATHER COMFORTS

APPLE-BUTTERNUT SQUASH SOUP

This absolutely winning combination boasts a smooth and creamy butternut squash purée flavored with the essence of apple and redolent with nutmeg. Nutmeg is an exotic spice, native to Grenada in the West Indies, sporting a sweet, nutty flavor and woody scent. This makes delectable food for the Thanksgiving feast.

2 tablespoons butter
1 large yellow onion, chopped
2 large Granny Smith apples, peeled and chopped
2 to 2¼ pound butternut squash, peeled and chopped
3 cups chicken broth
salt and pepper to taste
generous ¾ teaspoon nutmeg
½ cup light cream

1. Heat the butter in a large saucepan. Add the onion and cook over low heat for 15 minutes until soft.

2. Add the apples, squash, broth, and seasonings.

3. Bring to a boil, cover, lower the heat, and simmer for 20 minutes until the apples and squash are tender.

4. Remove the soup in batches to a food processor or blender and purée. Return the purée to the saucepan, stir in the cream, and heat gently until hot. Serve at once.

6 to 8 appetizer portions; 3 to 4 luncheon portions

PARSNIP AND PEAR SOUP

This creamy soup features the melting together of two aromatic flavors—the natural sweetness of the parsnip coupled with the buttery perfume of the pear. The parsnip shows its true illustrious colors in this slightly sweet, heavenly soup. The parsnip is actually a starchy vegetable, high in carbohydrates. This root vegetable was once the primary source of starch in Europe centuries ago before the arrival of the potato. The potato pushed the parsnip out of the limelight, and it has never regained its stature. However, once sampled, once savored, and much prized!

2 tablespoons butter
4 shallots, peeled and chopped
1 pound parsnips, peeled and chopped
2 ripe pears, peeled, cored, and chopped
1 quart chicken broth
1/2 cup dry white wine
salt and pepper to taste
1/4 teaspoon nutmeg
1/2 cup sour cream

1. Heat the butter in a large stockpot. Add the shallots, parsnips, and pears, and sauté over medium-high heat for 10 minutes until tender.

2. Add the chicken broth, wine, and seasonings.

3. Bring to a boil, cover, lower the heat, and simmer for 20 minutes until the parsnips are soft.

4. Remove the soup in batches to a food processor or blender and purée. Return the purée to the stockpot and stir in the sour cream.

5. Heat the soup gently until piping hot. Serve at once.

6 to 8 portions

WINTER DINNER

Parsnip and Pear Soup
· · ·
Baked Scrod with
Lobster Crumbs
· · ·
Vegetable Rice Pilaf
· · ·
Green Beans Caesar
· · ·
Chocolate-Banana
Bread Pudding

DINNER MENU

Orange-Fennel Soup
. . .
Lamb Chops
. . .
Herbed Orzo Pilaf
. . .
Green Beans,
Prosciutto, and
Parmesan
. . .
Chocolate Mousse◆

ORANGE-FENNEL SOUP

The anise flavor of the beautiful, aromatic fennel bulb is tempered by the sweet taste of orange essence. This is a delightful soup for both cold and warm weather.

¹/₂ cup olive oil
3 large cloves garlic, minced
1 large Spanish onion, chopped
3 fennel bulbs (about 2 pounds), tops removed, and coarsely chopped
2 large carrots, chopped
salt and freshly ground pepper to taste
1 tablespoon grated orange peel
2 cups orange juice
28-ounce can Italian plum tomatoes, broken up with their juice
3 cups chicken broth

1. Heat the olive oil in a large stockpot. Add the garlic, onion, fennel, and carrots and sauté over medium heat until soft, about 15 minutes.

2. Add the remaining ingredients and simmer uncovered for 30 minutes. Serve piping hot.

8 to 10 portions

WILD MUSHROOM SOUP

For those who like earthy and robust flavor, these meaty, wild mushrooms are rich and fragrant treasures, enhanced with thyme and the sweetness of Port wine.

1/2 cup butter
2 medium-size red onions, chopped
1 large clove garlic, minced
2 pounds assorted wild mushrooms, sliced
   (shiitake, oyster, and cremini)
1 teaspoon dried thyme
freshly ground pepper to taste
2 tablespoons all-purpose flour
4 cups canned beef consommé
2 cups water
1 cup Port wine
freshly grated Parmesan cheese for garnish

LIGHT SUPPER

Wild Mushroom Soup
. . .
French Bread
. . .
Grilled Chicken
Caesar Salad
. . .
Frozen Yogurt

1. Heat the butter in a large sauté pan. Add the onions and garlic and sauté over medium-high heat for 10 to 15 minutes until the onions are lightly golden.

2. Add the mushrooms and season with thyme and pepper. Sauté for 15 minutes stirring occasionally, until the mushrooms are browned.

3. Sprinkle the flour over all and mix well. Transfer the sautéed vegetables to a large stockpot.

4. Add the consommé, water, and wine. Bring to a boil, cover, reduce the heat, and simmer for 30 minutes.

5. To serve, ladle the hot soup into individual bowls and garnish each portion with freshly grated cheese.

6 to 8 portions

CREAM OF ONION SOUP

What could be more comforting than a triple-onion indulgence in a light cream stock? This heavenly potage is redolent with sautéed onions, leeks, and garlic, laced with sweet vermouth, and scented with tarragon.

4 tablespoons butter
3 large cloves garlic, minced
4 cups chopped Spanish or Vidalia onions
3 leeks, chopped (white part only)
1 teaspoon dried tarragon
salt and pepper to taste
4 cups chicken broth
1/2 cup sweet vermouth
1 cup light cream

1. Heat the butter in a large saucepan. Add the garlic, onions, leeks, tarragon, salt, and pepper. Sauté over medium heat for 20 to 25 minutes until the onions are soft and lightly golden. Stir occasionally.

2. Stir in the chicken broth and vermouth. Bring to a boil, lower the heat, and simmer for 10 minutes.

3. Using a slotted spoon, remove 1 cup of the solids from the soup to a food processor or blender and purée. Return the purée to the saucepan and mix well.

4. Add the cream and heat gently until hot. Serve at once.

6 to 8 portions

ORIENTAL PEA SOUP

Easy, colorful, and delicate, this Oriental-flavored chicken stock is teeming with peas, peapods, baby shrimp, and water chestnuts.

2 cups fresh or frozen peas
1 cup peapods, cut in half on the diagonal
1/2 cup sliced water chestnuts
2 scallions, cut into 1/4-inch thick slices
4 cups chicken broth
1 tablespoon soy sauce
1 tablespoon dry white wine
freshly ground pepper to taste
1/4 pound cooked small shrimp
1 teaspoon Oriental sesame oil

ORIENTAL STIR-FRY

Oriental Pea Soup
. . .
Minced Chicken with
Pine Nuts
. . .
Beef and Broccoli with
Oyster Sauce
. . .
White Rice
. . .
Flambéed Bananas

1. Place the peas, peapods, water chestnuts, scallions, chicken broth, soy, wine, and pepper in a large saucepan and bring to a boil.

2. Add the shrimp, stir in the sesame oil, and serve at once.

4 portions

ROOT VEGETABLE SOUP

Peasant root vegetables provide gourmet pleasures in this soul-soothing comfort food. A medley of roots—leeks, carrots, parsnips, turnips, sweet potatoes, and red potatoes—all come together with a delicate blending of flavors, accented by dill.

3 tablespoons olive oil
2 large cloves garlic, minced
2 large yellow onions, chopped
1 cup chopped leeks (white part only)
2 cups peeled and diced carrots
2 cups peeled and diced parsnips
2 cups peeled and diced turnips
2¹/₂ cups peeled and diced sweet potatoes
2 cups diced red potatoes
2 quarts chicken broth
salt to taste
¹/₂ teaspoon black pepper
¹/₄ cup chopped fresh dilll

1. Heat the oil in a large stockpot. Add the garlic, onions, and leeks and sauté over medium heat for 10 to 15 minutes until lightly golden.

2. Add the remaining ingredients. Bring to a boil, lower the heat, cover, and simmer for 20 minutes until the vegetables are tender.

3. Remove 3 cups of the soup to a food procesor or blender and purée. Return the purée to the stockpot and mix well.

4. Heat until piping hot. Serve at once.

8 to 10 portions

ORIENTAL MANHATTAN CLAM CHOWDER

This East meets West zesty version of the distinguished tomato-based clam soup is spiked with horseradish, Tabasco and Worcestershire sauces, and flavored with soy sauce and gingerroot.

1 quart tomato juice
28-ounce can Italian plum tomatoes, coarsely chopped with their juice
3 dozen littleneck clams, steamed and shelled
1 cup reserved clam broth
³/₄ cup dry white wine
2 large stalks celery, minced
¹/₃ cup thinly sliced scallions
¹/₄ cup lemon juice
3 tablespoons prepared white horseradish
1 teaspoon Worcestershire sauce
¹/₄ teaspoon Tabasco sauce
1 tablespoon grated fresh gingerroot
1 tablespoon soy sauce
¹/₄ teaspoon black pepper

1. Combine all of the ingredients in a large stockpot.
2. Heat gently until piping hot. Serve at once.

6 to 8 appetizer portions; 3 to 4 main-course portions

WINTER SOUP PARTY

Mixed Green Salad with Balsamic Vinaigrette◆
. . .
Oriental Manhattan Clam Chowder
. . .
Southwestern Corn Chowder
. . .
Assorted Breads
. . .
Rum-Raisin Rice Pudding

CRAB-CORN CHOWDER

Corn chowder is one of my favorites. This rendition is composed of the best of ingredients with subtle flavors—crab, potatoes, corn, and sautéed red onion in a light cream broth.

3 tablespoons butter
2 large red onions, chopped
¹/₄ cup all-purpose flour
4 cups chicken broth
2 small red-skinned potatoes, cut into ¹/₂-inch cubes (about 2 cups)
1 bay leaf
1 teaspoon dried thyme
salt and pepper to taste
1¹/₂ cups corn kernels, fresh or frozen
1 pound crabmeat, cut into chunks
2 cups half and half

1. Heat the butter in a large saucepan. Add the onions and sauté over medium-high heat until lightly browned, about 10 minutes.

2. Add the flour and cook for 5 minutes more, stirring constantly.

3. Add the broth, potatoes, and seasonings. Simmer for 5 to 10 minutes until the potatoes are tender.

4. Add the corn, crab, and half and half, and simmer for 2 to 3 minutes more until heated through. Serve piping hot.

6 to 8 portions

SCALLOP CHOWDER

This thick, chunky soup is rich with scallops, onions, and potatoes, surrounded by a light ginger-infused cream base. It's absolutely divine and real cold weather comfort food.

4 tablespoons butter
2 large yellow onions, chopped
2 large Russet or Idaho potatoes, cut into 1/2-inch cubes
2 cups light cream
2 cups milk
1 pound sea scallops
3 tablespoons grated gingerroot
salt and freshly ground pepper to taste

1. Heat the butter in a large saucepan. Add the onions and cook until soft and translucent.

2. Add the potatoes, cream, and milk, and heat gently until the potatoes are tender, about 10 to 15 minutes.

3. Add the scallops and seasonings and let simmer for 5 to 6 minutes until the scallops are cooked through and opaque. Never let the soup boil! Serve piping hot.

6 to 8 portions

LUNCHEON
MENU

Bacon and
Orange Salad
· · ·
Country Bread
· · ·
Scallop Chowder
· · ·
Strawberry Bread

CHICKEN NOODLE SOUP

No cookbook would be complete without a recipe for chicken soup. It has actually been established that chicken soup cures certain maladies, besides the fact that it tastes so good. This version uses chicken feet, rather than a whole bird, which produces a rich, clear, and very flavorful stock. If your market does not display chicken feet, ask the butcher to save them for you.

1 pound chicken feet
1 large yellow onion, chopped
3 large carrots, peeled and cut into 2-inch lengths
2 parsnips, peeled and cut into 2-inch lengths
3 large ribs celery, cut into 2-inch lengths
2 tablespoons chopped fresh parsley
1¹/₂ teaspoons dried basil
1¹/₂ teaspoons salt
freshly ground pepper to taste
10 cups water
1 pound boneless, skinless chicken breasts, cut into 3-inch long
    julienne pieces
¹/₄ pound dry vermicelli, broken in half
¹/₃ cup sliced scallions

1. Place the chicken feet, onion, carrots, parsnips, celery, parsley, basil, salt, pepper, and water in a large soup pot. Bring to a boil, reduce the heat, and simmer uncovered for 1 hour.

2. Remove the chicken feet from the soup and discard. (Up to this point may be done several hours in advance.) When ready to serve, add the chicken, vermicelli, and scallions. Boil gently until the chicken and pasta are cooked, about 3 to 4 minutes. Adjust seasonings if necessary. Serve piping hot.

6 portions

BLACK BEAN SOUP

Assertive Mexican flavors dominate this robust soup. Black beans are set against a background of assorted vegetables and seasoned with oregano, cumin, orange peel, and crushed red pepper.

2 cups dried black turtle beans, pre-soaked (see page 319,
    How to Cook Dried Beans)
1/4 cup olive oil
4 large cloves garlic, crushed
1 large Spanish onion, chopped
3 stalks celery, chopped
2 large carrots, chopped
1 leek, chopped (white part only)
1 teaspoon dried oregano
1 teaspoon ground cumin
1 teaspoon crushed red pepper flakes
2 bay leaves
1 tablespoon grated orange peel
salt and freshly ground pepper to taste
1/4 cup chopped Italian parsley
1 cup orange juice
1/2 cup dry red wine
8 cups chicken broth

MEXICAN DINNER

Black Bean Soup
· · ·
Chicken Fajitas
· · ·
Pineapple Freeze

1. Heat the olive oil in a large stockpot. Add the garlic, onion, celery, carrots, and leek. Sauté for 15 to 20 minutes over medium heat until the vegetables are tender.

2. Add the drained beans, seasonings, orange juice, wine, and chicken broth.

3. Bring to a boil, reduce the heat, and simmer uncovered for 1 1/2 hours.

4. Remove 1/3 of the soup to a food processor or blender and purée. Return the purée to the stockpot and stir well. Heat through and serve at once.

8 soup portions; 4 to 6 main-course portions

SOUTHWESTERN CORN CHOWDER

Corn kernels star in a light cream stock that's chock full of onions and sweet potato. It's seasoned with a Southwestern chili accent and garnished with cornbread croutons.

3 x 5-inch wedge of cornbread, cut into 3/4-inch cubes
2 tablespoons butter
2 medium-size yellow onions, chopped
1 large clove garlic, minced
4 slices bacon, cooked until crisp and coarsely chopped
1 large sweet potato, peeled and cut into 1/2-inch cubes
4 cups chicken broth
salt and pepper to taste
1 bay leaf
1 1/2 teaspoons chili powder
4 cups fresh or frozen corn kernels
1 cup light cream

1. Make the cornbread croutons. Preheat the oven to 400°F. Bake the cornbread cubes on a cookie sheet for 10 minutes. Turn the pieces over and bake for 5 minutes more until golden. Set aside to cool.

2. Heat the butter in a large saucepan. Add the onions and garlic and sauté over medium heat until the onions are golden.

3. Add the bacon, sweet potato, chicken broth, and seasonings.

4. Bring to a boil, lower the heat, and simmer for 10 minutes until the potatoes are tender.

5. Stir in the corn and cream and heat gently until piping hot.

6. To serve, ladle spoonfuls of hot chowder into bowls, garnishing each with cornbread croutons.

6 to 8 portions

LENTIL SOUP

Lentils are the one type of legume that do not require pre-soaking, as they cook in a relatively short amount of time as compared to other beans. This soup is a light, yet chunky, aromatic vegetable potage embellished with lentils. Unlike most lentil soups that are a thick purée, this presentation will surprise and delight you. I guarantee it will appeal to those who aren't lentil fans!

WINTER SOUP PARTY

Root Vegetable Soup
. . .
Lentil Soup
. . .
Pasta and Bean Soup
. . .
Assorted Breads
. . .
Apple Crisp

1/4 cup olive oil
1 large clove garlic, crushed
2 large yellow onions, chopped
2 large carrots, peeled and chopped
1 large stalk celery, chopped
1 bay leaf
1 teaspoon dried thyme
1/2 teaspoon dried marjoram
salt and freshly ground pepper to taste
28-ounce can Italian plum tomatoes with their juice
5 cups chicken broth
1 cup dry brown lentils

1. Heat the olive oil in a large stockpot. Add the garlic, onions, carrots, and celery and sauté over medium heat until the vegetables are soft, about 10 to 15 minutes.

2. Add the seasonings and tomatoes, breaking them into pieces. Stir in the chicken broth and lentils.

3. Bring the soup to a boil, cover, lower the heat, and simmer until lentils are tender, about 40 minutes. Serve piping hot.

6 to 8 portions

APRÉS SKI LUNCH

Mushroom-Barley
Soup
· · ·
French Rolls
· · ·
Greens with
Walnut Vinaigrette
· · ·
Cream Cheese
Brownies◆

MUSHROOM-BARLEY SOUP

This is a hearty, peasant soup, teeming with an assortment of vegetables—onions, carrot, celery, and mushrooms—and the much acclaimed grain, barley. Barley's bland flavor is complemented by the herbal seasonings and vegetable embellishment.

2 tablespoons olive oil
2 large yellow onions, chopped
2 large cloves garlic, crushed
1 large carrot, peeled and chopped
1 large stalk celery, chopped
1 pound fresh cultivated mushrooms, sliced
1/2 cup pearl barley
6 cups beef broth
1 cup dry white wine
1/4 cup chopped Italian parsley
1 bay leaf
1 1/2 teaspoons dried marjoram
salt and pepper to taste

1. Heat the olive oil in a large stockpot. Add the onions, garlic, carrot, celery, and mushrooms and sauté over medium heat stirring occasionally, until vegetables are soft, about 15 minutes.

2. Add the remaining ingredients and bring to a boil. Reduce the heat and simmer partially covered for 50 minutes.

3. Serve the soup piping hot. The soup will thicken upon standing.

6 to 8 portions

TUSCAN WHITE BEAN SOUP

Even though wholesome and hearty, this soup is light and vegetarian in theme. It's almost like a white minestrone. Chicken broth is brimming with escarole, onion, garlic, leeks, fennel, celery, parsnips, and the Great Northern bean, and fragrantly scented with a potpourri of herbs.

1 cup dry Great Northern beans, pre-soaked (see page 319,
    How to Cook Dried Beans)
1/4 cup olive oil
1 large yellow onion, chopped
3 large cloves garlic, minced
2 parsnips, peeled and chopped
2 large stalks celery, chopped
1 cup chopped fennel
1 large leek, chopped (white part only)
1 bay leaf
1 tablespoon dried basil
1 teaspoon dried thyme
1/2 teaspoon dried oregano
3 tablespoons chopped fresh parsley
1 1/2 teaspoons salt
1/2 teaspoon black pepper
7 cups chicken broth
1 head escarole, coarsely chopped
1/2 cup grated Parmesan cheese

1. Heat the olive oil in a large stockpot. Add the onion, garlic, parsnips, celery, fennel, and leek and sauté over medium heat until the onion is soft and translucent, about 10 minutes.

2. Add the beans, seasonings, and broth.

3. Bring to a boil, reduce the heat, cover, and simmer for 1 hour until the beans are tender.

4. Add the escarole, mixing well. Cover and simmer for 10 minutes more until the escarole is soft. Stir in the cheese and serve at once.

6 to 8 soup portions; 4 main-course portions

**COLD WEATHER
COMFORT FOOD**

Hunter's Salad
. . .
Sourdough Bread
. . .
Tuscan White
Bean Soup
. . .
Apple Crisp

PASTA AND BEAN SOUP

Robust, Italian peasant-style soups brim with exciting flavor. This slow-simmering, one-dish meal boasts a small pasta shell and Great Northern bean base woven with the characteristic smoky taste of baked ham, fresh vegetables, and the pine-like aroma of rosemary. Finished with pesto, this makes for memorable eating!

1 cup dry Great Northern beans or cannelli beans, pre-soaked
    (see page 319, How to Cook Dried Beans)
1/4 cup olive oil
1 large clove garlic, minced
1 large yellow onion, chopped
1 large stalk celery, chopped
2 large carrots, chopped
1/4 pound slice of baked ham, diced
1 cup chopped plum tomatoes
1 teaspoon dried rosemary
2 bay leaves
1/4 cup chopped Italian parsley
salt and pepper to taste
8 cups chicken broth
1 cup dry small pasta shells
3 tablespoons Pesto (see page 15)

1. Heat the olive oil in a large stockpot. Add the garlic, onion, celery, and carrots and sauté over medium heat until the onion is soft and translucent, about 10 to 15 minutes.

2. Add the drained beans, ham, tomatoes, seasonings, and chicken broth.

3. Bring to a boil, reduce the heat, and simmer partially covered for 1 hour until the beans are tender.

4. Add the pasta and simmer for 10 minutes more.

5. Stir in the pesto and serve at once.

6 to 8 soup portions; 4 main-course portions

SPLIT PEA SOUP

Hearty, thick, and flavorful describe this split pea soup that is distinguished by chunky vegetables and the smoky flavor of Canadian bacon. The longer the soup cooks, the thicker it gets.

¼ cup vegetable oil
1 pound Canadian bacon, cut into ½-inch cubes
1 large yellow onion, chopped
2 medium-size carrots, chopped
2 large stalks celery, chopped
2 large cloves garlic, minced
1 tablespoon grated gingerroot
½ teaspoon black pepper
8 cups chicken broth
1 pound split peas

1. Heat the oil in a large stockpot. Add the Canadian bacon, onion, carrots, celery, garlic, ginger, and pepper and sauté over medium heat until the vegetables are soft, about 10 minutes.

2. Add the chicken broth and peas. Bring to a boil, reduce the heat, and simmer partially covered for 1¼ hours. Stir well and serve piping hot.

6 portions

SOUPS ON

Split Pea Soup
. . .
Cobb Salad
. . .
Peasant Bread
. . .
Peanut Butter-
Chocolate Chip
Cookies

**SOUP 'N SALAD
SUPPER**

Succotash Chowder
. . .
Tarragon-Roasted
Chicken with
Mixed Greens
. . .
Sourdough Bread
. . .
Pound Cake
with Ice Cream

SUCCOTASH CHOWDER

Born of corn and lima beans, this light cream soup is distinguished by zucchini, cilantro, and the hickory flavor of bacon.

2 tablespoons butter
1 large yellow onion, chopped
1 medium-size zucchini, chopped
2 cups corn kernels, fresh or frozen
10-ounce package frozen baby lima beans
4 slices bacon, cooked and coarsely chopped
4 cups chicken broth
2 tablespoons finely chopped fresh cilantro
salt and freshly ground pepper to taste
1 cup light cream

1. Heat the butter in a large saucepan. Add the onion and sauté until soft and translucent.

2. Add the zucchini, corn, lima beans, bacon, chicken broth, cilantro, salt, and pepper. Bring to a boil, lower the heat, and simmer for 5 minutes.

3. Add the cream and heat through. Serve piping hot.

6 to 8 portions

HOT WEATHER COOLERS

CHILLED BLUEBERRY SOUP

Fruit soups provide a refreshing meal alternative on the dog days of summer. This one offers the taste of blueberry pie à la mode all packed into a chilled soup.

1 pint blueberries
2 cups water
1 cup sour cream
1/4 cup packed light brown sugar
1/4 cup Port wine
2 tablespoons lemon juice
1/2 teaspoon vanilla
pinch cinnamon

1. Bring the berries and water to a boil in a saucepan and simmer for 3 minutes. Remove from the heat and let cool. Purée the mixture in batches in a blender or food processor.

2. In a large bowl, combine the sour cream and brown sugar. Add the wine, lemon juice, vanilla, and cinnamon and mix well. Stir in the blueberry purée. Cover and refrigerate until well chilled.

3. To serve, ladle the chilled soup into bowls.

4 to 6 portions

MANGO SOUP

A creamy mango purée is enhanced by lime juice, cilantro, chives, and pineapple juice, lending a taste of the tropics that's both comforting and delectable.

2 ripe mangoes, peeled and cut into chunks
3 tablespoons fresh lime juice
2 tablespoons honey
1/2 cup sour cream
1 cup unsweetened pineapple juice
1 tablespoon chopped fresh cilantro
2 tablespoons snipped chives
thin slices of lime for garnish

1. Place the mangoes, lime juice, and honey in the bowl of a food processor and purée.

2. Remove the purée to a soup tureen. Stir in the sour cream, mixing until well blended.

3. Add the pineapple juice, cilantro, and chives. Cover and chill until serving time.

4. To serve, stir the soup and ladle into bowls. Garnish each with a slice of lime.

4 portions

SUMMER DINNER

Mango Soup
. . .
Grilled Trout
. . .
Pasta with
Grilled Vegetables◆
. . .
Chocolate Angel
Food Cake with
Assorted Berries

TROPICAL ISLAND DINNER

Piña Colada Soup
. . .
Shrimp Margarita
. . .
Caribbean
Melon Salad
. . .
Grilled Corn
on the Cob
. . .
Assorted Sherbets

PIÑA COLADA SOUP

Enjoy a taste of the Islands with the tropical flavors of pineapple, coconut, and rum, all blended into this thick, creamy soup.

4 cups fresh pineapple chunks
1/2 cup sweetened, shredded coconut
1/2 cup sugar
1/2 cup sour cream
1/2 cup light rum
1 1/2 cups unsweetened pineapple juice

1. Put the pineapple, coconut, and sugar into the bowl of a food processor and purée.

2. Add the sour cream, rum, and pineapple juice and process until blended.

3. Transfer the soup to a bowl, cover, and chill until serving time.

4. When ready to serve, stir the soup, and ladle into bowls.

6 portions

RHUBARB SOUP

Savor the brilliance of spring with the quintessential spring perennial, rhubarb. The pink, sweet, tart, and fruity rhubarb purée is
scented with orange essence and a hint of nutmeg. To extend your
enjoyment of this exceptional plant, freeze 1-inch chunks of rhubarb
in containers for use in the off-season.

6 cups rhubarb, cut into 1-inch chunks
2¹/₂ cups water
³/₄ cup sugar
¹/₃ cup Triple Sec
1 cup orange juice
1 tablespoon finely grated orange peel
¹/₂ teaspoon nutmeg

1. Combine the rhubarb, water, and sugar in a large saucepan.
Bring to a boil, reduce the heat, and simmer uncovered until tender,
about 30 minutes. Stir occasionally.

2. Transfer the soup to a bowl, and mash any large pieces. Add the
remaining ingredients and stir well.

3. Cover and refrigerate until ready to serve.

4. To serve, ladle the well-chilled soup into bowls.

6 portions

**LIGHT
LUNCHEON**

Rhubarb Soup
. . .
Mixed Greens with
Chèvre Vinaigrette
. . .
French Bread
. . .
Poppy Seed
Butter Cookies

ICED STRAWBERRY SOUP

This delightful, cold soup struts a strawberries and cream theme. It makes an elegant first course for a summer dinner party, and a light, tasty, luncheon repast.

1 quart strawberries, hulled and puréed
1 cup sour cream
¼ cup light brown sugar
½ cup dry white wine
1 cup cranberry juice

1. In a large bowl, combine the strawberries and sour cream, stirring until evenly blended.

2. Add the sugar, white wine, and juice, and mix well.

3. Cover and chill until serving time. (This may be made 24 hours in advance, allowing the flavors to mellow.)

4. To serve, ladle the well-chilled soup into bowls and present.

4 to 6 portions

BRUNCH

Iced Strawberry Soup
· · ·
Lobster and
Tortellini Salad
· · ·
Mixed Green Salad◆
· · ·
French and
Sourdough Breads
· · ·
World's Best Sour
Cream Coffeecake

STRAWBERRY-BANANA DAIQUIRI SOUP

Born from the classic drink, this soup is light and ever so refreshing on a hot day. Strawberries, bananas, lime, and rum are all whirled together in the blender for a taste of the tropics.

1 pint strawberries, hulled
1 large banana, peeled
1/2 cup fresh lime juice
1 teaspoon finely grated lime zest
1/2 cup sugar
1/2 cup cold water
1/4 cup light rum

Garnishes:
1/2 cup sliced strawberries
1/2 cup sliced banana

1. Place the berries, banana, and lime juice in the bowl of a food processor and purée.

2. Add the lime zest, sugar, water, and rum. Pulse to blend. Remove the soup to a tureen.

3. Stir in the sliced fruit garnish. Cover and chill the soup until serving time.

4. To serve, ladle the well-chilled soup into bowls and present.

4 appetizer portions; 2 to 3 luncheon portions

SUMMER LUNCHEON

Strawberry-Banana
Daiquiri Soup
. . .
Mussels, Tomatoes,
and Arugula
. . .
Assorted Rolls
. . .
Honeydew Freeze

BEET GAZPACHO

This thick purée addresses the best of both worlds. It's a subtle melding of borscht and gazpacho, resulting in a blast of flavor!

4 medium-size beets, boiled 35 to 40 minutes until tender, and peeled
2 cups reserved beet cooking liquid
1 medium-size red pepper
1 large pickling cucumber
1/2 medium-size red onion
3 large cloves garlic, crushed
1 tablespoon prepared red horseradish
3 tablespoons balsamic vinegar
2 tablespoons olive oil
salt and freshly ground pepper to taste

Garnishes:
1 large pickling cucumber, diced
1/2 medium-size red onion, diced
sour cream

1. Put all of the ingredients in the bowl of a food processor and purée. Transfer the soup to a tureen.

2. Cover and refrigerate for at least 3 to 4 hours, or even overnight, allowing the flavors to blend.

3. When ready to serve, ladle into individual bowls. Garnish each portion with a spoonful of cucumber, onion, and a dollop of sour cream.

4 to 6 portions

CURRIED CREAM OF BROCCOLI SOUP

The fresh flavor of broccoli is enhanced by curry and garlic in this thick and creamy puréed soup. Aside from its sound nutritional value, broccoli is available year-round, making this a soup for all occasions.

2 tablespoons butter
4 large cloves garlic, minced
1 small Spanish onion, coarsely chopped
1 pound broccoli, heavy ends trimmed and stalks peeled
3 cups chicken broth
salt and pepper to taste
1 tablespoon lemon juice
1¹/₂ teaspoons curry powder
¹/₂ teaspoon Worcestershire sauce
1 cup sour cream

1. Heat the butter in a large saucepan. Add the garlic and onion and sauté over low heat until the onion is soft and translucent, about 10 minutes.

2. Coarsely chop the broccoli. Add the broccoli, chicken broth, salt, pepper, and lemon juice to the saucepan. Bring to a boil, cover, and simmer for 10 to 15 minutes until the broccoli is very tender. Remove from the heat and let cool.

3. Place the soup in batches in the bowl of a food processor and purée until smooth. Transfer the purée to a large bowl.

4. Stir in the curry powder, Worcestershire, and sour cream. Cover and refrigerate until chilled, at least 4 hours. Serve cold.

6 portions

LUNCHEON FARE

Cheddar-Chutney
Wonton Cups
. . .
Curried Cream of
Broccoli Soup
. . .
Marinated Cherry
Tomatoes
. . .
Assorted Cookies

GREEN GAZPACHO

Unlike its tomato-based counterpart that is of Spanish origin, this version boasts a thick purée of dill-scented green garden vegetables and grapes. Bruschetta spread with chèvre provide a magical garnish.

**HOT WEATHER
COOLER**

Green Gazpacho
. . .
Grilled Swordfish
. . .
Bulgar Pilaf
. . .
Mango and Red
Pepper Salad
. . .
Pear Ice

10 ounces cooked spinach
2 medium-size pickling cucumbers
1 large green pepper
1 cup green grapes
1/2 cup chopped scallions
2 tablespoons white wine vinegar
3 tablespoons chopped fresh parsley
1 teaspoon dried dill
salt to taste
1/4 teaspoon pepper
3 cups chicken broth
1 cup sour cream

Garnish:
toasted French bread slices spread with chèvre

1. Put the spinach, cucumbers, green pepper, grapes, scallions, vinegar, parsley, dill, salt, pepper, and 1 cup chicken broth in the bowl of a food processor and purée.

2. Transfer the soup to a tureen, and add the remaining 2 cups broth and sour cream. Chill for at least 1 to 2 hours and as much as overnight, allowing the flavors to blend.

3. When ready to serve, stir the soup, and ladle it into bowls. Garnish each portion with a chèvre crouton.

6 portions

MEXICAN-STYLE GAZPACHO

South-of-the-Border ingredients—black beans, corn, tomatoes, avocado, and red onion—come together in this upbeat, chunky, cold soup that's spiked with cilantro.

15-ounce can black beans, rinsed and drained
1²/₃ cups corn kernels (fresh or frozen), blanched
2 large tomatoes, diced
1 large ripe avocado, peeled, pitted, and diced
1 small red onion, diced
¹/₄ cup finely chopped fresh cilantro
1 large clove garlic, crushed
4 to 5 drops Tabasco sauce
salt to taste
¹/₄ teaspoon black pepper
2 tablespoons red wine vinegar
2 tablespoons olive oil
2 cups beef broth
2¹/₂ cups tomato juice

1. Place all of the ingredients in a large soup tureen and mix well. Cover and chill for several hours or overnight, so that the flavors have a chance to mellow.

2. When ready to serve, stir the soup and present chilled.

6 to 8 portions

MEXICAN MEDLEY

Chili-Cheese Puffs
· · ·
Mexican-Style Gazpacho
· · ·
Burgers with Jen's Salsa
· · ·
Grilled Bread
· · ·
Watermelon

**FOURTH OF JULY
CELEBRATION**

Sweet Potato
Vichyssoise
. . .
Greens with
Walnut Vinaigrette
. . .
Herb-Roasted Salmon
and Linguine with
Tomato-Corn Relish
. . .
Deep-Dish Blueberry-
Nectarine Pie

SWEET POTATO VICHYSSOISE

The sweet potato gives a stellar performance in this rendition of the classic cold potato-leek potage. It's smooth, thick, creamy, and very satisfying.

4 tablespoons butter
4 cups sliced leeks (white part only)
2 pounds sweet potatoes, peeled and coarsely chopped
4 cups chicken broth
salt and pepper to taste
1/2 cup light cream
2 tablespoons thinly sliced scallions for garnish

1. Melt the butter in a large saucepan. Add the leeks and sauté until soft and translucent, stirring occasionally.

2. Add the potatoes, broth, salt, and pepper. Bring to a boil, reduce the heat, and simmer uncovered until the potatoes are tender, about 10 to 15 minutes. Let cool.

3. When cooled, purée the soup in batches in a food processor.

4. Remove the purée to a soup tureen and add the cream.

5. Refrigerate several hours, or as much as overnight.

6. Serve chilled or at room temperature, garnished with the sliced scallions.

6 to 8 soup portions

CREAM OF TOMATO SOUP

Simple in preparation, yet elegant in presentation, this cold, creamy tomato-base soup is accented with dill. It's low in calories and refreshingly delicious.

   1 quart tomato juice
   1/2 cup sour cream or yogurt
   1 clove garlic, crushed
   1 teaspoon dried dill
   1/4 cup thinly sliced scallions
   salt and freshly ground pepper to taste

   1. In a large bowl, combine all of the ingredients, stirring until evenly blended.

   2. Cover and refrigerate for 1 to 2 hours, allowing the flavors to mellow.

   3. To serve, ladle the chilled soup into bowls.

4 portions

**DINNER PARTY
FOR 6**

Cream of
Tomato Soup
. . .
Grilled Salmon
. . .
Mixed Greens with
Balsamic Vinaigrette◆
. . .
Pasta with Peas, Ham,
and Parmesan
. . .
Fruit Tart

SMOKED SALMON SOUP

The buttermilk base provides an elusive flavor to this summertime soup. It's teeming with smoked salmon and chopped vegetables, and is delicately seasoned with dill. This is actually better if prepared ahead of time, allowing the flavors to mellow.

SUMMER LUNCH

Smoked Salmon Soup

· · ·

Spice Bread with
Cream Cheese

· · ·

Watermelon,
Cantaloupe, and
Honeydew Slices

1 quart buttermilk
1 cup sour cream
1/2 pound sliced smoked salmon, cut into 1/2-inch wide strips
1/4 cup thinly sliced scallions
1 large pickling cucumber, peeled and chopped
2 large plum tomatoes, diced
1/2 cup sliced black olives
1/4 cup chopped fresh dill
1 tablespoon prepared white horseradish
salt and freshly ground pepper to taste

1. Combine all of the ingredients in a soup tureen and mix well.

2. Cover and refrigerate for 6 to 8 hours (and as much as overnight).

3. To serve, ladle the well-chilled soup into bowls.

6 appetizer portions; 4 main-course portions

PASTA FARE

Pasta has become the object of much attention in American cuisine. In the past decade, we have seen a culinary awareness and appreciation for pasta. It has risen from being a humble staple to unusual gastronomic heights.

Young and old alike are hooked on this adaptable foodstuff we have come to love. Pasta is served up daily in homes and restaurants across the country, being economical, extremely versatile, easy to prepare, nutritious, and above all, delicious. It can be served with a myriad of toppings from simple olive oil and butter with grated cheese to elaborate sauces rich with seafood and vegetables.

Pasta cuisine is here to stay. It's one of the world's most favored foods, providing satisfying, comforting fare. Make every pasta meal an exciting culinary adventure.

Note—Unless specified, the pasta called for in a recipe is dried. With regard to servings, the portion size refers to a side accompaniment.

APRICOT NOODLE PUDDING

Noodle pudding is real comfort food. This sweet baked noodle custard is laced with apricot preserves and Amaretto and crowned with cornflakes. The combination of the apricot and almond flavoring is absolutely divine, making this an all occasion dish— for brunch, luncheon, side dish, buffet, appetizer, or dessert.

1 pound wide egg noodles
1 pound cottage cheese
1 cup sour cream
4 eggs, beaten
¹/₃ cup sugar
¹/₂ cup butter, melted
³/₄ cup apricot preserves
¹/₄ cup Amaretto
¹/₂ teaspoon salt
1 cup coarsely crushed cornflakes

1. Preheat the oven to 350°F. Grease a 9 x 13-inch pan.

2. Cook the noodles for 5 minutes and drain well.

3. In a large mixing bowl, combine the cottage cheese, sour cream, eggs, sugar, butter, apricot preserves, Amaretto, and salt. Stir until well mixed.

4. Add the noodles and mix until evenly blended. Turn the pudding into the prepared pan.

5. Sprinkle the top with the crushed cornflakes. (Up to this point may be prepared 6 to 8 hours in advance and refrigerated; return to room temperature before baking.)

6. Bake for 45 minutes until golden. Cut into squares and serve hot or at room temperature.

15 or more portions

PASTA FONTINA

This new-wave rendition of the classic macaroni and cheese is sure to be a crowd pleaser. Fontina cheese lends a smooth, buttery taste to the pasta that's punctuated with roasted garlic and sautéed mushrooms.

3 tablespoons butter
1 pound fresh cultivated mushrooms, cut in half
12 ounces wide egg noodles
1 large head garlic, roasted (see page 37, How to Roast Garlic)
3/4 cup light cream
3/4 pound fontina cheese, grated
salt and pepper to taste

1. Preheat the oven to 350°F. Grease a 2½ to 3-quart casserole dish.

2. Heat the butter in a large skillet. When hot, add the mushrooms and sauté them over medium heat until browned. Set aside.

3. Cook the pasta according to the package directions and drain well.

4. While the pasta is cooking, prepare the cheese sauce. Remove the garlic pulp from the skin. In a small saucepan, combine the garlic pulp, cream, cheese, salt, and pepper, Heat over low until the cheese melts, stirring occasionally. Remove from the heat.

5. Combine the freshly cooked noodles, mushrooms, and cheese sauce in a large bowl and mix well. Turn the mixture into the prepared dish. (Up to this point may be done in advance and refrigerated; return to room temperature before proceeding.)

6. Bake for 30 minutes. Serve piping hot.

8 or more side portions; 4 to 6 main-course portions

OLD-FASHIONED GOODNESS

Tomato Bisque◆
. . .
Pasta Fontina
. . .
Green Salad
. . .
Butterscotch Meringues

ITALIAN NOODLE BAKE

ITALIAN DINNER PARTY

Shredded Greens with
Strawberry Vinaigrette
. . .
Chicken Rustica
. . .
Slow-Roasted
Tomatoes
. . .
Italian Noodle Bake
. . .
Lemon Ice◆
. . .
Assorted Cookies

This recipe is a fusion of flavors—a cross between noodle pudding and spinach quiche. The ricotta-base pudding is dotted with raisins and pine nuts and infused with Parmesan cheese, lending an Italian accent. This dish is sure to delight you and makes wonderful buffet food.

12 ounces wide egg noodles
1 pound ricotta cheese
6 eggs, beaten
3 cups milk
1/4 cup butter, melted and cooled
2/3 cup Parmesan cheese
10-ounce package frozen, chopped spinach, thawed and
  squeezed of its liquid
1/2 cup raisins
1/4 cup pine nuts, toasted
salt and pepper to taste

1. Preheat the oven to 375°F. Grease a 9 x 13-inch pan.

2. Cook the noodles according to the package directions and drain well.

3. While the noodles are cooking, prepare the custard. In a large mixing bowl, combine the ricotta cheese, eggs, milk, butter, Parmesan, spinach, raisins, pine nuts, salt, and pepper. Stir until well mixed. (Up to this point may be prepared 4 to 6 hours in advance and refrigerated; return to room temperature before baking.)

4. Add the freshly cooked noodles and mix well. Turn the mixture into the prepared pan. Bake for 40 minutes. Serve hot.

12 portions

PUMPKIN LASAGNE

Lasagne continues to be a favorite of most. This recipe originated in the northern region of Italy, and showcases a vegetarian, triple cheese-pumpkin filling perfumed with nutmeg, that's rich, flavorful, and satisfying. Butternut squash purée may be substituted for the pumpkin.

15-ounce can pumpkin purée
1 pound ricotta cheese
1¹/2 cup Parmesan cheese
2 eggs, beaten
1 teaspoon nutmeg
¹/2 teaspoon ginger
salt and pepper to taste
1 pound lasagne noodles
3 cups grated mozzarella cheese
2 tablespoons butter, melted

1. Preheat the oven to 350°F. Grease a 9 x 13-inch baking dish.

2. Combine the pumpkin, ricotta cheese, 1 cup Parmesan cheese, eggs, nutmeg, ginger, salt, and pepper in a large mixing bowl.

3. Cook the lasagne noodles according to the package directions and drain well.

4. Arrange 2 layers of lasagne noodles in the bottom of the prepared pan. Spread half of the pumpkin filling over the lasagne. Sprinkle with 1 cup mozzarella. Repeat the layers of noodles, filling, and cheese. Top with the remaining noodles.

5. Brush the top with the melted butter and sprinkle with the remaining 1/2 cup Parmesan and 1 cup mozzarella.

6. Bake for 30 to 35 minutes until lightly golden. Serve at once.

8 portions

ITALIAN FARE

Pita with Olivada
· · ·
Pumpkin Lasagne
· · ·
Autumn Salad
· · ·
Chocolate-Almond
Biscotti

BASQUE-STYLE PASTA AND EGGS

The cuisine of the Basque country of Spain favors spicy mixtures of onions, peppers, and olive oil. This pasta dish keys in on this theme, featuring a spinach fettuccine base and a sautéed onion and roasted pepper-scrambled egg topping.

12 ounces fresh spinach fettuccine
1/4 cup olive oil
1 large clove garlic, crushed
1 large yellow onion, chopped
2 large red peppers, roasted and sliced into julienne strips
1 large green pepper, roasted and sliced into julienne strips
2 ripe plum tomatoes, chopped
salt and freshly ground pepper to taste
6 eggs, beaten
1/2 cup shaved Parmesan cheese

1. Cook the pasta according to the package directions and drain well. Transfer to a large serving bowl or platter.

2. While the fettuccine is cooking, prepare the topping. Heat the olive oil in a large skillet. Add the garlic and onion and sauté over medium heat until the onion is golden.

3. Add the roasted peppers and tomatoes. Season with salt and pepper, and simmer for 10 minutes.

4. Add the eggs and cook, stirring constantly until the eggs are set, for about 1 minute. Remove from the heat and add to the freshly cooked pasta. Sprinkle with the Parmesan cheese, mix well, and serve.

3 to 4 main-course portions

PASTA MARINARA

Long strands of pasta luxuriate in this simple, yet lush tomato sauce, redolent with garlic and basil and finished with a splash of vodka. For a truly sumptuous meal, add cooked lobster meat to the sauce just before serving!

1/4 cup extra-virgin olive oil
1 large clove garlic, minced
1/3 cup diced shallots
35-ounce can Italian plum tomatoes, coarsely crushed with their juice
1/4 cup chopped fresh basil
1/4 cup chopped fresh parsley
salt and freshly ground pepper to taste
1/2 cup vodka
1 pound spaghetti

1. Heat the olive oil in a large saucepan. Add the garlic and shallots and cook until lightly golden.

2. Add the tomatoes, basil, parsley, salt, pepper, and vodka.

3. Bring to a boil, reduce the heat, and simmer for 30 minutes.

4. While the sauce is cooking, prepare the pasta according to the package directions. Drain well.

5. Pour the sauce over the freshly cooked pasta, toss well, and serve.

6 to 8 side portions; 3 to 4 main-course portions

ITALIAN-INSPIRED
MENU

Pasta Marinara
· · ·
Antipasto◆
· · ·
Onion Crostini
· · ·
Cannoli

HERBED LINGUINE

Teeming with a potpourri of fresh herbs and rippled with goat cheese, this pasta dish is heavenly.

6 ounces goat cheese
1 large clove garlic, crushed
1/3 cup snipped chives
1 cup coarsely chopped Italian parsley
1 teaspoon dried thyme
1 teaspoon dried tarragon
1 teaspoon dried savory
1/2 teaspoon dried sage
salt to taste
1/4 teaspoon black pepper
2 tablespoons balsamic vinegar
1/3 cup virgin olive oil
9 ounces fresh linguine

1. In a small bowl, combine the goat cheese, garlic, chives, parsley, thyme, tarragon, savory, sage, salt, pepper, vinegar, and olive oil and mix well.

2. Cook the linguine according to the package directions and drain well. Transfer the pasta to a serving bowl.

3. Mix the sauce into the freshly cooked pasta, stirring until evenly blended. Serve at once.

4 side portions; 2 to 3 main-course portions

PASTA WITH BLACK OLIVE PESTO

This recipe gives new definition to pesto. It's fragrant with basil and enriched with black olives, capers, and sun-dried tomatoes, adding a Mediterranean touch. Any extra pesto can be used atop bruschetta, as a sauce for grilled tuna, or as a garnish for baked potatoes.

1 cup pitted ripe black olives
½ cup sun-dried tomatoes, plumped in hot water for 15 seconds
   and drained
1 cup packed fresh basil
½ cup pine nuts, toasted
2 large cloves garlic
1 tablespoon capers
black pepper to taste
1 cup virgin olive oil
1 pound linguine

ITALIAN FEST

Tomatoes and
Pine Nuts
. . .
Chicken Piccata
. . .
Spinach Romano
. . .
Pasta with Black
Olive Pesto
. . .
Chocolate Chip-
Ricotta Cheesecake

1. Place the olives, sun-dried tomatoes, basil, pine nuts, garlic, capers, and black pepper in the bowl of a food processor. Process until the mixture is a paste.

2. With the motor running, add the olive oil in a slow, steady stream until all the oil is incorporated. Transfer the pesto to a bowl. (This may be prepared up to 1 week in advance and refrigerated until needed. Return to room temperature before using.)

3. Cook the pasta according to the package directions and drain well. Toss the freshly cooked pasta with 1½ cups pesto and present warm or at room temperature.

2 cups of pesto; 4 to 6 portions

LINGUINE WITH RED PEPPER PESTO

A pesto of different sorts adorns strands of linguine. A thick purée of roasted red peppers, pine nuts, and garlic is highlighted by cayenne pepper, chives, and the essence of orange peel for added flavor.

2 large red peppers, roasted
1/4 cup pine nuts, toasted
1 large or 2 small cloves garlic
3 tablespoons snipped chives
2 teaspoons finely grated orange peel
1/4 teaspoon cayenne pepper
salt and freshly ground pepper to taste
3/4 cup extra-virgin olive oil
1 pound linguine

1. Place the peppers, pine nuts, garlic, chives, orange peel, cayenne, salt, and pepper in the bowl of a food processor and purée.

2. With the motor running, add the olive oil in a slow, steady stream until it is completely incorporated. (The pesto may be refrigerated at this point for 2 to 3 days; return to room temperature to use.)

3. Cook the linguine according to the package directions and drain well. Spoon the pesto over the freshly cooked pasta and toss well. Serve warm or at room temperature.

1³/₄ to 2 cups of pesto; 6 to 8 portions

FARFALLE WITH SUN-DRIED TOMATO PESTO

I have updated the pesto theme with the concentrated flavor of sun-dried tomatoes. Try it over grilled bread, shrimp, or steak. It also makes a marvelous filling for stuffed burgers or chicken breasts.

1 cup well-packed sun-dried tomatoes, plumped in hot water
for 15 seconds and drained
1 cup packed fresh basil
2 large cloves garlic
½ cup pine nuts, toasted
salt and pepper to taste
¾ cup virgin olive oil
1 pound farfalle (bow-tie pasta)

1. Put the sun-dried tomatoes, basil, garlic, ¼ cup pine nuts, salt, and pepper in the bowl of a food processor and process until the mixture is a paste.

2. With the motor running, add the olive oil in a slow, steady stream until all the oil is incorporated. Transfer the pesto to a bowl. (The pesto may be made up to 1 week in advance and refrigerated until needed; return to room temperature before using.)

3. Cook the pasta according to the package directions and drain well. Cover the pasta with 1 cup pesto, sprinkle with the remaining ¼ cup pine nuts, and mix well. Serve warm or at room temperature.

1¼ cups of pesto; enough sauce to cover 1¼ pounds pasta; 6 to 8 portions

DINNER FARE

Salad Lucia
. . .
Veal Chops Tonnato
. . .
Farfalle with Sun-Dried Tomato Pesto
. . .
Lemon Ice◆

PASTA WITH GREEN OLIVE TAPENADE

Piquant flavors dominate this uncooked pasta sauce. The tapenade is lush with chopped green olives, capers, and onion, accented with anchovy paste, and tempered by a basil purée.

1/2 cup packed fresh basil
1/2 cup virgin olive oil
1/2 cup coarsely chopped pimento-stuffed green olives
1/2 cup finely chopped red onion
3 tablespoons capers, rinsed and drained
2 large cloves garlic, minced
1 teaspoon anchovy paste
freshly ground black pepper to taste
8 ounces ziti

1. Put the basil and olive oil in the bowl of a food processor and purée. Transfer the purée to a small bowl.

2. Add the olives, onion, capers, garlic, anchovy paste, and pepper and mix well. (Up to this point may be prepared 3 to 4 days in advance and stored in the refrigerator until needed; return to room temperature before using.)

3. Cook the pasta according to the package directions and drain well. Pour the olive sauce over the pasta and toss until evenly mixed. Serve warm or at room temperature.

3 to 4 portions

PASTA GREMOLATA

Parsley, lemon zest, garlic, ground walnuts, and olive oil all come together harmoniously in this delicate, nutty, pesto-like sauce.

9 ounces fresh linguine
1 large clove garlic, minced
1 tablespoon finely grated lemon zest
2/3 cup finely chopped fresh parsley
1/3 cup ground walnuts
1/2 to 2/3 cup extra-virgin olive oil
salt and pepper to taste

1. Cook the pasta according to the package directions and drain well.

2. While the pasta is cooking, prepare the sauce. In a small bowl, mix the garlic, lemon zest, parsley, walnuts, olive oil, salt, and pepper.

3. Pour the sauce over the freshly cooked pasta and toss well. Serve warm or at room temperature.

4 to 6 side portions; 2 to 3 main-course portions

ITALIAN MENU

Chicken Portobello
. . .
Salad Lucia
. . .
Pasta Gremolata
. . .
Chocolate-Almond
Biscotti

PASTA WITH BLACK BEAN-CORN SALSA

Corkscrew shaped pasta is daubed with charred corn kernels, roasted red and yellow peppers, and black beans and dressed in a light, balsamic vinaigrette. The subtle flavors make for addictive eating.

> 3 to 4 ears of corn (enough to yield 2 cups kernels), brushed with
> 2 tablespoons olive oil
> 15-ounce can black beans, rinsed and drained
> 1 large red pepper, roasted, and cut into 1/4-inch pieces
> 1 large yellow pepper, roasted, and cut into 1/4-inch pieces
> 1 pound rotini, freshly cooked
> 1 large clove garlic, crushed
> 3 tablespoons balsamic vinegar
> 3/4 cup extra-virgin olive oil
> salt and freshly ground pepper to taste

1. Broil the ears of corn, 4 inches from the heat source, until lightly browned, about 5 minutes per side. Let cool and then remove the kernels from the cob.

2. In a large bowl, combine the corn, black beans, roasted peppers, and pasta.

3. In a separate small bowl, whisk together the garlic, vinegar, oil, salt, and pepper. Pour the vinaigrette over the pasta and toss well until evenly coated. Serve at room temperature.

8 or more portions

PASTA MARINO

This dish was conceived for pizza lovers. The composition is distinguished by pizza ingredients—sautéed onion, mushrooms, green pepper, and tomatoes with a dusting of Parmesan cheese—atop strands of fettuccine.

10 ounces fresh fettuccine
¼ cup olive oil
2 tablespoons butter
1 medium-size clove garlic, smashed
12 ounces fresh cultivated mushrooms, thinly sliced
1 large Spanish onion, thinly sliced
1 large green pepper, thinly sliced
salt and pepper to taste
3 large, ripe plum tomatoes, coarsely chopped
¼ cup freshly grated Parmesan cheese

1. Cook the pasta according to the package directions and drain well. Transfer to a large serving bowl.

2. While the pasta is cooking, prepare the topping. Heat the olive oil and butter in a large skillet. Add the garlic, mushrooms, onion, green pepper, salt, and pepper. Sauté over medium-high heat until the vegetables are lightly golden.

3. Add the tomatoes and cook for 3 to 4 minutes more, stirring occasionally.

4. Spoon the sautéed vegetables over the freshly cooked pasta and sprinkle with the Parmesan. Toss well and serve.

4 to 6 portions

MID-WEEK DINNER

Pasta Marino
. . .
Salad Lucia
. . .
Garlic Bread
. . .
Pot de Crème♦

LINGUINE WITH RED ONION RELISH

Slow-cooked, caramelized onions, sweet raisins, aromatic rosemary, and heady goat cheese compose a complex contrast of textures and flavors for this pasta topping. Don't be alarmed by the large amount of onions, as they cook down. Also try the relish as a topping for grilled burgers, roasted pork, or chicken.

1/2 cup olive oil
2 pounds red onions, thinly sliced
2 tablespoons sugar
2 teaspoons dried rosemary
1/2 cup raisins
salt and pepper to taste
1 pound linguine
5 to 6 ounces goat cheese, crumbled

1. Heat the olive oil in a large skillet. Add the onions and sauté over medium-low heat until soft, about 10 minutes.

2. Add the sugar, rosemary, and raisins. Season with salt and pepper and mix well. Sauté over medium heat until the onions are lightly browned and caramelized, about 45 minutes, stirring occasionally. (This can be made ahead and refrigerated for up to 2 days; return to room temperature before proceeding.)

3. Cook the pasta according to the package directions and drain well. Transfer the linguine to a large serving bowl.

4. Top the freshly cooked pasta with the onion relish and garnish with the goat cheese. Toss well and serve warm or at room temperature.

5 to 6 main-course portions

PASTA AND BLUE CHEESE

Blue cheese lovers will bask in the glory of this dish. The noble, characteristic tang of blue cheese is coupled with toasted walnuts, adding pizzazz to this creamy, uncooked pasta topping.

12 ounces medium-size pasta shells
3 ounces blue cheese, crumbled
³/4 cup sour cream
2 tablespoons butter, melted
1 small clove garlic, minced
salt and freshly ground pepper to taste
¹/3 cup walnuts, toasted and coarsely chopped

1. Cook the pasta according to the package directions and drain well.

2. While the pasta is cooking, prepare the sauce. In a small bowl, combine the blue cheese, sour cream, butter, garlic, salt, pepper, and walnuts and mix well.

3. Pour the blue cheese dressing over the freshly cooked pasta and serve.

6 side portions; 3 main-course portions

**EASY SUMMER
MENU**

Grilled Steaks
. . .
Pasta and Blue Cheese
. . .
Sliced Garden
Tomatoes
. . .
Assorted Berries and
Ice Cream

FEZ'S PASTA WITH FRESH TOMATO SAUCE

Tubes of pasta are dressed in a fresh cherry tomato sauce that is dominated by Greek flavors—black olives, feta cheese, mint, lemon juice, and olive oil.

1 pound ziti
3 cups quartered cherry tomatoes
6 ounces feta cheese, crumbled
1 cup sliced ripe black olives
1/2 cup thinly sliced scallions
1 tablespoon dried mint
salt and freshly ground pepper to taste
2 tablespoons lemon juice
1/2 cup extra-virgin olive oil

1. Cook the pasta according to the package directions and drain well. Transfer the ziti to a large serving bowl.

2. While the pasta is cooking, prepare the sauce. In a medium-size bowl, combine the tomatoes, feta, black olives, scallions, mint, salt, pepper, lemon juice, and olive oil and mix well. (This may be made in advance and refrigerated until needed; return to room temperature before proceeding.)

3. Pour the sauce over the freshly cooked pasta and toss well. Serve warm or at room temperature.

6 to 8 side portions

PASTA WITH PEAS, HAM, AND PARMESAN

Classically called hay and straw, this pasta combination has a blast of flavor from hickory-smoked ham, Parmesan cheese, peas, and a hint of nutmeg. It's a real crowd pleaser.

1 pound spaghetti
10 ounces fresh or frozen peas, steamed 1 minute
1/4 pound hickory-smoked ham, sliced 1/8-inch thick,
*   cut into 1/2-inch pieces*
6 tablespoons butter, melted
freshly ground pepper to taste
generous pinch of nutmeg
1/2 cup freshly grated Parmesan cheese

1. Cook the pasta according to the package directions and drain well.

2. While the pasta is cooking, prepare the topping. In a small bowl, combine the peas, ham, butter, pepper, and nutmeg.

3. Pour the sauce over the freshly cooked pasta. Sprinkle with the Parmesan and toss well. Serve at once.

6 to 8 portions

**DINNER PARTY
FOR 6**

Cream of
Tomato Soup
. . .
Grilled Salmon
. . .
Mixed Greens with
Balsamic Vinaigrette◆
. . .
Pasta with Peas, Ham,
and Parmesan
. . .
Fruit Tart

PASTA PORTOBELLO

The earthy and meaty, giant portobello mushrooms star in this pasta presentation. Roasted to a turn, they are hearty, rich, and savory.

1 pound portobello mushrooms, stems removed and saved
olive oil
salt and pepper to taste
12 ounces rotini
2 ripe plum tomatoes, diced
1/4 cup diced red onion
1/3 cup coarsely chopped Italian parsley
1 clove garlic, minced
3 tablespoons balsamic vinegar
1/2 cup virgin olive oil

1. Preheat the oven to 400°F. Grease a large roasting pan with olive oil.

2. Brush the mushrooms and their stems with olive oil. Season with salt and pepper. Roast the mushrooms for 20 minutes. Cut the giant fungi into 1-inch chunks.

3. Cook the pasta according to the package directions and drain well. Transfer to a large serving bowl.

4. While the pasta is cooking, prepare the topping. In a medium-size mixing bowl, combine the roasted portobellos, plum tomatoes, red onion, parsley, garlic, vinegar, and 1/2 cup olive oil. Season with salt and pepper.

5. Pour the mushroom sauce over the freshly cooked pasta and toss well. Serve warm or at room temperature. (This may be made in advance and refrigerated until needed; return to room temperature before serving.)

8 side portions; 4 main-course portions

SPAGHETTI WITH SPINACH, BACON, AND PINE NUTS

Bacon has a marvelous affinity for spinach. Sautéed spinach and bacon team up for a burst of savory flavor, accented by toasted pine nuts in this soul-soothing pasta dish.

> *12 ounces spaghetti*
> *6 tablespoons olive oil*
> *2 large cloves garlic, minced*
> *10 ounces fresh spinach, heavy stems removed and coarsely chopped*
> *salt and pepper to taste*
> *1/4 pound bacon, cooked until crisp and coarsely chopped*
> *1/4 cup pine nuts, toasted*

1. Cook the pasta according to the package directions and drain well. Transfer to a large serving bowl.

2. While the pasta is cooking, prepare the sauce. Heat the olive oil in a large skillet. Add the garlic and cook for 1 minute.

3. Add the spinach and season with salt and pepper. Cover and cook over medium heat for 3 minutes.

4. Uncover, add the bacon and pine nuts, and stir well. Cook for 1 minute more. Pour the sauce over the freshly cooked pasta, toss well, and serve.

6 side portions; 4 main-course portions

DINNER MENU

Grilled Swordfish
. . .
Spaghetti with
Spinach, Bacon,
and Pine Nuts
. . .
Slow-Roasted
Tomatoes
. . .
Grapes and Cookies

PENNE AMATRICIANA

The simplest of ingredients—tomatoes, onion, and bacon—complement each other in this ever popular Italian pasta sauce. The hickory flavor of the bacon lends a slight smoky taste to this glorious Roman dish.

1 tablespoon olive oil
1 medium-size Spanish onion, chopped
1/4 pound bacon, coarsely chopped
2 large cloves garlic, minced
35-ounce can Italian plum tomatoes, coarsely chopped with their juice
1/2 cup dry red wine
1/4 to 1/2 teaspoon crushed red pepper flakes
salt and freshly ground pepper to taste
1 pound penne

1. Heat the olive oil in a large saucepan. Add the onion, bacon, and garlic and sauté over medium heat until the bacon is lightly golden.

2. Add the tomatoes, wine, and red pepper flakes. Season with salt and pepper. Simmer, uncovered, for 30 minutes, stirring occasionally.

3. Cook the pasta according to the package directions and drain well. Transfer the pasta to a large serving bowl. Pour the sauce over the freshly cooked penne, mix well, and serve.

4 to 6 main-course portions

WEEKNIGHT FARE

Grilled Scallops
· · ·
Caesar Salad◆
· · ·
Penne Amatriciana
· · ·
Lemon Sherbet

PASTA ANNA

A symphony of Mediterranean flavors abounds in this pasta dish. Rotini are coated with a mushroom-tomato sauce, rippled with Pesto and garnished with the heady taste of goat cheese.

2 tablespoons olive oil
1 large yellow onion, chopped
1 large clove garlic, minced
1 pound fresh cultivated mushrooms, sliced
28-ounce can Italian tomatoes, coarsely chopped with their juice
1 bay leaf
salt and pepper to taste
1/3 cup sweet vermouth
1 pound rotini
1/2 cup Pesto (see page 15)
5 ounces chèvre, crumbled

1. Heat the olive oil in a large saucepan. Add the onion, garlic, and mushrooms and sauté over medium-high heat until the mushrooms are golden.

2. Add the tomatoes, bay leaf, salt, pepper, and wine. Simmer for 20 minutes.

3. While the sauce is cooking, prepare the pasta according to the package directions and drain well.

4. When the sauce is cooked, remove from the heat and stir in the Pesto. Pour over the freshly cooked pasta and sprinkle with the goat cheese. Toss well until evenly coated and the cheese is melted. Serve at once.

6 to 8 portions

VEGETARIAN DINNER

Tuscan White
Bean Soup
· · ·
Pasta Anna
· · ·
Bruschetta with
Roasted Garlic
· · ·
Cantaloupe and
Ice Cream

INTIMATE DINNER FOR 6

Pita with Olivada
· · ·
Veal Chops Tonnato
· · ·
Pasta Piperade
· · ·
Tomatoes and
Pine Nuts
· · ·
Tiramisu Cake

PASTA PIPERADE

Thin strands of linguine are embellished with a colorful melange of roasted peppers and capers in a light, white wine sauce.

1 large red pepper, roasted and sliced into julienne strips
1 large orange pepper, roasted and sliced into julienne strips
1 large yellow pepper, roasted and sliced into julienne strips
1 large green pepper, roasted and sliced into julienne strips
12 ounces linguine
6 tablespoons olive oil
2 large cloves garlic, minced
1½ tablespoons capers
salt and freshly ground pepper to taste
1 teaspoon dried oregano
½ cup dry white wine

1. Place the peppers in a bowl so that the juices they exude can accumulate.

2. Cook the pasta according to the package directions and drain well. Transfer to a large bowl.

3. While the pasta is cooking, prepare the topping. Heat the olive oil in a large skillet. Add the garlic and sauté until lightly browned.

4. Add the peppers with their juice, capers, salt, pepper, oregano, and wine. Simmer for 3 minutes. Pour the sauce over the freshly cooked pasta, toss well, and serve.

3 to 4 portions

LINGUINE WITH SUN-DRIED TOMATO CREAM

The purest of ingredients—cream, wine, sun-dried tomatoes, and Parmesan cheese—come together in this luscious pasta dish that's decadent and outrageous! This recipe may be doubled easily.

1 cup all-purpose whipping cream
1/3 cup dry white wine
2/3 cup coarsely chopped sun-dried tomatoes
8 ounces linguine
1/4 cup freshly grated Parmesan cheese

1. Put the cream and wine in a saucepan. Bring to a boil and simmer until the sauce is reduced by about one-third.

2. Add the tomatoes and simmer for 2 to 3 minutes more.

3. Cook the pasta according to the package directions and drain well.

4. Pour the sauce over the freshly cooked pasta. Sprinkle with the Parmesan, toss well, and serve.

4 to 5 side portions; 3 to 4 main-course portions

SHELLS UMBERTO

This recipe was born out of my son's love for creamy red sauce. It's an easy dish to prepare and real comfort food.

> 3 tablespoons butter
> 1 medium-size yellow onion, chopped
> 28-ounce can Italian plum tomatoes, broken up into chunks
>   with their juice
> 1 teaspoon dried basil
> salt and pepper to taste
> 1 pound medium-size shells
> 1 cup sour cream
> 1/4 cup Parmesan cheese

1. Heat the butter in a medium-size saucepan. Add the onion and sauté until it is soft and translucent.

2. Add the tomatoes, basil, salt, and pepper and simmer for 15 minutes.

3. While the sauce is simmering, cook the pasta according to the package directions and drain well.

4. Add the sour cream and Parmesan to the sauce, stirring until well blended. Heat through and pour over the freshly cooked pasta. Serve at once.

6 to 8 portions

ITALIAN DINNER

Veal Chops Columbia
. . .
Salad Aromatica
. . .
Shells Umberto
. . .
Red and Green Grapes

HERBED ORZO PILAF

Orzo is a rice-shaped pasta that lends itself well to pilaf. This type of pasta makes a perfect partner for the melange of aromatic spices, all gently cooked in chicken broth.

2 tablespoons butter
1 medium-size yellow onion, chopped
1 large clove garlic, minced
1 cup orzo
2 cups chicken broth
1½ teaspoons dried basil
1 teaspoon dried thyme
½ teaspoon dried rosemary
salt to taste
2 tablespoons chopped fresh parsley

1. In a medium-size saucepan, melt the butter. Add the onion and garlic and sauté over medium heat until the onion is soft and translucent.

2. Stir in the orzo, chicken broth, and seasonings.

3. Cover, bring to a boil, reduce the heat to low, and simmer for 17 to 18 minutes until all the liquid is absorbed. Remove the pan from the heat and let stand for 5 minutes. Stir well and serve.

6 portions

DINNER MENU

Orange-Fennel Soup
. . .
Lamb Chops
. . .
Herbed Orzo Pilaf
. . .
Green Beans,
Prosciutto, and
Parmesan
. . .
Chocolate Mousse♦

SHELLS BOLOGNESE

The classic, slow-simmering, Southern Italian sauce is probably my family's favorite. Fragrant with herbs and rich with flavor, it is a most glorious pasta dish. To achieve the best results, use very lean, fresh chopped sirloin, and allow enough time for the sauce to cook. It can be prepared a day in advance and reheated; it also freezes well.

1 tablespoon virgin olive oil
1 large yellow onion, chopped
2 scallions, coarsely chopped
1 large clove garlic, minced
1 pound extra-lean chopped sirloin
28-ounce can crushed Italian tomatoes
1 tablespoon tomato paste
1 cup dry red wine
salt to taste
1/4 teaspoon freshly ground black pepper
1 1/2 teaspoons dried basil
1 teaspoon dried oregano
1 bay leaf
1/4 cup finely chopped fresh parsley
1 pound medium-size shells
3/4 cup freshly grated Parmesan cheese

1. Heat the olive oil in a large saucepan. Add the onion and scallions and sauté over medium heat for 10 minutes, stirring occasionally, until the onion is soft but not brown. Add the garlic and cook for 1 minute.

2. Add the chopped sirloin, stirring to break up any chunks. Continue to sauté over medium-high heat until the meat is browned.

3. Add the tomatoes, tomato paste, wine, salt, pepper, basil, oregano, bay leaf, and parsley. Bring the sauce to a boil, reduce the heat to low, and simmer for 1 hour, stirring occasionally.

4. Cook the pasta according to the package directions and drain well. Divide the shells among four bowls and top each with spoonfuls of sauce. Sprinkle with the cheese and serve at once.

4 portions

PASTA NIÇOISE

Pantry ingredients—tuna, capers, and black olives—are harmoniously combined in this easy-to-fix Mediterranean-inspired pasta dish. It's great for lunch, picnics, and buffets.

8 ounces rotini
13-ounce can tuna, drained
3/4 cup ripe black olives, sliced
3 tablespoons capers
1 teaspoon dried basil
1 large clove garlic, minced
1/3 cup coarsely chopped Italian parsley
freshly ground pepper to taste
2/3 cup extra-virgin olive oil

1. Cook the rotini according to the package directions and drain well.

2. While the pasta is cooking, prepare the sauce. In a medium-size mixing bowl, combine the tuna, black olives, capers, basil, garlic, parsley, pepper, and olive oil. Mix well.

3. Pour the sauce over the freshly cooked pasta and toss until evenly combined. Serve warm or at room temperature. (This may be refrigerated for later use; return to room temperature to present.)

4 to 5 side portions; 3 main-course portions

BROWN-BAG-IT LUNCH

Pasta Niçoise
. . .
Marinated Cherry Tomatoes
. . .
Oranges
. . .
Chocolate-Almond Biscotti

PASTA AND SALMON SEVICHE

This is a new interpretation of the Latin American classic, seviche, or "fish cooked in citrus juice." The pasta topping is a composition of chopped, lime-marinated salmon filet, diced cucumber and red onion, delicately scented with cilantro for a Mexican influence.

3/4 pound salmon filet, cut into 1/2-inch pieces
1/4 cup lime juice
1/2 teaspoon coarsely ground black pepper
1/2 teaspoon coarse salt
1/4 cup diced red onion
1/2 large English cucumber, diced
2 tablespoons finely chopped fresh cilantro
1/2 teaspoon crushed red pepper flakes
2/3 cup extra-virgin olive oil
1 pound ziti or penne

1. In a glass dish, combine the salmon, lime juice, black pepper, and coarse salt. Cover and refrigerate for 2 hours so that the fish can cook in the citrus juice.

2. In a small bowl, combine the red onion, cucumber, cilantro, red pepper flakes, and olive oil. Add the "cooked" salmon and mix gently.

3. Cook the pasta according to the package directions and drain well. Transfer to a large serving bowl. Top the pasta with the seviche, toss gently, and serve at room temperature.

5 to 6 main course portions

KUNG PAO SHRIMP AND NOODLES

The peanut is the ingredient indigenous to Kung Pao, particular to Szechuan cuisine. This pasta, shrimp, and vegetable medley stir-fry is presented with a spicy Chinese sauce and garnished with peanuts.

ORIENTAL FARE

Oriental-Glazed
Cornish Hens
. . .
Kung Pao Shrimp
and Noodles
. . .
Sesame Sugar
Snap Peas
. . .
Fresh Pineapple
. . .
Fortune Cookies

$^1/_3$ *cup hoisin sauce*
3 tablespoons soy sauce
3 tablespoons mirin (sweet rice wine)
$^1/_2$ *teaspoon crushed red pepper flakes*
1 pound linguine
$^1/_4$ *cup vegetable oil*
2 large cloves garlic, minced
2 tablespoons grated gingerroot
1 bunch scallions, cut into 1-inch lengths
1 medium-size yellow pepper, cut into $^1/_8$-inch wide julienne strips
1 medium-size red pepper, cut into $^1/_8$-inch wide julienne strips
$^3/_4$ *cup unsalted, roasted peanuts*
1 pound raw large shrimp, shelled

1. Combine the hoisin sauce, soy sauce, mirin, and red pepper flakes in a small bowl. Set aside.

2. Cook the linguine according to the package directions and drain well. Transfer the pasta to a large serving bowl.

3. Heat the oil in a wok or a large skillet over high heat. Add the garlic and ginger and stir-fry for 1 minute.

4. Add the vegetables and peanuts and stir-fry for 2 minutes. Add the shrimp and continue to stir-fry for 2 to 3 minutes more until the shrimp turn pink and are no longer translucent.

5. Add the sauce and stir-fry for 1 minute. Spoon the mixture over the freshly cooked pasta. Toss well and serve hot or at room temperature.

8 side portions; 6 main-course portions

DINNER PARTY

Tuscan Salad
· · ·
Fettuccine with
Grilled Scallops,
Leeks, and Fennel
· · ·
Bruschetta with
Roasted Garlic
· · ·
Tomatoes Provençal◆
· · ·
Chocolate Chip-
Ricotta Cheesecake

FETTUCCINE WITH GRILLED SCALLOPS, LEEKS, AND FENNEL

Grilled scallops are immersed in a light wine-cream sauce brimming with sautéed leeks and fennel. The fennel lends a delicate anise flavor to the sauce.

1¹/₂ pounds sea scallops
2 tablespoons olive oil
salt and pepper to taste
1 pound fettuccine
4 tablespoons butter
4 cups julienne-sliced leeks (white part only)
2 cups thinly sliced fennel
1 cup dry white wine
1 cup light cream

1. Toss the scallops with the olive oil and season with salt and pepper. Grill over hot coals until charred, about 3 to 4 minutes per side. (This may be done several hours in advance and refrigerated; return to room temperature before proceeding.)

2. Cook the fettuccine according to the package directions and drain well. Transfer to a large serving bowl.

3. While the pasta is cooking, prepare the sauce. Heat the butter in a large skillet. Add the leeks and fennel and sauté over medium heat until the vegetables are soft, about 5 to 10 minutes.

4. Season with salt and pepper. Add the wine and cream and simmer for 4 minutes. Add the grilled scallops and heat through. Pour the sauce over the freshly cooked pasta, toss, and present.

6 main-course portions

LINGUINE AND SHRIMP WITH CHARRED TOMATO SAUCE

Long strands of pasta are adorned with shrimp in a charred plum tomato sauce that's fragrant with rosemary. This simple combination has outstanding results.

PASTA PARTY

Ziti with Sausage
and Broccoli
· · ·
Linguine and
Shrimp with Charred
Tomato Sauce
· · ·
Pasta Portobello
· · ·
Sourdough Bread
· · ·
Green Salad
· · ·
Chocolate Chip-
Ricotta Cheesecake

*2 (28-ounce) cans Italian plum tomatoes, broken into coarse chunks
   with their juice*
2 large cloves garlic, crushed
2 teaspoons dried rosemary
1¹/₂ teaspoons coarsely ground black pepper
¹/₄ cup plus 2 tablespoons olive oil
2 teaspoons sugar
1 pound linguine
1¹/₂ pounds raw large shrimp, shelled

1. Preheat the oven to 450°F.

2. Put the tomatoes in a 9 x 13-inch pan. Season with the garlic, rosemary, and black pepper, and drizzle with ¹/₄ cup olive oil. Sprinkle with the sugar.

3. Roast for 30 minutes. Then broil, 4 inches from the heat source, until the tomatoes are well charred, about 6 to 7 minutes.

(This may be done several hours in advance and refrigerated until needed; return to room temperature before proceeding.)

4. Cook the linguine according to the package directions and drain well. Transfer to a large serving bowl.

5. While the pasta is cooking, sauté the shrimp. Heat 2 tablespoons olive oil in a large skillet. Add the shrimp and sauté over medium-high heat until pink. Add the charred tomato sauce and heat through. Pour over the freshly cooked pasta, toss well, and serve.

4 to 6 main-course portions

FETTUCCINE WITH SHELLFISH IN TOMATO-CREAM SAUCE

Treasures from the sea—mussels, shrimp, and scallops—sit atop fettuccine noodles covered with a delicate, creamy tomato sauce that's laced with white wine. This is a seafood lover's dream dish!

2 tablespoons butter
4 shallots, diced
1 medium-size clove garlic, minced
8 canned plum tomatoes, drained and coarsely chopped
1½ cups dry white wine
1 teaspoon dried thyme
salt and pepper to taste
¾ cup light cream
1 pound mussels, scrubbed and debearded
½ pound raw large shrimp, shelled
½ pound scallops
9 ounces fresh fettuccine noodles

1. Heat the butter in a large saucepan. Add the shallots and garlic and cook over medium heat for 1 minute.

2. Add the tomatoes, wine, and thyme. Season with salt and pepper. Bring the mixture to a boil, reduce the heat, and simmer for 20 minutes.

3. Add the cream and simmer for 5 minutes more.

4. Add the mussels, shrimp, and scallops. Cover and simmer for 5 to 6 minutes until the mussels open, the shrimp turn pink, and the scallops are no longer translucent.

5. While the sauce is simmering, cook the pasta according to the package directions and drain well. Transfer to a large serving bowl. Pour the seafood topping over the freshly cooked pasta, toss until evenly combined, and serve at once.

4 main-course portions

LINGUINE AND SQUID PUTTANESCA

Puttanesca is a robust sauce. It is typified by a subtle mingling of distinctive, strong Niçoise flavors—garlic, capers, anchovies, tomatoes, and black olives. As the sauce cooks, the flavors blend and take on special character. This version is teeming with squid, a favorite Italian seafood. In order for squid to be tender, it should either be cooked for a very brief time of only several minutes, or for an extended time of at least 45 minutes—any time in between will cause the squid to be rubbery.

¹/₄ cup olive oil
3 large cloves garlic, minced
6 anchovy filets, finely chopped
28-ounce can Italian plum tomatoes, drained and coarsely chopped
2 tablespoons capers
1 cup ripe black olives, coarsely chopped
¹/₄ teaspoon crushed red pepper flakes
freshly ground black pepper to taste
1 pound squid, sliced into ¹/₂-inch wide rings
12 ounces fresh linguine

1. Heat the olive oil, garlic, and anchovies in a large saucepan over medium heat. Using a wooden spoon, mash the anchovies to a paste.

2. Add the tomatoes, capers, black olives, red pepper flakes, and black pepper. Reduce the heat to low and simmer, uncovered, for 45 minutes.

3. Add the squid and simmer for 3 to 4 minutes longer.

4. Cook the linguine according to the package directions and drain well. Transfer to a large serving bowl. Pour the puttanesca sauce over the pasta, toss well, and serve at once.

4 portions

ITALIAN REPAST

Linguine and Squid
Puttanesca
· · ·
Bruschetta with
Artichoke Pesto
· · ·
Greens with
Walnut Vinaigrette
· · ·
Spumoni

TAIL-GATING
PARTY

Pasta and Sausages
with Plum Salsa
· · ·
French Bread with
Assorted Cheeses
· · ·
Roasted Pepper Salad
· · ·
Red and Green Grapes
· · ·
Orange Thins

PASTA AND SAUSAGES WITH PLUM SALSA

A refreshing yellow pepper and Plum Salsa laced with cilantro and gingerroot adds sparkle to pasta and grilled sausages. For a change of pace, try the salsa as a relish with other grilled or roasted meats or poultry.

1 pound ziti or rotini
1¹/₂ pounds sweet or hot sausages (or a combination), grilled or
    broiled, and sliced into ¹/₂-inch thick rounds
Plum Salsa (recipe follows)

  1. Cook the pasta according to the package directions and drain well. Transfer to a large serving bowl.

  2. Add the sausages to the freshly cooked pasta. Cover with the salsa and toss until evenly mixed. Serve warm or at room temperature.

5 to 6 portions

Plum Salsa:
3 large, ripe plums, pitted and diced
1 large yellow pepper, diced
¹/₂ cup chopped red onion
2 tablespoons finely chopped fresh cilantro
1 tablespoon grated gingerroot
2 tablespoons plum jam or preserves
2 tablespoons virgin olive oil
2 tablespoons lime juice
salt and freshly ground pepper to taste

  In a small bowl, combine all of the salsa ingredients and mix well. Set aside and let marinate for 1 to 2 hours and as much as overnight in the refrigerator.

ZITI WITH SAUSAGE AND BROCCOLI

A medley of complex tastes and textures tantalize the senses in this pasta recipe. Sautéed broccoli, grilled sausages, and tubes of ziti are laced with Parmesan and redolent with garlic. For a change of pace, you may substitute grilled boneless breasts of chicken, cut into bite-size chunks for the sausages.

1 pound ziti
2/3 cup olive oil
5 cups broccoli flowerets
4 large cloves garlic, minced
salt and pepper to taste
1 pound sweet Italian sausage, broiled or grilled, and cut into
    1/2-inch thick rounds (I use chicken sausage to cut down on
    fat and cholesterol.)
1 cup freshly grated Parmesan cheese

1. Cook the pasta according to the package directions and drain well.

2. Heat the olive oil in a large, deep saucepan. Add the broccoli, garlic, salt, and pepper. Stir-fry over high heat for 2 to 3 minutes until the broccoli is tender-crisp.

3. Add the sausage and freshly cooked ziti. Heat through, tossing gently. Sprinkle with the Parmesan, stir through, and serve at once.

6 to 8 side portions; 4 to 6 main-course portions

PASTA PARTY

Ziti with Sausage
and Broccoli
· · ·
Linguine and
Shrimp with Charred
Tomato Sauce
· · ·
Pasta Portobello
· · ·
Sourdough Bread
· · ·
Green Salad
· · ·
Chocolate Chip-
Ricotta Cheesecake

MAIN ATTRACTIONS

When the day is over and it's time to unwind, an expansive dinner for family and friends is most welcome. It's a time to share ideas, feelings, and food with unabashed enthusiasm. Whether it's a sit-down dinner or a casual buffet, it should be a celebration of the season—a feast of grilled, roasted, or sautéed meat, poultry, or seafood. Subtleties of flavors should reflect an interesting blend of herbs and spices which makes for exciting eating.

It doesn't take much effort to dress up a meal and make it look special. Use fruit and flower garnishes, take advantage of the fresh offerings of the season, and turn the meal into an extraordinary occasion.

SAVORY MEATS

BURGERS WITH VIDALIA ONION MARMALADE

This slow-simmering caramelized onion relish turns burgers into a gourmet meal. It's also fabulous atop pizza, bruschetta, poultry, fish, and steak. If Vidalia onions are unavailable, use Spanish onions.

Onion Marmalade:
¹/₄ cup olive oil
2 pounds Vidalia onions, thinly sliced
salt and pepper to taste
¹/₄ cup balsamic vinegar

8 chopped sirloin burgers (5 to 6 ounces each)

1. In a large non-stick skillet, heat the olive oil. Add the onions, season with salt and pepper, cover, and cook over medium heat until the onions are translucent, about 10 minutes. Stir occasionally.

2. Uncover, add the vinegar, and simmer until the onions are caramelized, about 45 minutes, stirring often. Transfer to a bowl. (The marmalade may be prepared 2 to 3 days in advance and refrigerated until needed; return to room temperature before serving.) Any extra marmalade will keep for 1 week refrigerated.

3. When ready to serve, broil or grill the burgers over hot coals; rare = 3 minutes per side, medium-to-well = 4 minutes per side. When cooked, transfer the burgers to a platter and top with spoonfuls of the Onion Marmalade.

About 1¹/₂ cups marmalade; 8 portions

SLOW-ROASTED TEXAS BRISKET

Texas-style brisket is rubbed with a chili-flavored barbecue spice mix and slow-roasted for 8 hours, resulting in melt-in-the-mouth tenderness and rich flavor. It's a real crowd-pleaser and easy to prepare. It also makes delectable sandwiches.

1 teaspoon garlic powder
1 teaspoon salt
1/2 teaspoon black pepper
1 tablespoon chili powder
1 1/2 tablespoons paprika
2 teaspoons dry mustard
1/2 teaspoon ground cumin
3 tablespoons dark brown sugar
4- to 5-pound brisket

WINTER FARE

Slow-Roasted
Texas Brisket
. . .
Cornbread
. . .
Carrots and
Turnips Gilbert
. . .
Assorted Cookies

1. Preheat the oven to 200°F.

2. In a bowl, combine the garlic powder, salt, pepper, chili powder, paprika, mustard, cumin, and brown sugar. Rub the mixture into both sides of the brisket, coating generously.

3. Place the meat fat side up on a large piece of heavy duty foil. Wrap tightly and place in a roasting pan.

4. Bake for 8 hours. Slice and serve with the pan juices.

8 to 10 portions

BEEF CARBONNADE

**SUNDAY NITE
WINTER SUPPER**

Winter Salad with
Walnut Pesto
· · ·
Beef Carbonnade
· · ·
Buttered Noodles
· · ·
Chocolate-Banana
Bread Pudding

This thick, rich, Belgian-style beef stew is typified by meat and lots of caramelized onions simmered in beer and beef broth. It's a great company dish—hearty fare that reheats well. Serve it atop buttered noodles.

4 pounds chuck steak, trimmed of heavy fat, cut into 1 1/2-inch cubes
1/4 cup all-purpose flour
2 tablespoons butter
3 tablespoons vegetable oil
4 large cloves garlic, minced
2 pounds Spanish onions, cut into 1/2-inch thick rings
2 tablespoons light brown sugar
2 tablespoons red wine vinegar
1 tablespoon tomato paste
2 cups beef broth
24 ounces beer
2 bay leaves, crumbled
1 teaspoon dried thyme
1/4 cup chopped fresh parsley
salt and pepper to taste

1. Dredge the meat in the flour. In a large Dutch oven, heat 1 tablespoon butter and 2 tablespoons oil. Brown the meat in the hot fat; then remove from the pan and set aside.

2. Add the remaining butter and oil to the pan. When hot, add the garlic, onions, and brown sugar. Cook over medium-high heat, stirring occasionally until the onions are lightly browned.

3. Add the vinegar, tomato paste, beef broth, and beer, stirring to remove any browned bits.

4. Return the meat along with any accumulated juices to the pan. Add the bay leaves, thyme, and parsley, and season with salt and pepper. Cover tightly and place in a preheated 350°F oven for 2 to 2 1/2 hours until fork tender. Serve piping hot. (This is actually better if made a day in advance and refrigerated, allowing the flavors to mellow; return to room temperature before reheating in a 350°F oven for 30 minutes.)

8 portions

GRILLED HUNAN BEEF

The Asian flavors of soy, ginger, molasses, and curry dominate the savory marinade in this grilled beef dish.

2 pounds sirloin tip steak, trimmed of heavy fat
¹/₄ cup soy sauce
¹/₄ cup dry red wine
2 tablespoons vegetable oil
1 tablespoon molasses
2 teaspoons curry powder
1 tablespoon grated gingerroot

1. In a bowl, combine the soy sauce, wine, oil, molasses, curry, and gingerroot. Pour the sauce over the beef and let marinate for 1 to 2 hours and as much as overnight.

2. When ready to serve, grill the meat over hot coals, 4 inches from the heat source, 4 minutes per side for rare to medium-rare. Slice into chunks and serve with rice.

6 portions

CHINESE DINNER

Grilled Hunan Beef
. . .
Fried Wild Rice
. . .
Sesame Sugar
Snap Peas
. . .
Fresh Pineapple
Wedges

BEEF AND BROCCOLI WITH OYSTER SAUCE

This famous Asian recipe pairs two dynamic foods, beef and broccoli. Quickly stir-fried and finished with an oyster-flavored sauce, this authentic Oriental dish is sure to garner praise. Present it with a bed of white rice.

1-pound sirloin tip steak, cut into ¹/₂-inch wide slices
1 large clove garlic, smashed
2 teaspoons grated gingerroot
freshly ground pepper to taste
1 tablespoon soy sauce
1 tablespoon mirin* or cream sherry
1 to 2 tablespoons cornstarch
3 tablespoons vegetable oil
2 scallions, cut into 1-inch pieces
4 cups broccoli flowerets, poached for 2 minutes
Oyster Sauce (recipe follows)

1. Place the meat in a glass baking dish.

2. Combine the garlic, ginger, pepper, soy sauce, and mirin. Add the seasonings to the meat and mix well. Let marinate for 1 to 2 hours.

3. Sprinkle the meat with the cornstarch, mixing to coat evenly.

4. Heat 1 tablespoon oil in a wok or large skillet. Add the scallions and broccoli and stir-fry over high heat for 2 minutes until the broccoli is tender. Remove the vegetables to a plate.

5. Add the remaining 2 tablespoons oil to the wok. When hot, add the meat and stir-fry over high heat until the meat is browned on both sides, about 2 to 3 minutes. Return the cooked vegetables to the wok. Add the Oyster Sauce, stir-fry for 1 minute more, and serve at once.

4 portions

Oyster Sauce:
2 tablespoons oyster sauce*
3 tablespoons mirin* or cream sherry
1 teaspoon Oriental sesame oil

Combine all of the sauce ingredients and mix well. Refrigerate until needed. (The sauce may be prepared a day in advance.)

*Available in Oriental markets

HOISIN-GLAZED RACK OF LAMB

Hoisin sauce, the celebrated Chinese bean sauce, is a mixture of soybeans, garlic, chili peppers, and various spices, lending a sweet and spicy flair to roasted rack of lamb. This is an elegant, easy, and gustatory dish.

2 racks of lamb (8 or 9 chops each), cut in half
¹/₄ cup hoisin sauce
1 tablespoon honey

1. Preheat the oven to 400°F.
2. Place the racks of lamb in a roasting pan.
3. Combine the hoisin sauce and honey. Paint all surfaces of the lamb with the sauce.
4. Roast for 25 minutes for rare to medium-rare. Slice into individual chops and serve.

4 to 6 portions

FORMAL DINNER PARTY FOR 6

Apple-Butternut
Squash Soup
· · ·
Hoisin-Glazed Rack
of Lamb
· · ·
Chèvre Mashed
Potatoes

Oven-Roasted
Asparagus
· · ·
Asian Pear Tart

BRAISED LAMB SHANKS

**WINTER
COMFORT FOOD**

Braised Lamb Shanks
· · ·
Chèvre Mashed
Potatoes
· · ·
Green Beans
· · ·
Maple-Pecan
Pound Cake

This hearty lamb stew will warm the cockles of your heart. Seared shanks are surrounded by a riot of herbs and vegetables and braised slowly until fork tender. Mashed potatoes make a sumptuous accompaniment.

6 lamb shanks, heavy fat and sinew removed
flour for dredging
3 tablespoons olive oil
2 large cloves garlic, minced
salt and pepper to taste
1 bay leaf
1 teaspoon dried thyme
1 teaspoon dried marjoram
2 large yellow onions, chopped
3 large carrots, coarsely chopped
2 large stalks celery, coarsely chopped
28-ounce can Italian plum tomatoes, coarsely chopped with their juice
2 cups dry red wine

1. Dredge the lamb in flour. Heat the olive oil in a large Dutch oven. Add the lamb in batches, searing the shanks over high heat. When browned on all sides, remove the shanks to a plate. When all the shanks are browned, return them to the pot.

2. Preheat the oven to 350°F.

3. Add the garlic, salt, pepper, bay leaf, thyme, marjoram, onions, carrots, celery, tomatoes, and wine to the lamb. Stir through and remove from the heat. Cover and transfer to the oven.

4. Roast for 2 hours until the shanks are fork tender. Serve piping hot. (This may be prepared a day in advance and refrigerated; return to room temperature before reheating.)

6 portions

ROAST LAMB WITH MINT PESTO

Lamb and mint have a curious affinity, making it a most savory combination. Leg of lamb is encrusted with a thick Mint Pesto redolent with garlic and swirled with goat cheese. The result is heavenly!

5-pound leg of lamb, at room temperature, trimmed of heavy fat
  and sinew

Mint Pesto:
1 cup loosely packed fresh mint leaves
1/4 cup chopped scallions
1/4 cup chopped Italian parsley
2 large cloves garlic, crushed
1/2 teaspoon salt
freshly ground pepper to taste
3 ounces goat cheese
2 tablespoons balsamic vinegar
1/2 cup virgin olive oil

1. Make several slits in the meat so that the pesto flavors can permeate the lamb.

2. Prepare the mint pesto. Put all of the pesto ingredients in the bowl of a food processor and purée. (The pesto may be made 2 to 3 days in advance and refrigerated until needed.)

3. Coat the lamb generously with the pesto and let sit for 1 hour, allowing the meat to marinate.

4. Roast the lamb in a preheated 400°F oven for 1 1/4 hours for rare to medium-rare meat—15 minutes per pound. Remove to a platter and let rest for 10 minutes before slicing. Serve with the pan juices.

6 portions

MIDDLE EASTERN DINNER

Middle Eastern
Eggplant Spread
· · ·
Roast Lamb with
Mint Pesto
· · ·
Cracked Wheat and
Olive Salad
· · ·
Baklava

BARBECUED LEG OF LAMB

The hoisin-based barbecue sauce accented by ketchup, molasses, gingerroot, and soy adds a mouth-watering, Oriental taste and juicy, yet crusty quality to this glorious, grilled lamb. It's a great dish for an outdoor barbecue or summer get together. Once sampled, once savored!

5-pound boned leg of lamb, butterflied (weight after boned)

Hoisin Marinade:
1/3 cup hoisin sauce
1/2 cup ketchup
1 tablespoon molasses
1 tablespoon grated gingerroot
2 tablespoons rice vinegar
1 tablespoon soy sauce
2 tablespoons vegetable oil
1/2 teaspoon Oriental hot oil
lots of freshly ground black pepper

1. Trim the lamb of any heavy fat.

2. Combine all of the marinade ingredients. Pour the marinade over the lamb and let sit for 1 to 2 hours for flavors to develop. (You may let it marinate as much as overnight in the refrigerator; return to room temperature before grilling.)

3. Grill the lamb over hot coals, 4 inches from the heat source, 5 to 6 minutes per side for medium-rare, basting with the reserved marinade. Serve hot off the grill, carving into thin slices.

8 portions

PORK CHOPS WITH BLUEBERRY SAUCE

Pork chops are glazed in a reduced balsamic sauce spiked with blueberries. The fruity sauce has a distinctive tang that complements the succulent pork. When blueberry season abounds, freeze several extra pints for winter use.

6 pork chops, 1 to 1¼ inches thick
salt and pepper to taste
2 tablespoons olive oil
1 large clove garlic, minced
1¼ cups blueberries (fresh or frozen*)
½ cup balsamic vinegar

1. Season the pork with salt and pepper. In a large skillet, heat the olive oil. Add the garlic and pork and sauté over medium-high heat, about 4 minutes per side for medium. Remove the chops to a platter and keep warm.

2. Add the blueberries and balsamic vinegar to the pan. Raise the heat to high and cook until the sauce is syrupy and somewhat reduced, about 3 to 4 minutes. Pour the sauce over the pork and serve at once.

6 portions

*If using frozen berries, let them thaw for 30 minutes before adding to the sauce.

DINNER MENU

Pork Chops with
Blueberry Sauce
· · ·
Sweet Potatoes and
Red Onions
· · ·
Parsnip Chips
· · ·
Chocolate Cake

JAMAICAN-SPICED PORK LOIN

A savory blend of intriguing flavors, particular to Jamaican jerk, seasons boneless pork that is marinated and then barbecued, leaving you craving for more of this fiery island dish.

$2^1/2$ pound boneless pork roast
2 large cloves garlic, crushed
$^1/2$ teaspoon salt
$^1/2$ teaspoon black pepper
$^1/2$ teaspoon chili powder
1 teaspoon ground allspice
1 teaspoon cinnamon
$^1/4$ teaspoon cayenne pepper
1 bay leaf, crushed
1 tablespoon tomato paste
$^1/2$ cup dark brown sugar
$^1/2$ cup red wine vinegar
$^1/4$ cup olive oil

1. Butterfly the pork roast, removing any excess fat.

2. In a bowl, whisk together the garlic, salt, pepper, chili powder, allspice, cinnamon, cayenne pepper, bay leaf, tomato paste, brown sugar, vinegar, and olive oil.

3. Coat the pork with the sauce, rubbing it into the meat. Cover and refrigerate for 2 to 3 hours and as much as overnight.

4. Return the pork to room temperature. Grill over hot coals, 4 inches from the heat source, 4 to 5 minutes per side for medium, basting with the marinade. The meat should be pink on the inside so that it remains juicy. Slice and serve.

6 portions

ROASTED PORK TENDERLOIN WITH FIG SAUCE

The choicest cut of pork, the tenderloin, is marinated in an orange-scented dressing, roasted to a turn, and finished with a full-bodied dried fig and Port wine sauce.

> 1 large clove garlic, crushed
> 1/2 teaspoon dried orange peel
> 1/8 teaspoon cayenne pepper
> salt and pepper to taste
> 2 tablespoons orange juice
> 2 tablespoons olive oil
> 3 pork tenderloins, about 3/4 pound each
> Fig Sauce (recipe follows)

1. In a bowl, whisk together the garlic, orange peel, cayenne pepper, salt, pepper, orange juice, and olive oil.

2. Place the tenderloins in a roasting pan. Pour the sauce over the pork, cover, and let marinate in the refrigerator for 2 to 3 hours and as much as overnight. Return to room temperature before cooking.

3. Preheat the oven to 400°F.

4. Roast the tenderloin for 15 to 20 minutes, or until pink at the center when tested. Remove the pork from the oven and let sit for 10 minutes.

5. While the pork is roasting, prepare the Fig Sauce.

6. To serve, slice the pork into 1/2-inch thick pieces. Spoon the fig sauce over the slices and present.

6 portions

DINNER FARE

Roasted Pork
Tenderloin with
Fig Sauce
. . .
Julienne Sauté
. . .
Roasted New Potatoes
. . .
Rhubarb Crisp

Fig Sauce:
3 tablespoons butter
6 shallots, sliced in half lengthwise
1 large clove garlic, minced
¼ teaspoon dried thyme
freshly ground pepper to taste
6 dried figs, coarsely chopped
¾ cup Port wine

1. In a small saucepan, heat the butter. Add the shallots and sauté over medium heat until golden brown. Add the garlic and sauté for 1 more minute.

2. Add the thyme, pepper, figs, and wine. Simmer for 4 to 5 minutes and serve. (This may be prepared in advance and gently reheated.)

SAM'S MEMPHIS-STYLE RIBS

Straight from the deep South, these ribs are sure to set your taste buds dancing. A spicy, dry rub coats ribs that are slow-roasted in a very low oven for moist tenderness, and then charred over hot coals for a spectacular finish.

TEXAS BARBECUE

Sam's Memphis-
Style Ribs
· · ·
Cornbread
· · ·
Baked Beans
· · ·
Jicama Slaw
· · ·
Watermelon
· · ·
Triple Chocolate
Chunk Cookies

Barbecue Rub:
1 teaspoon salt
1 teaspoon black pepper
2 tablespoons dark brown sugar
1 tablespoon chili powder
1 teaspoon garlic powder
1 teaspoon onion powder
$1/2$ teaspoon cayenne pepper

3-pound rack of pork spareribs, trimmed of excess fat

1. Preheat the oven to 180°F.

2. Combine the ingredients of the spice mix. Rub both surfaces of the rack of ribs generously with the spices. Place on a baking sheet.

3. Roast for 3 hours. (This may be done a day in advance and refrigerated; return to room temperature before proceeding.)

4. When ready to serve, grill the rack over hot coals for 2 to 3 minutes per side until crusty. Slice into individual ribs and serve with cornbread and coleslaw.

3 to 4 portions

Note—this recipe doubles easily for a larger group.

VEAL CHOPS COLUMBIA

ITALIAN DINNER

Veal Chops Columbia
. . .
Salad Aromatica
. . .
Shells Umberto
. . .
Red and Green Grapes

I first sampled this delectable topping at my friends' the Columbias, and adapted the piquant Onion and Caper Relish for veal. It also performs magic atop pasta with freshly grated Parmesan and on grilled chicken or fish.

Onion and Caper Relish:
2 tablespoons olive oil
2 cups diced Spanish onions
freshly ground pepper to taste
¼ cup sweet vermouth
½ cup capers, rinsed and drained

4 loin or rib veal chops, 1-inch thick
olive oil
salt and pepper to taste

1. Prepare the relish. Heat the olive oil in a small skillet. Add the onions, season with pepper, and sauté over low heat until the onions are soft and translucent, about 10 minutes.

2. Add the vermouth and simmer for 2 to 3 minutes. Stir in the capers and heat through. (This may be prepared a day in advance and refrigerated; reheat before serving.)

3. Rub the chops with olive oil and season with salt and pepper. Grill (or broil) the chops over hot coals, 4 inches from the heat source, 4 to 5 minutes per side. Spoon the relish atop each chop and serve.

4 portions

VEAL CHOPS TONNATO

Veal chops are cloaked in a delicate tuna mayonnaise perfumed with lemon, basil, and capers. The sauce also works well over grilled or poached chicken.

Tuna Mayonnaise:
3¹/₂-ounce can tuna, drained
¹/₂ cup mayonnaise
1¹/₂ tablespoons lemon juice
1 tablespoon capers
1 teaspoon dried basil
freshly ground black pepper to taste

4 rib or loin veal chops, 1-inch thick
olive oil
salt and pepper to taste

1. Prepare the Tuna Mayonnaise. Put the tuna, mayonnaise, lemon juice, capers, basil, and pepper in the bowl of a food processor and purée. Transfer the purée to a bowl and set aside until needed. (This may be prepared 2 days in advance and refrigerated; return to room temperature to serve.)

2. Brush the veal chops with olive oil. Season with salt and pepper. Grill or broil the chops, 4 inches from the heat source, 4 minutes per side for medium-rare.

3. Top each chop with dollops of the Tuna Mayonnaise and serve.

4 portions

**INTIMATE
DINNER FOR 6**

Pita with Olivada
· · ·
Veal Chops Tonnato
· · ·
Pasta Piperade
· · ·
Tomatoes and
Pine Nuts
· · ·
Tiramisu Cake

VEAL CHOPS WITH TOMATO RELISH

The classic preparation of breaded veal is taken one step further in this exciting new presentation. The crispy, sautéed chops are then napped in a cool Tomato Relish spiked with chopped arugula and radicchio. Try adding chopped fresh mozzarella to the relish for a delightful salad.

4 rib or loin veal chops, ³/₄ to 1-inch thick
salt and pepper to taste
flour for dredging
1 egg, beaten
³/₄ cup plain bread crumbs
¹/₄ cup olive oil
Tomato Relish (recipe follows)

1. Season the chops with salt and pepper. Dredge in flour, dip in the beaten egg, and then coat with the bread crumbs.

2. Heat the olive oil in a non-stick skillet and sauté the chops until browned, about 3 to 4 minutes per side. Transfer the chops to a platter and top each with a large spoonful of Tomato Relish. Serve at once.

4 portions

Tomato Relish:
³/₄ cup chopped arugula
1 cup chopped radicchio
4 large or 5 medium-size ripe plum tomatoes, coarsely chopped
salt and freshly ground pepper to taste
2 tablespoons balsamic vinegar
1 tablespoon extra-virgin olive oil

Combine all of the relish ingredients and let marinate for 1 to 2 hours.

POULTRY PLEASERS

BERBER-SPICED GAME HENS

Cornish hens are encrusted with an exotic spice mix featuring typical Moroccan flavors—cumin, turmeric, ginger, cinnamon, and paprika—resulting in moist, succulent, and savory birds.

4 Cornish game hens
2 lemons, cut in half
1/4 cup olive oil
Berber Spice Mix (recipe follows)

1. Preheat the oven to 425°F.

2. Stuff the cavity of each hen with half a lemon. Rub the skin of each bird with 1 tablespoon olive oil.

3. Generously coat the exterior surfaces of the hens with the spice mixture. Place breast side up in a large roasting pan.

4. Roast for 50 to 60 minutes, basting occasionally with the pan juices. Remove to a platter and serve at once.

4 portions

Berber Spice Mix:
2 teaspoons ground cumin
1 teaspoon turmeric
1 teaspoon ground ginger
2 teaspoons paprika
1/2 teaspoon garlic powder
1/2 teaspoon cinnamon
1 teaspoon salt
1/2 teaspoon black pepper
1/4 teaspoon cayenne pepper

Combine all of the seasonings and mix well. This may be made up to a week in advance and stored in an airtight container.

ORIENTAL-GLAZED CORNISH HENS

A deep mahogany glaze coats these darling little hens that are richly flavored with ginger preserves, hoisin sauce, and scallions.

4 Cornish game hens
1 cup chopped scallions
4 large cloves garlic, thinly sliced
1/2 cup ginger preserves
1/4 cup hoisin sauce
1 tablespoon lemon juice

1. Preheat the oven to 400°F.

2. Stuff the cavity of each hen with 1/4 cup scallions and 1 clove sliced garlic.

3. Combine the ginger preserves, hoisin sauce, and lemon juice. Paint all surfaces of the hens with the glaze.

4. Place breast side up in a large roasting pan. Roast for 50 minutes. Serve at once with the pan juices spooned over each hen.

4 portions

ASIAN DELIGHT

Oriental-Glazed
Cornish Hens
· · ·
Thai Vegetable Salad
· · ·
Fried Wild Rice
· · ·
Sautéed Bananas

ROAST CHICKEN WITH FIG RELISH

This simple roasted chicken dish has a marvelous fruity embellishment. The dried fig relish is somewhat hot, somewhat spicy, and somewhat sweet, typical of a chutney. It is actually better if made 2 to 3 days in advance to allow the flavors to blend.

4- to 5-pound roasting chicken
2 tablespoons virgin olive oil
salt and pepper to taste
Fig Relish (recipe follows)

1. Preheat the oven to 375°F.

2. Rub the exterior of the roast with the olive oil. Season with salt and pepper. Place the chicken breast side up in a large roasting pan.

3. Set the roast in the oven for 1¼ to 1½ hours, basting occasionally with the pan juices. When the chicken is done, transfer the bird to a platter and carve the roast into serving pieces. Present with dollops of the Fig Relish.

6 portions

Fig Relish:
1 cup dried figs, coarsely chopped
¼ cup diced red onion
1 tablespoon minced crystallized candied ginger
1 teaspoon finely grated orange peel
1 large clove garlic, minced
⅛ teaspoon cayenne pepper
2 tablespoons orange juice
2 tablespoons red wine vinegar
2 tablespoons virgin olive oil

Combine all of the relish ingredients and mix well. Store in the refrigerator until needed. Return to room temperature to serve. The relish will keep for 3 weeks under refrigeration.

CHICKEN STUFFED WITH SPINACH AND CHÈVRE

Roasted chicken is plumped with a creamy spinach stuffing, heady with goat cheese and dotted with pine nuts and sun-dried tomatoes.

10 ounces fresh spinach, steamed 2 minutes
5 to 6 ounces chèvre
2 tablespoons pine nuts, toasted
6 sun-dried tomatoes, chopped
6- to 7-pound roasting chicken
1 tablespoon olive oil
1 teaspoon dried rosemary
salt and pepper to taste

1. Preheat the oven to 350°F.

2. Combine the spinach, chèvre, pine nuts, and sun-dried tomatoes. Stuff the cavity of the chicken with this mixture.

3. Rub the skin with the olive oil. Season with the rosemary, salt, and pepper.

4. Place breast side down in a large roasting pan. Place in the oven for 1 hour. Turn the chicken over and continue roasting, breast side up, for 1 to 1½ more hours until done. Baste occasionally with the pan juices.

5. Transfer to a platter and carve the roast into individual pieces. Serve with spoonfuls of the delectable stuffing and the pan juices.

6 to 8 portions

SUNDAY NIGHT SUPPER

Chicken Stuffed with
Spinach and Chèvre
· · ·
Deluxe Mashed
Potatoes
· · ·
Slow-Roasted
Tomatoes
· · ·
Chocolate-Almond
Pound Cake◆

CHICKEN OLIVIA

I love to combine fruits with chicken when roasting—they impart a sweet, refreshing quality and new dimension to the poultry. The marinated and roasted chicken parts are surrounded by butternut squash, prunes, apricots, and shallots, resulting in a savory meal. Serve it accompanied by couscous. It makes a spectacular party dish.

2 whole broilers (2^1/$_2$ to 3 pounds each), quartered
^{1}/$_2$ cup virgin olive oil
^{1}/$_4$ cup red wine vinegar
1 cup Port wine
3 large cloves garlic, crushed
1 tablespoon dried thyme
^{3}/$_4$ cup dark brown sugar
salt and pepper to taste
1^1/$_2$ pound butternut squash, peeled and cut into 1-inch chunks
1 cup pitted prunes
1 cup dried apricots
20 whole shallots

1. Place the chicken in a large roasting pan.

2. In a bowl, whisk together the olive oil, vinegar, wine, garlic, thyme, brown sugar, salt, and pepper. Pour the marinade over the chicken and let marinate overnight in the refrigerator. Return to room temperature before proceeding.

3. Preheat the oven to 350°F.

4. Add the squash, prunes, apricots, and shallots to the chicken, mixing well to coat with the marinade.

5. Bake for 1 hour until tender and browned, basting occasionally with the marinade. Serve at once with the pan juices.

8 or more portions

CARIBBEAN CHICKEN

The sweet, crispy coconut crust enlivens these chicken tenders, lending a taste of the tropical islands. They're further dressed up with a fruity, rum-infused sauce.

1 pound chicken tenders
flour for dredging
salt and pepper to taste
1 egg, beaten
1¹/₃ cups sweetened, shredded coconut
5 tablespoons butter
Apricot Sauce (recipe follows)

1. Season the flour with salt and pepper; dredge the chicken in the flour mixture.

2. Dip the chicken in the egg, and then roll in the coconut to coat completely. Chill for 30 minutes to help the coconut adhere to the chicken.

3. Heat the butter in a large non-stick pan. Add the chicken and sauté over high heat, 2 to 3 minutes per side until golden brown. Serve at once with the Apricot Sauce.

4 portions

Apricot Sauce:
¹/₂ cup sour cream
2 tablespoons apricot preserves
1 tablespoon light rum
2 teaspoons finely grated lime zest

Combine all of the sauce ingredients and refrigerate until needed. Serve at room temperature.

HORS D'OEUVRE
PARTY FOR 24

Caribbean Chicken
· · ·
Grilled Shrimp and
Artichoke Hearts with
Cumin Mayonnaise
· · ·
Salmon Pâté
· · ·
Cured Beef Tenderloin
au Poivre
· · ·
White Bean Dip
with Crudités
· · ·
Grilled Fruits

CURRIED CHICKEN TENDERS WITH MANGO CHUTNEY

Curried chicken is enhanced by the intriguing, fruity, and spicy qualities of the outstanding mango condiment. The flavors of Indian cuisine are sophisticated, complex, and assertive.

1½ pounds chicken tenders
flour for dredging
salt and pepper to taste
5 tablespoons butter
1½ teaspoons curry powder
1 cup Mango Chutney (recipe follows)

1. Season the flour with salt and pepper; dredge the tenders in the flour mixture.

2. Heat the butter in a large skillet. Add the chicken and sprinkle with the curry. Sauté over high heat until browned, about 2 minutes per side. Add the chutney, stir well, and heat for 1 to 2 minutes more. Serve at once with rice.

6 portions

Mango Chutney:
2 medium-size ripe mangoes, peeled, pitted, and chopped
1 medium-size yellow onion, chopped
⅓ cup raisins
¼ cup diced green pepper
1 large clove garlic, crushed
1 tablespoon grated gingerroot
⅛ teaspoon cayenne pepper
1 cup lightly packed dark brown sugar
⅓ cup white vinegar

1. Put all of the ingredients in a large saucepan. Bring to a boil, lower the heat, and simmer until thick, about 1½ hours, stirring occasionally.

2. Pack into sterile jars. Refrigerate after opening. The chutney will keep for 3 weeks once opened.

2½ cups of chutney

CHICKEN FAJITAS

The Mexican fajita has taken Americans by storm—it's an easy, tasty, and satisfying meal in a roll-up. Tortillas are stuffed with a composition of grilled chicken tenders, onions, and a trio of peppers and garnished with a variety of toppings—salsa, chopped avocado, sour cream, grated cheese, and shredded romaine. They're for young and old alike.

2 large cloves garlic, minced
salt and pepper to taste
1/4 cup chopped fresh cilantro
6 tablespoons lime juice
1/2 cup extra-virgin olive oil
2 pounds chicken tenders
1 large red pepper, cut into 1/2-inch wide strips
1 large yellow pepper, cut into 1/2-inch wide strips
1 large orange pepper, cut into 1/2-inch wide strips
2 medium-size Vidalia or red onions, cut into 1/2-inch thick rings
12 to 14 (8-inch) flour tortillas, warmed

Garnishes:
1/2 pint sour cream
2 cups Salsa (see page 29)
1 avocado, peeled and chopped
2 cups grated Monterey Jack cheese
1 small head shredded romaine

1. In a small bowl, whisk together the garlic, salt, pepper, cilantro, lime juice, and 1/4 cup olive oil. Pour the marinade over the chicken and let sit for 30 minutes.

2. Put the peppers and onions in a large pan and toss with the remaining 1/4 cup olive oil. Season with salt and pepper.

3. Grill the chicken over hot coals, 4 inches from the heat source, 2 minutes per side until cooked and charred. Remove to a platter.

4. Grill the peppers and onions until charred, about 5 minutes per side. Remove the grilled vegetables to the platter.

5. To serve, place a tortilla on each plate. Fill with 1 to 2 pieces of chicken and several pieces of pepper and onion. Top with your choice of garnishes—be daring and try them all! Roll-up carefully and enjoy.

6 portions

MEXICAN DINNER

Black Bean Soup
. . .
Chicken Fajitas
. . .
Pineapple Freeze

ITALIAN SUPPER

Chicken Bernard
· · ·
Couscous Niçoise
· · ·
Broccoli Rabe
· · ·
Tiramisu Cake

CHICKEN BERNARD

Breaded, sautéed breasts are layered with Pesto, prosciutto, and provolone cheese and run under the broiler until browned, bubbly, and seductively delicious. This makes a great company dish.

3 large boneless, skinless chicken breasts, split in half
flour for dredging
salt and pepper to taste
2 eggs, beaten
³/₄ cup plain bread crumbs
¹/₄ cup olive oil
6 tablespoons Pesto (see page 15)
¹/₈ pound thinly sliced prosciutto
¹/₄ pound sliced provolone cheese

1. Preheat the broiler. Grease a large baking sheet.

2. Season the flour with salt and pepper; dredge the chicken in the flour mixture.

3. Dip the chicken pieces in the egg and then coat with the bread crumbs.

4. Heat the olive oil in a large non-stick skillet. Add the chicken and sauté over medium-high heat, 3 to 4 minutes per side until browned. Transfer the chicken to the prepared baking sheet.

5. Spread 1 tablespoon of Pesto on each breast. Distribute the slices of prosciutto evenly atop the chicken. Cover with the slices of provolone. (Up to this point may be prepared in advance and refrigerated; return to room temperature before proceeding.)

6. Run under the broiler for 2 minutes until the cheese is browned and bubbly. Serve at once.

6 portions

CHICKEN BREASTS ST. MICHELLE

Spirals of chicken breasts are stuffed with tender, mild-flavored leeks and served with a delicate roasted Red Pepper Relish. This is definite party fare.

DINNER PARTY MENU

Shredded Greens with Strawberry Vinaigrette
. . .
Chicken Breasts St. Michelle
. . .
Bulgur with Walnut Gremolata
. . .
Asparagus with Mustard Butter◆
. . .
Grand Dame Cake◆

> 6 tablespoons butter
> 4 large leeks (white part only), sliced lengthwise into quarters, and well rinsed
> 1/4 teaspoon dried thyme
> salt and pepper to taste
> 3 large boneless, skinless chicken breasts, split in half
> flour for dredging
> Red Pepper Relish (recipe follows)

1. Heat 3 tablespoons butter in a large skillet. Add the leeks and season with the thyme, salt, and pepper. Sauté over medium heat until soft and lightly golden. Remove the leeks to a plate.

2. Pound the chicken breasts with a meat pounder until 1/2-inch thick. Season with salt and pepper.

3. Place a spoonful of sautéed leeks on each breast and roll up. Dredge each breast in flour.

4. Heat the remaining 3 tablespoons butter in the same pan. Add the chicken breasts and sauté until cooked and browned, 4 to 5 minutes per side. Remove the breasts to a platter. With a sharp knife, slice each roll into thirds. Present the spirals of stuffed breasts on their side with dollops of Red Pepper Relish.

4 to 6 portions

> *Red Pepper Relish:*
> 1 large red pepper, roasted and coarsely chopped
> 3 large, ripe plum tomatoes, diced
> salt and pepper to taste
> 1/4 teaspoon dried thyme
> 3 tablespoons minced fresh parsley
> 1 tablespoon extra-virgin olive oil

Combine all of the relish ingredients and mix well.

CHICKEN WITH THREE CHEESE MELT

This is a lighter, new-wave version of the traditional chicken parmigiana. Boneless breasts are marinated in a fresh basil vinaigrette, grilled, and crowned with sliced plum tomatoes and a trio of grated cheeses.

4 large boneless, skinless chicken breasts, split in half
1 large clove garlic, crushed
salt and pepper to taste
1/4 cup chopped fresh basil
1 tablespoon red wine vinegar
1/4 cup virgin olive oil
3 ripe plum tomatoes, thinly sliced
1/3 cup grated mozzarella cheese
1/3 cup grated provolone cheese
1/3 cup freshly grated Parmesan cheese

1. Place the chicken in a large pan.

2. In a bowl, whisk together the garlic, salt, pepper, basil, vinegar, and olive oil. Pour the dressing over the chicken and let marinate for 1 to 2 hours.

3. Grill (or broil) over hot coals, 4 inches from the heat source, 3 to 4 minutes per side. Transfer the breasts to a large baking sheet.

4. Top with the sliced tomatoes.

5. Mix the three cheeses together. Sprinkle the cheese mixture over each breast, covering completely.

6. Run under a hot broiler for 1 to 2 minutes until the cheeses are browned and bubbly. Serve at once.

8 portions

CHICKEN WITH GINGER-PEACH CHUTNEY

Peach chutney is infused with ginger preserves that glazes the chicken breasts and lends a flavor and perfume that's lively, fruity, high in flavor, and low in fat.

3 large boneless, skinless chicken breasts, split in half
flour for dredging
salt and pepper to taste
3 tablespoons butter
Ginger-Peach Chutney (see page 11)

1. Season the flour with salt and pepper; dredge the chicken in the flour mixture.

2. Heat the butter in a large skillet. Add the chicken and sauté over high heat, 3 to 4 minutes per side until lightly browned.

3. Add the chutney and continue to simmer, spooning the chutney over the chicken until the sauce thickens and glazes the breasts, about 5 minutes. Serve at once with a rice accompaniment.

6 portions

SIMPLE DINNER

Chicken with Ginger-
Peach Chutney
· · ·
Basmati Rice
· · ·
Julienne Sauté
· · ·
Glazed Lemon
Pound Cake◆

SPRING MENU

Chicken Gouda
· · ·
Linguine with
Red Pepper Pesto
· · ·
Spinach Romano
· · ·
Strawberries
and Cream

CHICKEN GOUDA

Grilled boneless breasts are covered with slices of smoked Gouda cheese, lending a delightful hickory flavor to this simple dish. You may substitute smoked mozzarella if you wish.

4 large, boneless, skinless chicken breasts, split in half
3 to 4 tablespoons olive oil
salt to taste
lots of freshly ground black pepper
1/4 pound smoked Gouda cheese, thinly sliced, at room temperature

1. Rub the chicken with the olive oil. Season with salt and pepper.

2. Cook the breasts over a hot grill, 4 inches from the heat source, for 3 minutes. Turn the breasts over and cover each breast with slices of cheese. Cover the grill and continue to cook 5 minutes more, until the chicken is done and the cheese is melted. Serve at once.

6 to 8 portions

HONEY-GLAZED WALNUT CHICKEN

Delicate and tasty with an Asian flair, stir-fried chunks of chicken are glazed in a Honey-Lemon Sauce and embellished with honey-roasted walnuts.

CHINESE MENU

Potstickers
· · ·
Honey-Glazed
Walnut Chicken
· · ·
White Rice
· · ·
Ginger Ice Cream
· · ·
Fortune Cookies

1 cup coarsely chopped walnuts
3 tablespoons honey
1¹/₂ pounds boneless, skinless chicken breasts, cut into ¹/₂-inch chunks
cornstarch for dredging
2 tablespoons vegetable oil
1 large clove garlic, minced
Honey-Lemon Sauce (recipe follows)

1. Preheat the oven to 350°F. Grease a cookie sheet.

2. Combine the walnuts and honey in a bowl and mix until evenly coated. Spread the nuts out in a single layer on the prepared pan. Bake for 10 minutes. Immediately remove the nuts to a plate, along with any extra glaze, and let cool. (If they seem sticky, place them in the freezer for 10 minutes.) When the glaze hardens, break the nuts into individual pieces. Set aside.

3. Dredge the chicken in cornstarch.

4. Heat the oil in a wok. Add the garlic and chicken and stir-fry over high heat for 4 minutes until the chicken is browned. Add the Honey-Lemon Sauce and stir-fry for 1 minute more until the sauce thickens and glazes the chicken.

5. Add the nuts, stir through, and serve at once with a rice accompaniment.

4 portions

Honey-Lemon Sauce:
2 tablespoons honey
2 tablespoons lemon juice
2 tablespoons soy sauce

Combine all of the sauce ingredients and set aside.

CHICKEN MADRAS

Distinctive Indian flavors dominate this tasty chicken entree. Sautéed breasts are simmered in a tomato-based curry sauce that's punctuated with ginger preserves and raisins. Serve this on a bed of Basmati rice.

4 boneless, skinless chicken breasts, split in half
flour for dredging
4 tablespoons butter
1 medium-size yellow onion, chopped
Curried Tomato Sauce (recipe follows)

1. Dredge the chicken in flour.

2. Heat the butter in a large non-stick skillet. Add the onion and sauté over medium-high heat until the onion is golden, about 10 minutes.

3. Add the chicken and sauté for 3 minutes per side until lightly brown. Add the sauce and simmer for 5 minutes more. Serve at once.

6 to 8 portions

Curried Tomato Sauce:
14-ounce can tomatoes, broken up into chunks with their juice
1/3 cup ginger preserves
2 tablespoons orange juice
3 tablespoons raisins
1 large clove garlic, minced
1 teaspoon curry powder
salt and pepper to taste

Combine all of the sauce ingredients and mix well. Set aside until needed.

CHICKEN MARSALA

This new version of the Italian classic showcases sautéed breasts surrounded by a riot of gourmet mushrooms and glazed in a honey and balsamic-flavored Marsala Sauce. The balsamic vinegar and lemon juice balance the otherwise cloyingly sweet taste of the Marsala wine.

ITALIAN-INSPIRED MEAL

Salad Asiago
. . .
Chicken Marsala
. . .
Pasta with Pesto
. . .
Romano-Crusted Eggplant
. . .
Melon Wedges

3 large boneless, skinless chicken breasts, split in half
flour for dredging
salt and pepper to taste
6 tablespoons butter
1 large clove garlic, minced
1 pound assorted gourmet mushrooms (shiitake, oyster, and cremini),
*   thickly sliced*
¼ cup chopped Italian parsley
Marsala Sauce (recipe follows)

1. Season the flour with salt and pepper; dredge the chicken in the flour mixture.

2. Heat 3 tablespoons butter in a large skillet. Add the garlic and mushrooms and season with salt and pepper. Sauté over medium-high heat until the mushrooms are nicely browned. Remove the mushrooms from the pan and set aside.

3. Heat the remaining 3 tablespoons butter in the same pan. Add the chicken and sauté over medium-high heat, 4 minutes per side. Add the sautéed mushrooms, parsley, and Marsala Sauce. Simmer for 2 to 3 minutes more until the sauce is reduced slightly, basting the chicken with the glaze. Serve at once.

6 portions

Marsala Sauce:
1 tablespoon honey
2 tablespoons lemon juice
3 tablespoons balsamic vinegar
½ cup Marsala wine

Combine all of the sauce ingredients and mix well.

**ORIENTAL
STIR-FRY**

Oriental Pea Soup
. . .
Minced Chicken
with Pine Nuts
. . .
Beef and Broccoli
with Oyster Sauce
. . .
White Rice
. . .
Flambéed Bananas

MINCED CHICKEN WITH PINE NUTS

This Oriental dish of stir-fried, diced chicken and vegetables with pine nuts is presented as a filling for lettuce roll-ups. The roll-ups also make an interesting appetizer for a Chinese meal.

2 tablespoons soy sauce
1 tablespoon dry sherry
1/2 teaspoon finely grated gingerroot
1 teaspoon sugar
2 boneless, skinless chicken breasts, cut into 1/2-inch cubes
1 tablespoon Oriental sesame oil
1 tablespoon cornstarch
2 tablespoons vegetable oil
1/2 cup diced red pepper
1/2 cup diced green pepper
1/2 cup diced celery
2 scallions, sliced into 1/4-inch thick pieces
1/3 cup pine nuts
1 head iceberg lettuce, core removed

1. In a medium-size bowl, combine the soy sauce, sherry, ginger, and sugar. Add the chicken, mix well, and let marinate for 30 minutes.

2. In a separate small bowl, mix the sesame oil and cornstarch together until smooth. Set aside.

3. Heat the vegetable oil in a wok. Add the red and green pepper, celery, scallions, and pine nuts and stir-fry over high heat for 1 minute.

4. Add the chicken and marinade and stir-fry for 2 to 3 minutes until the chicken is cooked. Pour the sesame sauce over all and continue stir-frying until the sauce thickens. Turn out onto a platter and present with the lettuce leaves.

5. To serve, place a leaf of lettuce on each plate and spoon about 1/3 cup of the chicken mixture atop the middle of the lettuce. Fold in the sides of the lettuce and roll-up, forming a cylinder.

10 to 12 roll-ups; 4 portions

CHICKEN MIRABELLE

I love the heavenly flavors that dominate this dish. Sautéed boneless breasts are luxuriously surrounded by mushrooms, leeks, sun-dried tomatoes, wine, and cream.

4 boneless, skinless chicken breasts, split in half
flour for dredging
salt and pepper to taste
1/2 cup dry white wine
1/2 cup light cream
1/2 cup butter
1/4 pound shiitake mushrooms, sliced
2 leeks (white part only), cut into 2-inch long julienne pieces
3/4 cup sun-dried tomatoes, julienned

1. Season the flour with salt and pepper; dredge the chicken in the flour mixture.

2. Combine the wine and cream and set aside.

3. Heat 3 tablespoons butter in a large skillet. Add the mushrooms, leeks, and sun-dried tomatoes and sauté until golden, about 10 minutes. Remove the vegetables from the pan and set aside.

4. Heat the remaining 5 tablespoons butter in the same pan. Add the chicken and sauté over high heat until browned, 3 to 4 minutes per side.

5. Return the sautéed vegetables to the pan. Add the cream sauce and simmer for 2 to 3 minutes more until the sauce is reduced to half its volume, basting the chicken with the glaze. Serve at once.

6 to 8 portions

DINNER FARE

Caesar Salad♦
· · ·
Chicken Mirabelle
· · ·
Buttered Noodles
· · ·
Roasted Broccoli
· · ·
Orange Sunshine Cake

**WEEK-DAY
QUICKIE**

Chicken with
Orange Cream
. . .
Buttered Noodles
. . .
Ribbons of Zucchini
and Summer Squash
. . .
Assorted Cookies

CHICKEN WITH ORANGE CREAM

Sautéed breasts are napped with a delectable light cream sauce laced with orange liqueur, reminiscent of the flavors of a creamsicle. This is a simple dish to prepare with heavenly results!

4 boneless, skinless chicken breasts, split in half
flour for dredging
salt and pepper to taste
1/2 cup orange juice
1/2 cup light cream
1/4 cup Triple Sec or Grand Marnier
4 tablespoons butter

1. Season the flour with salt and pepper; dredge the chicken in the flour mixture.

2. Combine the orange juice, cream, and Triple Sec and set aside.

3. Heat the butter in a large skillet. Add the chicken and sauté over high heat, 3 to 4 minutes per side until browned. Add the orange sauce and simmer for 2 minutes more until the sauce is reduced, spooning the glaze over the chicken as it cooks. Serve at once.

6 to 8 portions

PACIFIC RIM CHICKEN

For a taste of the tropics, try these sautéed chunks of chicken and bananas that are douced with a fresh Lime-Rum Sauce.

2 pounds boneless, skinless chicken breasts, cut into 1¹/₂-inch chunks
flour for dredging
salt and pepper to taste
6 tablespoons butter
3 medium-size bananas, cut into 1-inch chunks
Lime-Rum Sauce (recipe follows)

1. Season the flour with salt and pepper; dredge the chicken in the flour mixture.

2. Heat the butter in a large skillet. Add the chicken and sauté over medium-high heat for 3 to 4 minutes. Turn the chicken over, add the bananas and sauce, and sauté for 3 to 4 minutes more, stirring occasionally. Serve at once with a rice accompaniment.

6 portions

Lime-Rum Sauce:
¹/₃ cup dark rum
1 teaspoon finely grated lime zest
¹/₄ cup lime juice
2 tablespoons packed dark brown sugar

Combine all of the sauce ingredients and mix well. Set aside until needed.

**TROPICAL
TASTES**

Mango Soup
· · ·
Pacific Rim Chicken
· · ·
White Rice
· · ·
Butternut Squash
· · ·
Coconut Cake

**CASUAL
GET-TOGETHER**

Peanut-Crusted
Chicken
. . .
Rice with
Apple-Pear Chutney
. . .
Red Cabbage Slaw
. . .
Triple Chocolate
Chunk Cookies

PEANUT-CRUSTED CHICKEN

This dish is a peanut lover's delight. Boneless breasts are dipped in a honey-mustard, encrusted with chopped peanuts, and baked to a turn.

4 boneless, skinless chicken breasts, split in half
salt and pepper to taste
¹/₄ cup Dijon mustard
¹/₄ cup honey
2 tablespoons vegetable oil
2 cups unsalted peanuts, finely crushed

1. Preheat the oven to 375°F. Grease a large cookie sheet.

2. Season the chicken with salt and pepper.

3. Combine the mustard, honey, and oil and mix well.

4. Dip the chicken in the mustard mixture and then roll in the crushed peanuts, coating well.

5. Place the chicken on the cookie sheet; bake for 20 minutes. Serve hot or at room temperature.

6 to 8 portions

PEKING CHICKEN

This is one of my family's favorite stir-fry dishes. Chunks of chicken are surrounded by crisp red and yellow peppers and scallions, glazed with hoisin sauce, and garnished with cashew nuts. As is typical of wok cooking, the chicken and vegetables are all cut into uniform pieces so that all of the ingredients cook evenly.

ORIENTAL
DINNER

Mussels Oriental
. . .
Peking Chicken
. . .
Rice
. . .
Kai Seki Asparagus
. . .
Ginger Ice Cream♦

2 large boneless, skinless chicken breasts, cut into 3/4-inch cubes
cornstarch for dredging
3 tablespoons hoisin sauce
2 tablespoons mirin (sweet rice wine)*
1/4 cup vegetable oil
1 large red pepper, cut into 3/4-inch square pieces
1 large yellow pepper, cut into 3/4-inch square pieces
3 scallions, cut into 1-inch lengths
3/4 cup cashew nuts

1. Dredge the chicken in cornstarch.

2. In a small bowl, combine the hoisin sauce and mirin and set aside.

3. Heat 1 tablespoon oil in a wok. Add the red and yellow peppers and scallions and stir-fry over high heat for 2 minutes. Remove the vegetables to a plate.

4. Add the remaining 3 tablespoons oil to the wok. When hot, add the chicken and stir-fry for 2 to 3 minutes until cooked. Return the vegetables to the wok, add the hoisin sauce, and mix well.

5. Add the cashew nuts and stir-fry for 1 minute. Serve at once with a rice accompaniment.

4 portions

*Available at Oriental markets

FAMILY DINNER

Chicken with
Piccolini Sauce
. . .
Ribbons of Zucchini
and Summer Squash
. . .
Deluxe Mashed
Potatoes
. . .
Chocolate Sorbet

CHICKEN WITH PICCOLINI SAUCE

Italian in design, the relish features finely minced mushrooms, onions, and black and green olives, accented by the piquancy of capers and the fruitiness of olive oil. The blending of these distinct Mediterranean flavors makes it a splendid topping for pasta, veal, and grilled fish as well.

3 large boneless, skinless chicken breasts, split in half
3 tablespoons olive oil
salt and pepper to taste
Piccolini Sauce (recipe follows)

1. Brush the chicken with the olive oil. Season with salt and pepper.

2. Grill over hot coals, 4 inches from the heat source, 4 to 5 minutes per side. Serve hot or at room temperature with spoonfuls of the sauce atop each piece.

6 portions

Piccolini Sauce:
$^1/_4$ cup extra-virgin olive oil
$1^1/_4$ cups minced, fresh cultivated mushrooms
$^3/_4$ cup minced Spanish onion
$^1/_2$ cup minced ripe black olives
$^1/_3$ cup minced pimiento-stuffed green olives
$^1/_4$ cup capers, rinsed and drained

1. Heat the olive oil in a medium-size skillet. Add the mushrooms and onion and sauté over low heat only until the onion is soft and translucent.

2. Add the black and green olives and capers and heat through. Remove to a bowl and serve at once or let cool to room temperature. (Any unused sauce will keep refrigerated for 3 to 4 days; return to room temperature before using.)

About $2^1/_4$ cups of sauce

CHICKEN PICCATA

Hailed from Italy, this classic dish is light and delicate, lavished with lemon juice, parsley, and capers. For a truly delicious indulgence, sprinkle the cooked chicken with freshly grated Parmesan just before removing from the heat.

4 boneless, skinless chicken breasts, split in half
flour for dredging
salt and pepper to taste
3 tablespoons lemon juice
¼ cup dry white wine
3 tablespoons capers
4 tablespoons butter
2 tablespoons olive oil
¼ cup chopped fresh parsley

ITALIAN FEST

Tomatoes and
Pine Nuts
. . .
Chicken Piccata
. . .
Spinach Romano
. . .
Pasta with
Black Olive Pesto
. . .
Chocolate Chip-
Ricotta Cheesecake

1. Season the flour with salt and pepper; dredge the chicken in the flour mixture.

2. In a bowl, combine the lemon juice, wine, and capers and set aside.

3. Heat the butter and olive oil in a large skillet. Add the chicken and sauté over high heat, 3 to 4 minutes per side until evenly browned. Add the lemon sauce and sprinkle with the parsley. Simmer for 2 to 3 minutes more until the sauce is reduced, spooning the glaze over the chicken. Serve at once.

6 to 8 portions

GRILLED CHICKEN WITH PINEAPPLE, MANGO, AND PAPAYA SALSA

The tropical fruits of this refreshing salsa are enlivened by fresh lime juice and cilantro. Used sparingly, cilantro has a wonderful affinity for fruits, especially in relishes and salsas.

3 large boneless, skinless chicken breasts, split in half
3 tablespoons olive oil
salt and pepper to taste
Pineapple, Mango, and Papaya Salsa (recipe follows)

1. Brush the chicken breasts with the olive oil. Season with salt and pepper.

2. Grill over hot coals, 4 inches from the heat source, 4 to 5 minutes per side. Serve hot off the grill or at room temperature with spoonfuls of the salsa atop each piece.

6 portions

Pineapple, Mango, and Papaya Salsa:
1 cup diced pineapple
1 cup peeled and diced mango
1 cup peeled, seeded, and diced papaya
1/4 cup diced red onion
1 jalapeño pepper, seeded and diced
1 teaspoon finely grated lime zest
2 tablespoons lime juice
1 tablespoon honey
3 tablespoons chopped fresh cilantro
salt and pepper to taste

Combine all of the salsa ingredients and mix well. Refrigerate until needed; return to room temperature before serving.

About 31/2 cups of salsa

CHICKEN PORTOBELLO

The much-prized, giant portobello mushrooms impart a marvelous, rich, woodsy flavor to the garlicky tomato sauce that naps these sautéed breasts.

4 boneless, skinless chicken breasts, split in half
flour for dredging
salt and pepper to taste
6 tablespoons olive oil
1 pound portobello mushrooms, stems trimmed,
    cut into 1/2-inch thick slices
4 cloves garlic, minced
28-ounce can Italian plum tomatoes, well drained and
    coarsely chopped
1/4 cup brandy
1/4 cup finely chopped fresh parsley

1. Season the flour with salt and pepper; dredge the chicken in the flour mixture.

2. Heat 3 tablespoons olive oil in a large skillet. Add the mushrooms and sauté over medium-high heat until browned, about 5 to 6 minutes. Remove the mushrooms from the pan and set them aside.

3. Heat the remaining olive oil in the pan. Add the garlic and cook over medium-high heat for 1 minute. Add the chicken and sauté, 4 to 5 minutes per side until browned.

4. Add the tomatoes, mushrooms, brandy, and parsley. Season with salt and pepper. Simmer for 3 to 4 minutes more, basting the chicken with the sauce. Serve at once.

6 to 8 portions

ITALIAN MENU

Chicken Portobello
. . .
Salad Lucia
. . .
Pasta Gremolata
. . .
Chocolate-Almond
Biscotti

GRILLED CHICKEN WITH PLUM COULIS

The sweet-tart flavor of the juicy plum makes this blushing, puréed sauce divine. Try it over grilled duck breasts for a gourmet treat.

3 large, boneless, skinless chicken breasts, split in half
3 tablespoons olive oil
salt and pepper to taste
Plum Coulis (recipe follows)

1. Brush the chicken breasts with the olive oil. Season with salt and pepper.

2. Grill over hot coals, 4 inches from the heat source, 4 to 5 minutes per side. Serve hot or at room temperature with spoonfuls of coulis atop each piece.

6 portions

Plum Coulis:
3 large, ripe plums, peeled and pitted
2 tablespoons Creme de Cassis (black currant liqueur)
1 tablespoon lemon juice
1 tablespoon snipped chives
1 teaspoon finely grated gingerroot
salt and pepper to taste

Place all of the ingredients in the bowl of a food processor and purée. Transfer the coulis to a container and refrigerate until needed. (This may be prepared a day in advance.) Return to room temperature to serve.

RASPBERRY-GLAZED CHICKEN

Sautéed chunks of chicken are defined by a rich raspberry and fresh lime glaze, and crowned with chopped pistachio nuts.

2 pounds boneless, skinless chicken breasts, cut into 1½-inch chunks
flour for dredging
salt and pepper to taste
4 tablespoons butter
Raspberry Sauce (recipe follows)
¼ cup shelled and skinned pistachio nuts, coarsely chopped
*   for garnish*

1. Season the flour with salt and pepper; dredge the chicken in the flour mixture.

2. Heat the butter in a large skillet. Add the chicken and sauté over medium-high heat, 3 to 4 minutes per side until browned.

3. Add the Raspberry Sauce, raise the heat to high, and simmer for 3 to 4 minutes more until the sauce thickens, basting the chicken with the glaze. Remove the chicken to a platter and sprinkle with the pistachio nuts. Serve at once.

6 portions

Raspberry Sauce:
3 tablespoons raspberry preserves
½ cup sweet vermouth
2 tablespoons lime juice
3 tablespoons snipped chives

Combine all of the sauce ingredients and mix well. Set aside until needed.

SUMMER SOLSTICE MENU

Beet Gazpacho
· · ·
Raspberry-Glazed Chicken
· · ·
Mango and Red Pepper Salad
· · ·
Pilaf with Popped Wild Rice
· · ·
Down East Blueberry Cake

CHICKEN ROMESCO

Romesco is one of the great Spanish sauces from Catalan. It combines the best red peppers, tomatoes, garlic, almonds, and olive oil, all ground to a pastelike pesto. It's marvelous over chicken, and also makes a delectable topping for pasta or grilled fish.

4 large boneless, skinless chicken breasts, split in half
flour for dredging
salt and pepper to taste
4 tablespoons olive oil
Romesco Sauce (recipe follows)

1. Season the flour with salt and pepper; dredge the chicken in the flour mixture.

2. Heat the olive oil in a large skillet. Add the chicken and sauté over high heat, 4 to 5 minutes per side until cooked and browned. Remove to a platter and top with spoonfuls of Romesco Sauce. Serve warm or at room temperature.

6 to 8 portions

Romesco Sauce:
3 large red peppers, roasted
2 large, ripe plum tomatoes, peeled and seeded
4 large cloves garlic, crushed
1/2 cup blanched almonds, coarsely chopped
salt and pepper to taste
1/4 teaspoon crushed red pepper flakes
1/4 cup extra-virgin olive oil

1. Place the red peppers, tomatoes, garlic, almonds, salt, pepper, and red pepper flakes in the bowl of a food processor. Grind to a fine paste.

2. With the motor running, add the oil in a slow, steady stream until it is completely incorporated. Transfer the sauce to a container and store in the refrigerator; the sauce will keep for 3 to 4 days. Return to room temperature before using.

2 cups of sauce

CHICKEN RUSTICA

Gustatory flavors of the Mediterranean dominate this hearty chicken dish, resplendent with olives, capers, and sun-dried tomatoes in a Port wine sauce. This is glorious company fare as it can be made in advance and reheated.

4 boneless, skinless chicken breasts, split in half
flour for dredging
salt and pepper to taste
3 tablespoons butter
3 tablespoons olive oil
1 large clove garlic, minced
¼ cup diced shallots
1 teaspoon dried oregano
¾ cup coarsely chopped sun-dried tomatoes
⅔ cup ripe black olives
2 tablespoons capers
2 tablespoons lemon juice
1 cup Port wine

1. Season the flour with salt and pepper; dredge the chicken in the flour mixture.

2. Heat the butter and olive oil in a large skillet. Add the garlic and shallots and sauté over medium heat until the shallots are translucent, about 2 minutes.

3. Add the chicken and sprinkle with the oregano. Turn the heat to high and sauté for 3 to 4 minutes per side until golden.

4. Add the sun-dried tomatoes, olives, capers, lemon juice, and wine. Simmer for 3 to 4 minutes more until the sauce thickens and reduces to half its volume. Baste the chicken with the pan juices. Serve at once or let cool and refrigerate overnight. Return to room temperature; cover and reheat in a 350°F oven for 20 minutes until hot.

6 to 8 portions

ITALIAN DINNER PARTY

Shredded Greens with
Strawberry Vinaigrette
. . .
Chicken Rustica
. . .
Slow-Roasted
Tomatoes
. . .
Italian Noodle Bake
. . .
Lemon Ice◆
. . .
Assorted Cookies

CHICKEN SALTIMBOCCA

Simple and particular to Rome, the flavors of chicken, prosciutto, sage, and olive oil come together for dramatic effects. This is a new interpretation of the classic presentation.

4 boneless, skinless chicken breasts, cut into 1¹/₂-inch chunks
flour for dredging
salt and pepper to taste
¹/₄ pound prosciutto, sliced ¹/₈-inch thick
¹/₃ cup olive oil
2 tablespoons finely rubbed fresh sage
3 tablespoons lemon juice

1. Season the flour with salt and pepper; dredge the chicken in the flour mixture.

2. Cut the prosciutto into ¹/₂-inch square pieces.

3. Heat the olive oil in a large skillet. Add the chicken and season with the sage. Sauté over medium-high heat for 3 to 4 minutes. Turn the chicken over.

4. Add the prosciutto and drizzle with the lemon juice. Sauté for 5 minutes more, stirring occasionally, until the chicken is done. Serve at once.

6 portions

SOUTH-OF-THE-BORDER CHICKEN

South-of-the-border spices embrace boneless breasts, titillating the taste buds. The grilled breasts are then served with a zesty chili mayonnaise. For large parties, cut the grilled chicken into bite-size pieces and serve the Chili Mayonnaise as a dipping sauce.

1 teaspoon onion powder
1 teaspoon garlic powder
1 teaspoon ground cumin
2 teaspoons dried oregano
2 teaspoons paprika
1/4 teaspoon black pepper
salt to taste
2 tablespoons lime juice
1/4 cup virgin olive oil
4 boneless, skinless chicken breasts, split in half
Chili Mayonnaise (recipe follows)

1. In a bowl, combine the onion powder, garlic powder, cumin, oregano, paprika, black pepper, salt, lime juice, and olive oil and mix well.

2. Spread the marinade over the chicken and let sit at room temperature for 30 minutes.

3. Grill over hot coals, 4 inches from the heat source, 4 to 5 minutes per side. Serve hot off the grill or let cool to room temperature, spooning dollops of the Chili Mayonnaise atop each portion.

6 to 8 portions

Chili Mayonnaise:
1/2 cup mayonnaise
1 1/2 teaspoons chili powder
1/4 teaspoon cayenne pepper
1 1/2 teaspoons lemon juice

Combine all of the sauce ingredients and mix well. Store in the refrigerator until needed.

MEXICAN-INSPIRED PICNIC

Guacamole
. . .
South-of-the-Border
Chicken
. . .
Southwestern
Corn Salad
. . .
Red Cabbage Slaw
. . .
Chocolate-Chocolate
Chip Wafers

TARRAGON CHICKEN

This is one of my family's absolute favorites, especially when time is of the essence. Bite-size pieces of chicken are liberally seasoned with tarragon, blushing with paprika, and quickly sautéed in a garlic-infused butter. It's best served with pilaf.

2 pounds boneless, skinless chicken breasts, cut into ³/₄-inch chunks
flour for dredging
salt and pepper to taste
6 tablespoons butter
1 large clove garlic, minced
1¹/₂ teaspoons paprika
1 tablespoon dried tarragon

1. Season the flour with salt and pepper; dredge the chicken in the flour mixture.

2. Heat the butter in a large skillet. Add the garlic and let cook for 1 minute.

3. Add the chicken and sprinkle with the paprika and tarragon. Sauté over high heat for 3 minutes. Turn the chicken over and continue to sauté until the chicken is cooked, about 2 to 3 minutes more, stirring occasionally. Serve at once.

6 portions

CHICKEN WITH TOMATO SALSA

This dish gets spectacular results with basic ingredients. A fresh plum tomato relish fragrant with parsley and scallions and rich with balsamic vinegar glazes sautéed chicken breasts, imparting a sweet, woody flavor.

4 boneless, skinless chicken breasts, split in half
flour for dredging
salt and pepper to taste
4 large, ripe plum tomatoes, chopped
1 cup finely chopped Italian parsley
2/3 cup chopped scallions
1/2 cup balsamic vinegar
1/4 cup olive oil

1. Season the flour with salt and pepper; dredge the chicken in the flour mixture.

2. In a bowl, combine the tomatoes, parsley, scallions, and vinegar.

3. Heat the olive oil in a large skillet. Add the chicken and sauté over high heat, 3 to 4 minutes per side until browned. Add the tomato salsa. Simmer for 2 to 3 minutes more, basting the chicken with the sauce until the vinegar becomes syrupy and forms a glaze. Serve at once.

6 to 8 portions

FAMILY DINNER

Chicken with
Tomato Salsa
. . .
Barley-Corn Pilaf
. . .
Roasted Broccoli
. . .
Blondies✦

CHICKEN VERONIQUE

Lemon has a wonderful affinity for mint as evidenced in this marinated and grilled chicken dish. It's enrobed with a refreshing, light, and lemony Grape Relish seasoned with a whisper of mint.

2 large boneless, skinless chicken breasts, split in half
1 medium-size clove garlic, crushed
salt and pepper to taste
1/2 teaspoon dried mint
2 tablespoons lemon juice
2 tablespoons extra-virgin olive oil
Grape Relish (recipe follows)

1. Place the chicken in a glass dish.

2. In a separate bowl, whisk together the garlic, salt, pepper, mint, lemon juice, and olive oil. Pour the marinade over the chicken and let sit at room temperature for 1 to 2 hours.

3. Grill over hot coals, 4 inches from the heat source, 4 to 5 minutes per side until cooked and browned, basting with the marinade.

4. Serve hot off the grill or let cool to room temperature. Present with spoonfuls of the Grape Relish atop each piece.

4 portions

Grape Relish:
1 1/2 cups red and green grapes, cut in half
1/4 cup coarsely chopped Italian parsley
3 tablespoons snipped chives
salt and pepper to taste
1/2 teaspoon dried mint
1 teaspoon finely grated lemon zest
1 tablespoon lemon juice
2 tablespoons extra-virgin olive oil

Combine all of the relish ingredients and mix well. Refrigerate until needed; return to room temperature to serve.

CHICKEN WITH VINEGAR PEPPERS

The zesty tang of vinegar peppers enlivens sautéed breasts that are finished with a cream sherry-butter sauce. This is also delicious made with pork chops or pork tenderloins.

3 large, boneless, skinless chicken breasts, split in half
flour for dredging
salt and pepper to taste
6 tablespoons butter
the equivalent of 3 whole red and yellow vinegar peppers (see page 18)
¹/₂ cup cream sherry

1. Season the flour with salt and pepper; dredge the chicken in the flour mixture.

2. Heat the butter in a large skillet. Add the chicken and sauté over high heat until browned, about 5 minutes. Turn the chicken over and sauté for 3 minutes.

3. Add the vinegar peppers and cream sherry. Simmer for 2 minutes more. Serve at once with the pan juices spooned over the chicken.

6 portions

AN ITALIAN
AFFAIR

Bruschetta with
Artichoke Pesto
. . .
Chicken with
Vinegar Peppers
. . .
Roasted Potatoes
. . .
Romano-Crusted
Eggplant
. . .
Citrus Angel Food
Cake with Berries

CHICKEN WITH WHITE BEAN PURÉE

A flavorful, fashionable, and nutritious sauce tops grilled breasts that's sure to become a family favorite. The bean purée is fragrant with herbs and also makes a smashing dip with chunks of peasant bread and crudités.

3 large, boneless, skinless chicken breasts, split in half
3 tablespoons olive oil
salt and pepper to taste
White Bean Purée (recipe follows)

1. Brush the chicken with the olive oil. Season with salt and pepper.

2. Grill over hot coals, 4 inches from the heat source, about 4 to 5 minutes per side. Serve hot off the grill or at room temperature with dollops of the White Bean Purée.

6 portions

White Bean Purée:
1 cup canned cannelli beans, rinsed and drained
1 medium-size clove garlic, crushed
1 tablespoon lemon juice
2 tablespoons dry white wine
1½ teaspoons Dijon mustard
½ teaspoon dried rosemary
½ teaspoon dried thyme
¼ teaspoon ground ginger
salt and pepper to taste
1 tablespoon snipped chives
2 tablespoons extra-virgin olive oil

Place all of the ingredients in the bowl of a food processor and purée. Store in the refrigerator until needed; return to room temperature to serve.

TURKEY CHILI

Turkey may well become the food of the 90s, being inexpensive, flavorful, low in fat, and versatile. A boon to cooks, it replaces meat rather successfully in many dishes. This version of the all-American comfort food is unquestionably delicious and bold in flavor.

3 tablespoons olive oil
1 large yellow onion, chopped
2 large cloves garlic, minced
1 pound ground turkey
salt and pepper to taste
1 teaspoon dried oregano
1 teaspoon ground cumin
1 tablespoon chili powder
¹/₂ teaspoon crushed red pepper flakes
28-ounce can Italian plum tomatoes, coarsely crushed with their juice
2 cups cooked black beans

1. Heat the olive oil in a large saucepan. Add the onion and garlic and sauté until the onion is soft, about 5 minutes.

2. Add the turkey and stir-fry until it is browned. Season with the salt, pepper, oregano, cumin, chili powder, and red pepper flakes.

3. Add the tomatoes. Simmer uncovered for 30 minutes. Add the black beans and heat for 5 minutes. Serve piping hot. This reheats well.

4 to 5 portions

**SUPER BOWL
SUNDAY BASH**

Jen's Salsa with Chips
· · ·
Snake Bites
· · ·
Turkey Chili
· · ·
French Bread
· · ·
Green Salad with
Ranch Dressing
· · ·
Hermits

SEAFOOD TREASURES

BAKED BLUEFISH WITH WALNUT GREMOLATA

The strong flavor of bluefish makes it a delectable match for the assertive taste of the crusty, garlicky, walnut gremolata topping. Bluefish is one of the fishes with a high omega-3 fat content, making it a natural choice for those watching their cholesterol.

2 pounds bluefish filets
salt and pepper to taste
1/2 cup finely chopped fresh parsley
1 tablespoon grated lemon zest
4 medium-size cloves garlic, minced
1/2 cup ground walnuts
3/8 cup thinly sliced scallions
1/2 cup virgin olive oil

1. Preheat the oven to 400°F.

2. Place the bluefish in a baking dish. Season with salt and pepper.

3. In a bowl, combine the parsley, lemon zest, garlic, walnuts, scallions, and olive oil. Spread the gremolata evenly over the fish.

4. Bake for 30 minutes. Spoon the pan juices over the fish and serve at once.

5 to 6 portions

JERK-STYLE BLUEFISH

Jerk is a typical Jamaican barbecue style of cooking. The fish is marinated in an aromatic, spicy paste of allspice, bay leaves, scallions, and pepper, and then grilled to a turn.

Jerk Marinade:
2 large cloves garlic, crushed
¹/₂ cup finely chopped scallions
1¹/₂ teaspoons allspice
¹/₂ teaspoon cinnamon
¹/₄ teaspoon nutmeg
¹/₂ teaspoon crushed red pepper flakes
2 bay leaves, crushed
¹/₂ teaspoon salt
¹/₂ teaspoon black pepper
¹/₄ cup olive oil

2 pounds bluefish filets

1. Combine all of the ingredients of the Jerk Marinade. Spread the paste over the fish and let marinate at room temperature for 1 hour.

2. Grill over hot coals, 4 inches from the heat source, 5 minutes per side. Serve at once.

4 portions

**SIMPLE GRILLED
DINNER**

Jerk-Style Bluefish
. . .
Belmont Salad
. . .
Rice
. . .
Grilled Fruits
. . .
Lemon Ice◆

**LOUISIANA-STYLE
SUPPER**

Baked Catfish with
Cornbread Crumbs
· · ·
Bayou Rice and Corn
· · ·
Coleslaw◆
· · ·
Pecan Pie

BAKED CATFISH WITH CORNBREAD CRUMBS

With the advent of farm-raised seafood, catfish is becoming one of the most favored fishes, with its sweet flesh, medium-firm texture, versatility, and reasonable price.

2 pounds catfish filets
salt and pepper to taste
1/4 teaspoon cayenne pepper
1 cup cornbread crumbs
1 1/4 cups grated sharp cheddar cheese
6 tablespoons butter, melted

1. Preheat the oven to 400°F. Grease a baking dish.

2. Arrange the catfish in the prepared pan. Season with salt, pepper, and cayenne pepper.

3. Cover the filets with the cornbread crumbs and top with the grated cheese. Drizzle the melted butter over the fish.

4. Bake for 20 to 25 minutes. Spoon the pan juices over the catfish and serve at once.

6 portions

BERBER-SPICED ROASTED COD

The delicate, mild flavor of cod is enlivened with the high seasonings of Berber spices, indigenous to North African cuisine. The combination of these flavors is really both aromatic and exciting. I also use the spice mix on tuna, swordfish, and sirloin steak.

2 pounds cod filets
2 tablespoons olive oil

Berber Spice Mix:
1 teaspoon onion powder
2 teaspoons garlic powder
1 teaspoon salt
2 teaspoons paprika
1 teaspoon crushed red pepper flakes
1 teaspoon coarsely ground black pepper
$^1/_2$ teaspoon cinnamon
$^1/_2$ teaspoon allspice
$^1/_2$ teaspoon ground cloves
$^1/_2$ teaspoon ground coriander
1 teaspoon ground ginger
2 tablespoons all-purpose flour

A TASTE OF MOROCCO

Berber-Spiced
Roasted Cod
· · ·
Moroccan Grilled
Vegetables
· · ·
Couscous with
Dried Fruit
· · ·
Orange Wedges

1. Preheat the oven to 450°F. Grease a baking pan.

2. Place the fish in the prepared pan. Brush the cod filets with the olive oil.

3. Combine all of the Berber spices and flour and mix well. Sprinkle the spice mix over the fish, coating generously.

4. Bake for 20 to 25 minutes or until the fish flakes easily when tested with a fork. Serve at once.

6 portions

ORIENTAL CRAB CAKES

This "East meets West" crab presentation features cakes rich with crabmeat, spiked with the piquant Western influences of Dijon and Worcestershire, and flavored with the Oriental ingredients of ginger, scallions, and water chestnuts. Sautéed until golden, they're served with a Sesame Mayonnaise.

1 pound lump crabmeat
1 scallion, thinly sliced
$^1/_3$ cup chopped water chestnuts
$1^1/_2$ teaspoons grated gingerroot
$^1/_2$ teaspoon Worcestershire sauce
1 teaspoon Dijon mustard
freshly ground pepper to taste
1 egg, beaten
$^1/_2$ cup mayonnaise
1 cup plain bread crumbs
$^1/_4$ cup vegetable oil
Sesame Mayonnaise (recipe follows)

1. Combine the crabmeat, scallion, water chestnuts, ginger, Worcestershire sauce, Dijon, pepper, egg, mayonnaise, and $^1/_4$ cup bread crumbs.

2. Form the crab mixture into 8 equal-sized cakes. Dip each cake in the remaining bread crumbs, coating completely. Refrigerate for 1 to 2 hours.

3. Heat the oil in a large skillet. Sauté the cakes in the hot oil about 3 minutes per side until golden. Serve at once with dollops of the Sesame Mayonnaise.

4 portions

Sesame Mayonnaise:
1 cup mayonnaise
1 tablespoon soy sauce
$1^1/_2$ teaspoons Oriental sesame oil
1 tablespoon sesame seeds, toasted

Combine all of the ingredients and mix well. Store in the refrigerator until needed. (This will keep for 1 week.)

GRILLED SOFT-SHELL CRABS WITH RED PEPPER RELISH

Soft-shell crabs are indeed a delicacy, boasting sweet, tender, succulent flesh and shells. Their entire body is edible, including the main portion and the claws. Quickly grilled over hot coals, they are then crowned with a savory roasted red pepper relish, giving rise to an exquisite meal. This is sumptuous when served over a bed of freshly cooked linguine.

Red Pepper Relish:
3 red peppers, roasted and coarsely chopped
¹/₄ cup chopped sweet onion (preferably Vidalia or Texas;
*   if unavailable use red onion)*
1 tablespoon capers
¹/₂ teaspoon dried basil
2 tablespoons chopped fresh parsley
¹/₈ teaspoon freshly ground pepper
1 tablespoon balsamic vinegar
1 tablespoon extra-virgin olive oil

8 medium-size soft-shell crabs, cleaned
3 tablespoons olive oil
salt and pepper to taste

1. Prepare the relish. In a bowl, combine the roasted peppers, onion, capers, basil, parsley, pepper, vinegar, and olive oil. Mix well and let marinate for 1 to 2 hours. (This may be prepared up to 2 days in advance and refrigerated; return to room temperature to serve.)

2. Brush the crabs with the olive oil and season with salt and pepper.

3. Grill the crabs over hot coals, 4 inches from the heat source, 3 minutes per side until cooked and lightly charred. Serve hot off the grill with spoonfuls of the relish atop each crab.

4 portions

SUMMER'S
SUCCULENCE

Beet Gazpacho
. . .
Grilled Soft-Shell
Crabs with Red
Pepper Relish
. . .
Linguine

Grilled Corn
on the Cob
. . .
Deep-Dish Blueberry-
Nectarine Pie

SAUTÉED SOFT-SHELL CRABS

I look forward to crab season with great enthusiasm—it's one of the delights of summer. Soft-shell crabs are delicious any way you serve them, whether broiled, grilled, or sautéed. These plump, succulent shellfish tout a light cornmeal crust sautéed in garlic butter until crisp and golden.

1/2 cup all-purpose flour
1/2 cup cornmeal
1/2 teaspoon cayenne pepper
salt and pepper to taste
8 medium-size soft-shell crabs, cleaned
1/2 cup buttermilk
4 tablespoons butter
4 tablespoons vegetable oil
2 large cloves garlic, minced

1. Combine the flour, cornmeal, cayenne pepper, salt, and pepper in a large bowl.

2. Dip the crabs in the buttermilk and then coat them completely with the seasoned flour.

3. Heat the butter and oil in a large skillet. Add the garlic and crabs. Sauté over medium-high heat, 2 to 3 minutes per side until golden. (It may be necessary to cook the crabs in two batches; keep the first batch warm in a low oven while cooking the rest.) Serve at once.

4 portions

HADDOCK GENOVESE

The marriage of basil pesto and goat cheese is probably one of the great new flavor combinations. The sweet and mild tasting haddock filet is lavished with a Pesto and chèvre topping. This is also wonderful with scrod and cod.

2 pounds haddock filets
$^1/_2$ cup Pesto (see page 15)
4 ounces chèvre, crumbled

1. Preheat the oven to 350°F.

2. Place the haddock in a baking dish. Spread the Pesto over the fish. Sprinkle with the goat cheese.

3. Bake for 25 minutes. Serve at once with the pan juices spooned over the fish.

4 to 6 portions

COMPANY DINNER

Salad Aromatica
. . .
Haddock Genovese
. . .
Pilaf with
Popped Wild Rice
. . .
Tomatoes Provençal◆
. . .
Orange-Walnut Cake◆

HADDOCK WITH
RED PEPPER MAYONNAISE

Haddock filets are napped with a roasted red pepper mayonnaise which adds distinction and flavor to this mild, sweet fish.

2 pounds haddock filets, skinned
salt and pepper to taste
1 large red pepper, roasted and puréed
2/3 cup mayonnaise
1 tablespoon minced fresh basil
2 medium-size cloves garlic, crushed
pinch cayenne pepper

1. Preheat the oven to 350°F.

2. Place the haddock filets in a baking dish, tucking the thin ends under the filets for uniform thickness. Season with salt and pepper.

3. Combine the roasted pepper, mayonnaise, basil, garlic, and cayenne pepper. Spread the mixture over the filets, coating generously.

4. Bake for 25 minutes. Serve at once.

4 portions

HALIBUT DIJON

This is an easy and flavorful way to prepare halibut steaks. The sweet, firm flesh is covered with a creamy, double-mustard sauce and baked to perfection.

2 pounds halibut steaks, 1-inch thick
salt and pepper to taste
2 tablespoons Dijon mustard
2 tablespoons whole grain mustard
1/4 cup sour cream
2 tablespoons thinly sliced scallion
1 tablespoon lemon juice

1. Preheat the oven to 450°F.

2. Season the fish steaks with salt and pepper. Arrange in a baking pan.

3. In a separate bowl, mix the Dijon, whole grain mustard, sour cream, scallion, and lemon juice. Spread the sauce over the top and sides of the fish.

4. Bake for 15 to 20 minutes until the steaks are cooked through. Serve immediately.

4 to 6 portions

SIMPLE FISH DINNER

Halibut Dijon
. . .
Chopped Vegetables
with Ranch Dressing
. . .
Rice Pilaf◆
. . .
Coffee Ice

GRILLED MAHIMAHI WITH MANGO RELISH

I like to combine fresh fruits with fish, as they add sparkle and a sweet, refreshing twist to the dish. This tropical meaty fish is complemented by a savory mango relish that's spiked with cilantro and ginger. If mahimahi is unavailable, swordfish may be substituted.

2 pounds mahimahi filets
1/4 cup olive oil
salt and pepper to taste
Mango Relish (recipe follows)

1. Brush the fish with the olive oil and season with salt and pepper.

2. Grill the mahimahi over hot coals, 4 inches from the heat source, 5 to 6 minutes per side. Serve at once with the Mango Relish spooned over each portion.

4 to 6 portions

Mango Relish:
1 ripe mango, peeled, pitted, and diced
3/4 cup diced red pepper
1/4 cup diced red onion
1 tablespoon finely chopped fresh cilantro
1 tablespoon grated gingerroot
2 tablespoons lime juice
2 tablespoons extra-virgin olive oil

Combine all of the relish ingredients and let sit at room temperature for 1 to 2 hours for flavors to blend. (This may be prepared 24 hours in advance and refrigerated; return to room temperature to serve.)

MONKFISH WITH PLUM GLAZE

Sautéed medallions of monkfish are glazed with a savory Port wine-plum sauce.

 2 pounds monkfish
 flour for dredging
 salt and pepper to taste
 1 egg, beaten
 4 tablespoons butter
 1/4 cup diced shallots
 Plum Glaze (recipe follows)

1. Slice the monkfish into 3/4-inch thick medallions.

2. Season the flour with salt and pepper.

3. Dip the fish in the egg and then dredge in the seasoned flour.

4. Heat the butter in a large non-stick skillet. Add the shallots and sauté only until softened; do not brown.

5. Add the monkfish and sauté over medium-high heat, 3 minutes per side until golden. Pour the sauce over the fish and simmer for 1 minute more until thickened, spooning the glaze over the medallions. Serve at once.

4 to 6 portions

 Plum Glaze:
 3/4 cup Port wine
 2 tablespoons Damson plum jam

Combine the Port wine and jam and mix well.

CASUAL SUPPER

Orange-Beet Soup✦
. . .
Monkfish with
Plum Glaze
. . .
Basic Couscous
. . .
Dilled Carrots and
Zucchini Rounds
. . .
Fruit Tart

CHILI-ROASTED SALMON

Salmon filets are coated with a highly seasoned barbecue rub, infused with chili powder, paprika, and cayenne pepper and tempered with brown sugar for a blast of Texas flavor. The seasoning mix also works well on mahimahi.

1½ *pounds salmon filets*
1½ *tablespoons vegetable oil*

Spice Rub:
1 *tablespoon paprika*
1 *tablespoon dark brown sugar*
1½ *teaspoons chili powder*
½ *teaspoon ground cumin*
½ *teaspoon kosher or coarse salt*
½ *teaspoon black pepper*
½ *teaspoon cayenne pepper*

1. Preheat the oven to 400°F. Grease a baking dish.
2. Place the filets in the prepared pan. Brush with the vegetable oil.
3. Combine all of the ingredients of the spice rub. Sprinkle the rub evenly over the filets, covering completely.
4. Bake for 25 minutes. Serve at once.

4 portions

Note—This recipe doubles easily for a larger group.

HERB-ROASTED SALMON WITH TOMATO-CORN RELISH

Salmon filets are encrusted with a melange of fragrant herbs, baked to a turn, and embellished with a seductive, fresh plum tomato and corn relish. This makes a vibrant presentation. I serve the salmon with freshly cooked linguine and spoon the relish over both.

2 pounds salmon filets
2 tablespoons olive oil
salt and pepper to taste
2 teaspoons dried basil
1 teaspoon dried thyme
1 teaspoon dried tarragon
1 teaspoon dried sage
1 teaspoon dried marjoram
Tomato-Corn Relish (recipe follows)

1. Preheat the oven to 400°F. Grease a large baking dish.

2. Place the salmon in the prepared pan. Brush with the olive oil and season with salt and pepper.

3. In a small bowl, combine the basil, thyme, tarragon, sage, and marjoram, and mix well.

4. Sprinkle the herb mixture evenly over the salmon, coating completely.

5. Bake for 25 minutes. Serve each portion topped with spoonfuls of the relish.

6 portions

FOURTH OF JULY CELEBRATION

Sweet Potato
Vichyssoise
. . .
Greens with Walnut
Vinaigrette
. . .
Herb-Roasted
Salmon with
Tomato-Corn Relish
. . .
Linguine
. . .
Deep-Dish Blueberry-
Nectarine Pie

Tomato-Corn Relish:
5 or 6 large, ripe plum tomatoes, chopped
²/₃ cup fresh or frozen corn kernels, blanched
¹/₄ cup thinly sliced scallions
¹/₂ cup coarsely chopped Italian parsley
¹/₂ teaspoon dried basil
¹/₂ teaspoon dried thyme
salt to taste
¹/₄ teaspoon coarsely ground black pepper
1 tablespoon red wine vinegar
1 tablespoon extra-virgin olive oil

Combine all of the relish ingredients and mix well. Let sit at room temperature for 1 to 2 hours for flavors to blend. (This may be prepared up to 8 hours in advance and refrigerated; return to room temperature to serve.)

SALMON OLIVADA

Olivada, the dazzling Niçoise olive paste, gives new definition to salmon. Filets are coated with the olive spread and baked to a turn, creating a mouth-watering experience. This is just as tasty served at room temperature as it is hot out of the oven.

2 pounds salmon filets
½ cup Olivada (see page 14)
1 tablespoon balsamic vinegar

1. Preheat the oven to 400°F. Grease a baking pan.
2. Place the salmon in the prepared pan.
3. Combine the Olivada and balsamic vinegar, mixing well. Spread the olive paste evenly over the filet. (This may be done 6 to 8 hours in advance and refrigerated; return to room temperature before cooking.)
4. Bake for 25 minutes and serve.

4 to 6 portions

**DINNER PARTY
FOR 6**

Chèvre Turnovers
· · ·
Salmon Olivada
· · ·
Asparagus with
Balsamic Butter
· · ·
Pilaf with
Popped Wild Rice
· · ·
Fruit Tart

SALMON EN CROÛTE

This is an absolutely divine and impressive dish. Salmon filets are napped with Brie and toasted almonds, wrapped in a pastry crust, and baked until golden. This gets a 5-star rating in our house.

²/₃ pound Brie cheese, white rind removed
1 pound frozen puff pastry, thawed
1²/₃ pounds salmon filets
2 tablespoons butter, melted
salt and pepper to taste
¹/₂ cup sliced almonds, toasted
1 egg, beaten

1. Place the Brie in the freezer for 30 minutes; then slice it thinly with a cheese slicer.

2. Roll out the puff pastry on a board to form a rectangle 12 x 20-inches. Place it on a large cookie sheet and chill for 30 minutes.

3. Preheat the oven to 350°F.

4. Lay the salmon filet down the middle of the puff pastry. (It may be necessary to tuck the tip end under to fit.)

5. Drizzle the butter over the fish. Season with salt and pepper. Lay the cheese slices over the filet. Sprinkle with the sliced almonds.

6. Fold the dough over like a turnover, overlapping the sides. Crimp the ends together firmly to seal.

7. Brush the pastry with the beaten egg. Bake for 30 minutes. Cut into 6 equal pieces and serve at once.

6 portions

SEAFOOD FIESTA

Shellfish Remoulade
. . .
Salmon en Croûte
. . .
Watercress and
Strawberries
. . .
Down East
Blueberry Cake

HICKORY-GLAZED SCALLOPS

Scallops strut a delectable mustard-maple sauce that's highlighted by a slight hickory-smoked flavor.

2 pounds sea scallops
¹/₄ cup Dijon mustard
¹/₄ cup pure maple syrup
1 tablespoon soy sauce
1 teaspoon liquid smoke

1. Skewer the scallops.

2. Whisk together the Dijon, maple syrup, soy sauce, and liquid smoke. Pour the sauce over the scallops, turning to coat evenly.

3. Grill or broil the scallops, 4 inches from the heat source, 3 to 4 minutes per side until charred, basting with the sauce. Serve at once.

4 to 6 portions

**HORS D'OEUVRE
PARTY FOR 12**

Mediterranean
Pita Wedges
· · ·
Baked Stuffed Oysters
· · ·
Butternut Squash
Pillows
· · ·
Hickory-Glazed
Scallops
· · ·
Grilled Fruits

GRILLED SCALLOPS WITH MANGO COULIS

The simplicity of this dish makes it most appealing. Grilled scallops are set on a cold, sweet mango purée for a refreshing, delicate, and fruity effect. Try the coulis over almost any other grilled fish or chicken.

2¹/₂ pounds scallops
2¹/₂ tablespoons olive oil
salt and pepper to taste
Mango Coulis (recipe follows)

1. Skewer the scallops. Brush the shellfish with the olive oil and season with salt and pepper.

2. Grill over hot coals, 4 inches from the heat source, 3 to 4 minutes per side until charred and cooked through. Place large spoonfuls of the coulis on each plate, set a portion of scallops on the pool of sauce, and serve.

6 portions

Mango Coulis:
1 large, ripe mango, peeled, pitted, and puréed
1 tablespoon honey
1 teaspoon grated lime zest
1 tablespoon lime juice
1¹/₂ teaspoons grated gingerroot
salt and pepper to taste
2 tablespoons extra-virgin olive oil

Combine all of the ingredients of the coulis. Refrigerate until needed; return to room temperature before serving. (This may be prepared up to 2 days in advance.)

SAUTÉED SCALLOPS NIÇOISE

A symphony of Niçoise flavors—tomatoes, garlic, capers, basil, and thyme—embrace these succulent jewels from the sea.

¹/₄ cup plus 1 tablespoon olive oil
4 large, ripe plum tomatoes, chopped
2 tablespoons diced shallots
2 large cloves garlic, minced
2 tablespoons capers
freshly ground pepper to taste
1 teaspoon dried basil
¹/₂ teaspoon dried thyme
3 tablespoons chopped fresh parsley
2 pounds sea scallops
¹/₄ cup plain bread crumbs

1. Heat 1 tablespoon olive oil in a sauce pan. Add the tomatoes, shallots, garlic, capers, pepper, basil, thyme, and parsley. Simmer for 5 minutes. Set aside. (This may be prepared a day in advance and refrigerated; reheat before proceeding.)

2. Sprinkle the scallops with the bread crumbs.

3. Heat ¹/₄ cup olive oil in a large non-stick skillet. Add the scallops and sauté over high heat until golden, about 5 minutes, shaking the pan several times to turn the scallops. Add the tomato sauce, stir through until heated, and serve at once.

6 portions

DINNER MENU

Stuffed Shiitake
Mushrooms
· · ·
Sautéed Scallops
Niçoise
· · ·
Rice Pilaf♦
· · ·
Green Beans Olivada
· · ·
Pot de Crème♦

DINNER FARE

Mixed Greens with
Balsamic Vinaigrette◆
. . .
Scallops with
Crabmeat Crumbs
. . .
Buttered Wild Rice
. . .
Tomatoes Provençal◆
. . .
Down East
Blueberry Cake

SCALLOPS WITH CRABMEAT CRUMBS

Rich and extravagant, these sautéed treasures are coated with a crabmeat-crumb mixture that's divine. This goes one step beyond the traditional baked-stuffed presentation.

6 tablespoons butter
1 large clove garlic, minced
1 small yellow onion, diced
6 ounces crabmeat
1/2 cup French bread crumbs, lightly toasted
pinch cayenne pepper
1 pound sea scallops
salt and pepper to taste

1. Heat 4 tablespoons butter in a medium-size skillet. Add the garlic and onion and sauté until the onion is golden. Add the crab, bread crumbs, and cayenne. Sauté over medium-high heat, stirring constantly for 2 minutes. Set aside.

2. Heat the remaining 2 tablespoons butter in a large skillet. Add the scallops and season with salt and pepper. Sauté over high heat, 3 to 4 minutes per side until golden. Sprinkle with the crumb mixture, toss, and heat through. Serve at once.

4 portions

BAKED SCROD WITH LOBSTER CRUMBS

This is a new-wave version of the classic baked-stuffed fish. Scrod is elevated to gastronomic heights with a sumptuous lobster crumb topping. If scrod is unavailable, substitute cod or monkfish.

2 pounds scrod filets, 1-inch thick
salt and pepper to taste
1^1/$_2$ cups coarsely chopped cooked lobster meat
1^1/$_2$ cups fresh bread crumbs, from French bread
^{2}/$_3$ cup diced roasted red pepper
^{1}/$_2$ cup butter, melted

1. Preheat the oven to 400°F. Grease a baking dish.

2. Place the fish in the prepared pan. Season with salt and pepper.

3. Combine the lobster, bread crumbs, roasted pepper, and melted butter. Spread the mixture evenly over the fish.

4. Bake for 20 to 25 minutes or until the fish flakes easily when tested with a fork. Serve at once.

6 portions

WINTER FARE

Parsnip and Pear Soup
· · ·
Baked Scrod with
Lobster Crumbs
· · ·
Vegetable Rice Pilaf
· · ·
Green Beans Caesar
· · ·
Chocolate-Banana
Bread Pudding

SHRIMP DELMONICO

Shrimp are probably the most popular shellfish, being tasty, versatile, and easy to prepare. This dish features shrimp encrusted with a zesty sautéed vegetable and bacon bread topping that's baked until golden.

4 tablespoons butter
1 medium-size yellow onion, finely chopped
1 medium-size green pepper, finely diced
1 medium-size red pepper, finely diced
salt and pepper to taste
1½ teaspoons Worcestershire sauce
4 slices cooked bacon, chopped
¾ cup fresh bread crumbs
2 pounds raw extra-large shrimp, shelled

1. Preheat the oven to 400°F.

2. Heat the butter in a skillet. Add the onion and green and red peppers. Season with salt, pepper, and Worcestershire and sauté over medium until the vegetables are tender, about 5 minutes.

3. Add the bacon and bread crumbs and mix well. Remove the pan from the heat.

4. Place the shrimp in a large baking dish. Cover with the crumb mixture.

5. Bake for 15 minutes until golden. Serve at once.

6 portions

CORAL AND JADE SAUTÉ

The winning combination of shrimp and peapods shines in this delicate, colorful, and tasty Oriental stir-fry.

> 1 pound raw extra-large shrimp, shelled and deveined
> 2 tablespoons vegetable oil
> 1 large clove garlic, minced
> 1½ teaspoons grated gingerroot
> ½ pound snow peas or sugar snap peas
> salt to taste

1. Butterfly the shrimp. Use a sharp knife to split the shrimp almost in half, leaving them attached at the tail end. This allows the shrimp to spread open when cooked.

2. Heat the oil in a wok. When hot, add the garlic and ginger and stir-fry for 30 seconds.

3. Add the shrimp and snow peas. Season with salt. Stir-fry for 3 to 4 minutes until the shrimp turn pink. Serve at once with a white rice accompaniment.

3 to 4 portions

ORIENT EXPRESS

Oriental Crab Cakes
· · ·
Coral and Jade Sauté
· · ·
Soy-Dressed
Cucumbers◆
· · ·
White Rice
· · ·
Oranges

TROPICAL ISLAND DINNER

Piña Colada Soup
. . .
Shrimp Margarita
. . .
Caribbean
Melon Salad
. . .
Grilled Corn
on the Cob
. . .
Assorted Sherbets

SHRIMP MARGARITA

Fashioned after the tropical margarita drink, these shrimp are infused with Tequila, Triple Sec, and lime juice and grilled to a turn. They're stunning as an entree, and equally as dazzling as an hors d'oeuvre.

6 tablespoons Tequila
1/4 cup Triple Sec
1/4 cup lime juice
1 1/2 teaspoons grated lime zest
2 tablespoons honey
salt and pepper to taste
1/4 cup virgin olive oil
2 pounds raw extra-large shrimp, shelled

1. Whisk together the Tequila, Triple Sec, lime juice, lime zest, honey, salt, pepper, and olive oil.

2. Pour the marinade over the shrimp and let sit at room temperature for 1 hour.

3. Grill or broil the shrimp, 4 inches from the heat source, 2 to 3 minutes per side, basting with the marinade. Serve hot off the grill.

6 dinner portions; 12 hors d'oeuvre portions

MEXICAN-FLAVORED SHRIMP

The ever popular shellfish is covered with a sauce redolent with Mexican flavors—chili powder, oregano, orange juice, cinnamon, and tomato—for a South-of-the-border accent. Serve the dish with a white rice accompaniment. The sauce is also glorious over sautéed chicken breasts.

1/4 cup olive oil
1 medium-size yellow onion, chopped
1 1/2 pounds raw extra-large shrimp, shelled
Mexican-Flavored Sauce (recipe follows)

1. Heat the olive oil in a large skillet. Add the onion and sauté over medium-high heat until the onion is browned, about 10 minutes.

2. Add the shrimp and sauté 2 minutes per side until the shrimp turn pink. Add the Mexican sauce and simmer for 3 to 4 minutes more. Serve at once atop a bed of white rice.

4 portions

Mexican-Flavored Sauce:
1 ripe plum tomato, chopped
2 tablespoons raisins
1/2 cup orange juice
1 tablespoon chili powder
1 teaspoon dried oregano
1/4 teaspoon cinnamon
pinch ground cloves
salt to taste
1/4 teaspoon freshly ground black pepper

Combine all of the sauce ingredients and set aside.

MEXICAN MENU

Chili-Cheese Puffs
. . .
Mexican Caesar Salad
. . .
Mexican-Flavored
Shrimp
. . .
White Rice
. . .
Orange Freeze◆

GRILLED SHRIMP WITH ORANGE-TOMATO RELISH

Shrimp bask in the glory of a fragrant and fruity mandarin orange and plum tomato salsa that's spiked with toasted almonds.

1½ pounds raw extra-large shrimp, shelled
2 tablespoons olive oil
salt and pepper to taste
1 teaspoon dried orange peel
Orange-Tomato Relish (recipe follows)

1. Skewer the shrimp. Brush with the olive oil and season with salt, pepper, and orange peel.

2. Grill over hot coals, 4 inches from the heat source, 2 to 3 minutes per side. Spoon the relish over the shrimp and serve.

4 portions

Orange-Tomato Relish:
2 ripe plum tomatoes, chopped
11-ounce can mandarin oranges, drained
¼ cup diced red onion
¼ cup slivered almonds, toasted
1 teaspoon dried rosemary
salt and pepper to taste
1 tablespoon orange juice
1 tablespoon extra-virgin olive oil

Combine all of the relish ingredients and let marinate at room temperature for 1 to 2 hours. (This may be prepared a day in advance and refrigerated; return to room temperature to serve.)

PECAN-ENCRUSTED SOLE WITH SHRIMP SAUCE

Filet of sole, the sweetest of fishes, is quickly sautéed with a nutty, seasoned crumb coating and served with a tarragon-flavored mayonnaise, rich with chopped shrimp. The combination of flavors is complex and wonderful.

1 cup plain bread crumbs
salt and pepper to taste
generous pinch cayenne pepper
1 teaspoon dried thyme
1 cup finely chopped pecans
2 pounds filet of sole (6 filets)
2 eggs, beaten
¹/₂ cup butter
Shrimp Sauce (recipe follows)

1. Combine the bread crumbs, salt, pepper, cayenne pepper, thyme, and pecans in a pie plate.

2. Dip the fish in the beaten egg and then in the seasoned crumb mixture. Refrigerate for 30 minutes so crumbs will adhere.

3. In a large non-stick skillet, melt the butter. Add the filets and sauté over medium-high heat, 3 minutes per side until golden and cooked through. Remove to a platter, spoon dollops of the sauce over the filets, and serve at once.

6 portions

Shrimp Sauce:
1 cup mayonnaise
1 large clove garlic, minced
1 tablespoon lemon juice
1¹/₂ teaspoons Dijon mustard
salt and pepper to taste
generous pinch cayenne pepper
1 teaspoon dried tarragon
3 ounces cooked shrimp, chopped

Combine all of the sauce ingredients and mix well. Store in the refrigerator. (This may be prepared a day in advance.)

DINNER FARE

Warm Tomato and
Goat Cheese Salad
· · ·
Pecan-Encrusted Sole
with Shrimp Sauce
· · ·
Butter Wild Rice
· · ·
Sautéed Baby Squash
· · ·
Lemon Cake Roll

VENETIAN-STYLE SOLE

This sweet and sour cold fish dish is a classic of Venetian cuisine. It is traditionally prepared with smelts or sardines, but it works well with filet of sole or flounder. Fish filets are first sautéed in olive oil, then covered with a sweet-sour topping of balsamic-glazed, sautéed onions, pine nuts, raisins, and orange peel. Left to marinate overnight and served at room temperature, this is a splendid dish for buffets.

2 pounds filet of sole or flounder
salt and pepper to taste
flour for dredging
1/2 cup olive oil
2 medium-size yellow onions, sliced
1/4 cup pine nuts
1/4 cup raisins
3 tablespoons julienned orange peel
1 cup balsamic vinegar

1. Season the fish with salt and pepper and dredge in flour.

2. Heat the olive oil in a large skillet. Sauté the fish in batches over high heat until lightly browned. Remove the cooked filets to a pyrex dish.

3. Add the onions to the pan and sauté over medium-high heat until golden. Add the pine nuts, raisins, orange peel, and vinegar and cook for 2 to 3 minutes.

4. Spoon the onion mixture over the fish, cover, and refrigerate overnight. Return to room temperature to serve.

4 to 6 portions

HOT WEATHER FARE

Melon with Prosciutto
. . .
Venetian-Style Sole
. . .
Herbed Rice Salad
. . .
Slow-Roasted Tomatoes
. . .
Berries and Cream

SWORDFISH RUM RICKEY

Fashioned after the tropical drink, this meaty fish is embraced by the flavors of lime and rum.

3 tablespoons lime juice
¼ cup dark rum
1 medium-size clove garlic, crushed
3 tablespoons Dijon mustard
2 tablespoons soy sauce
1 tablespoon molasses
2 tablespoons vegetable oil
2½ pounds swordfish steaks, 1-inch thick

1. Whisk together the lime juice, rum, garlic, Dijon, soy sauce, molasses, and oil. Pour the dressing over the fish and let marinate at room temperature for 20 to 30 minutes.

2. Grill or broil the fish, 4 inches from the heat source, 4 to 5 minutes per side until cooked through, basting with the marinade. Serve at once.

6 portions

SIMPLE DINNER

Swordfish Rum Rickey
· · ·
White Rice
· · ·
Nectarines and
Tomatoes
· · ·
Grilled Fruits

**MEDITERRANEAN
FARE**

Warm Tomato and
Goat Cheese Salad
. . .
Sicilian-Roasted
Swordfish
. . .
Polenta
. . .
Sautéed Zucchini
. . .
Fresh Melon

SICILIAN-ROASTED SWORDFISH

Swordfish steaks are resplendent with a raisin, pine nut, bacon, and sautéed onion topping. The flavors all come together lending a sweet, rich, nutty, and slight hickory taste to this marvelous dish.

2 pounds swordfish steaks, 1¼-inches thick
3 tablespoons olive oil
freshly ground pepper to taste
1 medium-size yellow onion, chopped
¼ cup pine nuts
⅓ cup raisins
2 slices bacon, diced

1. Preheat the oven to 400°F. Grease a baking dish.

2. Place the swordfish in the prepared pan. Brush with 1 table-spoon olive oil and season with pepper.

3. Heat the remaining 2 tablespoons olive oil in a small skillet. Add the onion and sauté over medium heat until the onion is browned. Stir in the pine nuts, raisins, and bacon. Remove the pan from the heat. Spoon the mixture over the fish, spreading to cover the steaks completely.

4. Bake for 20 to 25 minutes. Serve at once.

4 to 6 portions

SWORDFISH AND MUSSELS IN TOMATO-LEEK SAUCE

Meaty swordfish pairs up with succulent mussels in a tomato sauce rich with leeks, garlic, and shallots. Serve this over a bed of freshly cooked linguine.

> 1/4 *cup olive oil*
> 1 *large clove garlic, crushed*
> 4 *shallots, diced*
> 3 *cups coarsely chopped leeks (white part only)*
> 28-*ounce can Italian plum tomatoes, coarsely chopped with their juice*
> *salt and pepper to taste*
> 1 *teaspoon dried thyme*
> 1/8 *teaspoon cayenne pepper*
> 1/2 *cup dry sherry*
> 1 *tablespoon capers*
> 1 1/3 *pounds swordfish, 1-inch thick, cut into 4 equal pieces*
> 1 1/2 *pounds mussels, scrubbed and debearded*

1. Heat the olive oil in a large skillet. Add the garlic, shallots, and leeks and sauté until the leeks are soft and translucent.

2. Add the tomatoes, salt, pepper, thyme, cayenne pepper, sherry, and capers. Simmer uncovered for 15 minutes. (This may be prepared 1 day in advance and refrigerated; reheat before proceeding.)

3. Add the swordfish and simmer for 10 minutes. Turn the swordfish pieces over, add the mussels, cover and simmer for about 5 minutes more until the swordfish is cooked and the mussels are fully opened. Serve at once atop freshly cooked pasta.

4 portions

ITALIAN-INSPIRED DINNER

Winter Salad with
Walnut Pesto
. . .
Swordfish and Mussels
in Tomato-Leek Sauce
. . .
Linguine
. . .
Romano-Crusted
Eggplant
. . .
Tiramisu Cake

GRILLED TROUT

SUMMER DINNER

Mango Soup
· · ·
Grilled Trout
· · ·
Pasta with Grilled
Vegetables◆
· · ·
Chocolate Angel
Food Cake with
Assorted Berries

Whole trout are resplendent with this highly seasoned presentation. The butterflied fish are grilled skin-side down, resulting in perfectly cooked, moist fish.

4 whole trout, head and bones removed
4 teaspoons olive oil
salt and pepper to taste
2 large cloves garlic, crushed
2 teaspoons dried rosemary
2 teaspoons dried thyme
2 tablespoons Worcestershire sauce
1/4 cup virgin olive oil

1. Brush the skin of each filet with 1 teaspoon olive oil. Spread open the fish and season the flesh with salt and pepper.

2. Whisk together the garlic, rosemary, thyme, Worcestershire sauce, and 1/4 cup olive oil.

3. Spread the marinade over the flesh of each fish.

4. Place the fish, skin side down on a hot grill. Cover the grill and cook for 4 to 5 minutes until done. Do not turn the fish. Serve at once.

4 portions

TUNA AU POIVRE

Thick, lean tuna steaks are seared quickly with an assertive, coarsely ground black pepper and mustard seed crust, and served with dollops of Mustard Mayonnaise. The tuna is rare and tender with a fiery coating.

1 tablespoon sugar
2 tablespoons coarsely ground black pepper
4 teaspoons mustard seeds
2 pounds tuna steaks, 1 to 1¹/₄-inches thick
¹/₄ cup olive oil
Mustard Mayonnaise (recipe follows)

1. Combine the sugar, pepper, and mustard seeds. Press the mixture firmly into each side of the tuna steaks, coating it thoroughly.

2. Heat the olive oil in a medium-size skillet, and sauté the tuna over high heat, 2 minutes per side until well-seared. Remove to a platter and slice thinly. Serve with dollops of the Mustard Mayonnaise.

4 to 6 portions

Mustard Mayonnaise:
²/₃ cup mayonnaise
1¹/₂ tablespoons Dijon mustard
1 tablespoon soy sauce

Combine all of the ingredients and mix well. Store in the refrigerator until needed. (This may be prepared 3 to 4 days in advance, and will keep for 1 week.)

SIMPLE SUPPER

Tuna Au Poivre
. . .
Linguine with
Red Onion Relish

Mixed Green Salad
with Herb-Dried
Cherry Tomatoes
. . .
Lemon Sorbet

KOREAN SESAME GRILLED TUNA

Bulgogi is the classic Korean-style barbecue dish. Traditionally it is made with thin slices of beef that have been marinated in a soy-sesame based sauce and grilled on a hibachi. I have adapted the flavors of bulgogi for tuna steaks resulting in more delicate fare.

1/2 cup finely chopped scallions
2 large cloves garlic, minced
1 tablespoon dark brown sugar
1/4 cup soy sauce
1/4 teaspoon freshly ground black pepper
1 tablespoon Oriental sesame oil
1 tablespoon dry sherry
1 tablespoon sesame seeds, toasted
2 pounds tuna steaks, 1 1/4-inches thick

1. Combine the scallions, garlic, brown sugar, soy sauce, pepper, sesame oil, sherry, and sesame seeds.

2. Pour the sauce over the tuna and let marinate at room temperature for 30 minutes.

3. Grill over hot coals, 4 inches from the heat source, 3 minutes per side for medium-rare. The tuna is much more delicate and succulent when pink in the middle. Serve hot off the grill or let cool to room temperature and present.

4 portions

GARDEN VEGETABLES

Vegetables should complement the meal. They should not overpower the main course, but should have their own identity and distinct flavor that adds to the dish.

Vegetables are best when freshly purchased—young, crisp, and tender. If you start with old, withered, dried-up, tough vegetables, you will have poor results. Keep in mind that the end product is only as good as its ingredients. I shop like a European and tend to buy only what I need or what looks enticing for the meals of that day. I realize you do not all have the luxury of shopping daily, but try to buy your produce every few days, rather than once a week. You'll find you have less waste, and will enjoy the marvelous, fresh flavor. Take advantage of seasonal offerings, indulging in the bounty of the harvest.

**SPRING DINNER
FOR 6**

Chèvre Turnovers
. . .
Salmon Olivada
. . .
Asparagus with
Balsamic Butter
. . .
Pilaf with
Popped Wild Rice
. . .
Fruit Tart

ASPARAGUS WITH BALSAMIC BUTTER

Asparagus is a harbinger of spring and a much prized vegetable. These slender, green stalks are accented by a splash of balsamic vinegar and the piquancy of capers.

1½ pounds asparagus, peeled and poached for 5 minutes
salt and pepper to taste
4 tablespoons butter
2 tablespoons balsamic vinegar
1 tablespoon capers

1. Arrange the asparagus spears in a serving dish. Season with salt and pepper.

2. Heat the butter, vinegar, and capers in a small saucepan over medium-high until syrupy. Pour over the asparagus and serve.

4 portions

OVEN-ROASTED ASPARAGUS

A simple oven-roasted presentation does justice to this perennial favorite.

2 pounds asparagus spears, peeled, tough ends removed
4 to 6 tablespoons olive oil
salt and freshly ground pepper to taste

1. Preheat the oven to 400°F. Grease a large baking dish.

2. Arrange the asparagus in the prepared pan. Drizzle with the olive oil and season with salt and pepper.

3. Roast for 20 minutes, until lightly brown, turning the stalks over after 10 minutes. Serve warm or at room temperature.

6 portions

**FORMAL DINNER
PARTY FOR 6**

Apple-Butternut
Squash Soup
. . .
Hoisin-Glazed Rack
of Lamb
. . .
Chèvre Mashed
Potatoes
. . .
Oven-Roasted
Asparagus
. . .
Asian Pear Tart

KAI SEKI ASPARAGUS

Poached asparagus take on an Oriental theme when dressed in a ginger-flavored hoisin vinaigrette and garnished with toasted sesame seeds.

> 2 pounds asparagus, peeled and poached until tender-crisp, about
>   5 minutes
> 2 scallions, thinly sliced
> 3 tablespoons hoisin sauce
> 6 tablespoons rice vinegar
> 1/4 cup Oriental sesame oil
> 2 tablespoons grated gingerroot
> 2 tablespoons sesame seeds, toasted

1. Arrange the asparagus in a serving dish. Sprinkle with the scallions.

2. In a small bowl, whisk together the hoisin sauce, vinegar, sesame oil, and gingerroot. Pour the vinaigrette over the asparagus. Sprinkle with the sesame seeds. Serve at once or let marinate for 1 to 2 hours and present at room temperature.

6 portions

ROASTED BEETS AND RED ONIONS

Roasted vegetables are definitely in vogue. The sweet flavor of ruby-hued beets is coupled with red onions, and delicately seasoned with a hint of orange peel in this roasted medley.

4 medium-size beets, peeled
3 medium-size red onions, peeled
1/3 cup olive oil
salt and freshly ground pepper to taste
1½ teaspoons finely grated orange peel

1. Preheat the oven to 400°F.

2. Quarter the beets and onions through their stems. Place the vegetables in a roasting pan.

3. Toss the beets and onions with the olive oil. Season with salt and pepper and sprinkle with the orange peel.

4. Cover and roast for 30 minutes. Uncover and roast for 30 minutes more. Serve at once.

4 portions

WINTER REPAST

Mushroom Pâté
· · ·
Roast Chicken with
Fig Relish
· · ·
Couscous
· · ·
Roasted Beets and
Red Onions
· · ·
Baked Apples

ROASTED BROCCOLI

Crispy flowerets of this nutritious vegetable are heady with garlic and splashed with lemon juice and olive oil for a light Mediterranean touch.

¹/₄ cup olive oil
1 tablespoon lemon juice
2 large cloves garlic, crushed
salt and freshly ground pepper to taste
5 cups broccoli flowerets, cut into reasonable serving-size pieces

1. Preheat the oven to 425°F.

2. In a large bowl, combine the olive oil, lemon juice, garlic, salt, and pepper.

3. Add the broccoli and toss until evenly coated. Turn the broccoli out into a large roasting pan in a single layer so that there is no overlapping.

4. Roast for 25 minutes, stirring the flowerets after 15 minutes. Serve hot or at room temperature.

4 portions

BRUSSELS SPROUTS GENOVESE

Of cabbages and their kin, the Brussels sprout is the diminutive member of the family. The sprouts bask in a lemon-infused pesto sauce that will charm and delight you.

1 pound Brussels sprouts, cut in half through the core
1/2 cup Pesto (see page 15)
2 tablespoons lemon juice
salt and pepper to taste

1. Poach the Brussels sprouts for about 7 minutes until they are tender-crisp; drain well. Transfer to a serving dish.

2. Combine the Pesto and lemon juice. Nap the cooked sprouts with the sauce and season with salt and pepper. Toss until evenly mixed. Serve hot or at room temperature.

4 portions

ROAST BEEF DINNER

Vermont Maple-
Walnut Salad
. . .
Roast Beef
. . .
Onion Pudding
. . .
Brussels Sprouts
Genovese
. . .
Chocolate Mousse◆

CARROTS AND TURNIPS GILBERT

The natural sweetness of these root vegetables shines in this creamy vegetable purée.

1 pound carrots, peeled and coarsely chopped
1 pound young white turnips, peeled and coarsely chopped
3 tablespoons butter
salt and pepper to taste

1. Bring a pot of water to a boil, and add the carrots and turnips. Cook until the vegetables are tender, about 15 minutes. Drain well.

2. Place the vegetables in the bowl of a food processor and purée. Add the butter, salt, and pepper and process about 15 seconds until evenly incorporated. Transfer the purée to a casserole and serve at once. (This may be made in advance and reheated in a microwave.)

4 to 6 portions

CORN SAUTÉ

Corn lovers take heed! This double-corn medley of sautéed corn kernels and baby corn is perfumed with the subtle anise flavor of dill butter.

4 tablespoons butter
1 large clove garlic, minced
3 cups corn kernels (fresh or frozen)
15-ounce can baby corn, drained
1/2 cup thinly sliced scallions
1 1/2 teaspoons dried dill
salt and freshly ground pepper to taste

1. Heat the butter in a large skillet. Add the garlic and cook for 1 minute for the garlic essence to be released.

2. Add the corn kernels, baby corn, scallions, and dill. Season with salt and pepper.

3. Sauté the vegetables over high heat for 2 to 3 minutes, stirring often. Serve at once.

6 to 8 portions

FAMILY DINNER

Baked Bluefish with
Walnut Gremolata
. . .
Corn Sauté
. . .
Herbed-Baked Red-
Skinned Potatoes◆
. . .
Citrus Angel
Food Cake

**TROPICAL ISLAND
DINNER**

Piña Colada Soup
. . .
Shrimp Margarita
. . .
Caribbean Melon
Salad
. . .
Grilled Corn
on the Cob
. . .
Assorted Sherbets

GRILLED CORN ON THE COB

Cobs of corn are in all their glory, simple and unadorned, grilled over hot coals until lightly charred. No one can eat just one! What better way to celebrate the warm weather than with this summer favorite.

8 ears of corn, husked
1/4 cup olive oil
salt and pepper to taste

1. Brush the corn with the olive oil. Season with salt and pepper.
2. Grill over hot coals, 4 inches from the heat source, for about 10 minutes, turning often until lightly charred. Serve hot off the grill, warm, or at room temperature.

4 to 6 portions

ROMANO-CRUSTED EGGPLANT

Thick rounds of eggplant sport a garlic and Romano cheese butter and are baked to a turn. The composed butter is very complimentary to the sliced eggplant, with a taste reminiscent of garlic bread.

4 tablespoons butter, at room temperature
2 tablespoons olive oil
6 tablespoons grated Romano cheese
2 large cloves garlic, crushed
freshly ground pepper to taste
2 (1 pound) eggplants, sliced into 1-inch thick rounds

1. Preheat the oven to 400°F.

2. In a small bowl, combine the butter, olive oil, Romano cheese, garlic, and pepper.

3. Spread the cheese mixture on both sides of the eggplant slices. Place the slices on cookie sheets so that they do not touch.

4. Bake for 30 minutes until the eggplant is tender and golden. Serve hot.

6 to 8 portions

ITALIAN-INSPIRED MEAL

Salad Asiago
· · ·
Chicken Marsala
· · ·
Pasta with Pesto
· · ·
Romano-Crusted Eggplant
· · ·
Melon Wedges

SIMPLE GRILLED
DINNER

Jerk-Style Bluefish
. . .
Belmont Salad
. . .
Rice
. . .
Grilled Fruits
. . .
Lemon Ice◆

GRILLED FRUITS

For a change of pace and an enticing accompaniment to a meal, try grilling rum-soaked fruits. You'll be surprised what a succulent garnish they make. My favorites are bananas, peaches, and pineapple, but mangoes, papayas, apples, and pears also make lush additions.

1 large banana, sliced into 3/4-inch thick rounds
2 large peaches or nectarines, cut into 6 wedges
2 cups fresh pineapple chunks
1/4 cup light rum
2 tablespoons dark brown sugar

1. Place the fruits in a large pan and drizzle with the rum. Let the fruits macerate for 30 minutes.

2. Skewer the fruits and sprinkle with the brown sugar.

3. Grill over hot coals (or broil), 4 inches from the heat source, for 4 to 5 minutes per side until caramelized. Serve hot off the grill or at room temperature, whatever your preference.

4 portions

GREEN BEANS CAESAR

A gutsy Caesar dressing redolent with garlic and a shade of anchovy paste gives these beans a zesty and dazzling dimension.

1 pound green beans, poached for 5 minutes until tender-crisp
2 large cloves garlic, crushed
2 tablespoons Dijon mustard
1 teaspoon anchovy paste
freshly ground pepper to taste
2 tablespoons Parmesan cheese
1 tablespoon balsamic vinegar
1 tablespoon red wine vinegar
1/2 cup virgin olive oil

1. Arrange the green beans in a serving dish.

2. In a small bowl, beat together the garlic, Dijon, anchovy paste, pepper, Parmesan, and balsamic and red wine vinegars.

3. Whisk in the olive oil until it is completely incorporated.

4. Pour the dressing over the green beans and serve warm or at room temperature. (This may be made in advance and refrigerated for up to 24 hours; return to room temperature to serve.)

4 to 6 portions

WINTER DINNER

Parsnip and Pear Soup
· · ·
Baked Scrod with
Lobster Crumbs
· · ·
Vegetable Rice Pilaf
· · ·
Green Beans Caesar
· · ·
Chocolate-Banana
Bread Pudding

**ANTIPASTO
PARTY FOR 24**

Spiced Mediterranean
Olives
. . .
Cherry Tomatoes
and Mozzarella
. . .
Oranges and
Red Onions
. . .
Green Beans Olivada
. . .
Bruschetta with
Artichoke Pesto
. . .
Marinated
Mushrooms♦
. . .
Roasted Pepper Salad
. . .
Melon Wrapped
with Prosciutto
. . .
White Bean Salad
. . .
Italian Pasta Salad♦
. . .
Focaccia and
Bread Sticks

GREEN BEANS OLIVADA

Green beans and black olives have a curious affinity. In this dish, poached green beans are sauced in a Niçoise-inspired olive paste.

1 pound green beans, poached for 5 minutes until tender-crisp
salt and pepper to taste
1 tablespoon lemon juice
1/2 cup Olivada (see page 14)

1. Arrange the beans in a serving dish. Season with salt and pepper.

2. In a small bowl, mix together the lemon juice and olivada and spoon the sauce over the beans. Toss well and serve warm or at room temperature.

4 to 6 portions

GREEN BEANS, PROSCIUTTO, AND PARMESAN

The salty, cured, imported Italian ham and mellow cheese are perfect accents for fresh green beans, lending a taste of Italy at its best. This dish is good as a meal opener, great as a salad or vegetable, and makes an important contribution to an antipasto.

1¹/₂ pounds green beans, poached 5 minutes until tender-crisp
¹/₂ pound prosciutto, sliced ¹/₈-inch thick, cut into 3-inch long matchstick pieces
1 cup freshly shaved Parmesan cheese (use a vegetable peeler)
1 teaspoon Dijon mustard
¹/₂ teaspoon crushed red pepper flakes
pinch of salt
generous ¹/₄ teaspoon freshly ground black pepper
3 tablespoons lemon juice
¹/₂ cup extra-virgin olive oil

1. Arrange the green beans in a serving dish. Top with the prosciutto and cheese.

2. In a small bowl, whisk together the Dijon, red pepper flakes, salt, pepper, lemon juice, and olive oil. Pour over the bean mixture and toss well. Serve warm or at room temperature. (This can marinate as much as 8 hours in the refrigerator; return to room temperature before serving.)

6 portions

DINNER MENU

Orange-Fennel Soup
. . .
Lamb Chops
. . .
Herbed Orzo Pilaf
. . .
Green Beans,
Prosciutto,
and Parmesan
. . .
Pot de Crème◆

**ROAST BEEF
DINNER**

Vermont Maple-
Walnut Salad
. . .
Roast Beef
. . .
Onion Pudding
. . .
Brussels Spouts
Genovese
. . .
Chocolate Mousse◆

ONION PUDDING

This is the best of both worlds, being a cross between a quiche and a souffle. The crustless onion custard is infused with goat cheese, fragrant with herbs, and baked until golden. It makes a grand luncheon statement, a marvelous meal opener, and an outstanding accompaniment to roasted poultry or meat.

2^1/$_2$ cups chopped yellow onions (Use Vidalia when available.)
3 tablespoons flour
1 cup whole milk
3 eggs, beaten
^{1}/$_4$ cup butter, melted
6 ounces goat cheese, crumbled
^{1}/$_2$ teaspoon salt
^{1}/$_2$ teaspoon coarsely ground black pepper
^{1}/$_2$ teaspoon dried thyme
^{1}/$_2$ teaspoon dried savory

1. Preheat the oven to 350°F. Grease a 2-quart casserole.

2. Put the onions in a medium-size bowl. Sprinkle with the flour and toss until evenly coated.

3. In a large bowl, mix together the milk, eggs, butter, cheese, and seasonings. Add the onions and stir well.

4. Turn the mixture into the prepared dish. Bake for 45 to 50 minutes until set and golden. Serve at once, cutting into squares.

6 to 8 side portions; 4 main-course portions

PARSNIP CHIPS

The sweetness of this root vegetable shines in these wafer crisps. They make for addictive eating, even better than potato chips!

1 pound parsnips, peeled and sliced into ¹/₈-inch thick rounds
2 tablespoons olive oil
salt and pepper to taste

1. Preheat the oven to 400°F. Grease a large baking sheet.

2. Toss the parsnip rounds with the olive oil. Season with salt and pepper.

3. Spread out in a single layer on the prepared pan so that the pieces are not touching. Bake for 15 to 18 minutes, removing chips as they brown. Let cool at least 5 minutes so that the chips crisp up.

2 to 3 portions

DINNER MENU

Pork Chops with
Blueberry Sauce
· · ·
Sweet Potatoes and
Red Onions
· · ·
Parsnip Chips
· · ·
Chocolate Cake

WINTER REPAST

Roast Chicken
· · ·
Wild Rice Stuffing
· · ·
Roasted Winter
Vegetables
· · ·
Apple Crisp

ROASTED WINTER VEGETABLES

A riot of roasted vegetables adds a splash of excitement to winter meals. This makes a splendid accompaniment to any roasted meat or poultry dish, and is fabulous for buffets. You may also try using turnips, rutabagas, and fennel.

3 large carrots, peeled and cut into 2-inch chunks
3 large parsnips, peeled and cut into 2-inch chunks
3 large leeks, white part only, sliced in half lengthwise
3 large ribs celery, cut into 2-inch lengths
³/₄ pound butternut squash, cut into 2-inch chunks
¹/₄ cup olive oil
1 cup chicken broth
salt and pepper to taste
¹/₂ teaspoon dried thyme

1. Preheat the oven to 400°F.

2. Put the vegetables in a large roasting pan.

3. Pour the olive oil and chicken broth over the vegetables and toss until evenly coated. Season with salt, pepper, and thyme.

4. Roast for 1 hour, stirring the vegetables every 15 minutes. Serve hot or at room temperature.

4 to 6 portions

JULIENNE SAUTÉ

A colorful melange of sautéed, julienned, Mediterranean vegetables are napped in a cream sherry-butter sauce and garnished with pine nuts.

1 medium-size red pepper
1 medium-size yellow pepper
1 medium-size zucchini
2 large carrots
1 fennel bulb, thick outer layer peeled
4 tablespoons butter
2 tablespoons pine nuts
salt and pepper to taste
1/2 cup cream sherry

1. Cut all of the vegetables into julienne matchstick pieces 3-inches long and 1/4-inch thick.

2. Heat the butter in a large skillet. Add the vegetables and pine nuts. Season with salt and pepper. Sauté over high heat for 3 minutes, stirring often, until the vegetables are tender-crisp.

3. Douse with the wine and sauté for 1 minute more. Serve at once.

6 portions

SIMPLE DINNER

Chicken in Ginger-
Peach Chutney
. . .
Basmati Rice
. . .
Julienne Sauté
. . .
Glazed Lemon
Pound Cake❖

ROASTED HOMESTYLE POTATOES

The potato takes on new character when roasted, providing a low-fat alternative to the fry.

4 Idaho potatoes, scrubbed
2 tablespoons olive oil
salt and pepper to taste
3 tablespoons Parmesan cheese

1. Preheat the oven to 400°F. Grease two cookie sheets.

2. Quarter each potato lengthwise, leaving on the skin. Cut each quarter into 2 long wedges.

3. Toss the potato wedges with the olive oil and season with salt and pepper. Arrange them on the baking sheets so that they are spread out in a single layer.

4. Roast for 15 minutes; turn the wedges over and bake for 15 minutes more.

5. Sprinkle with the Parmesan and run under the broiler until the cheese is browned and bubbly. Serve at once.

6 to 8 portions

CAJUN-SPICED ROASTED POTATOES

The mild-mannered potato is generously coated with a highly seasoned cajun spice mix and roasted to a turn.

2 pounds red-skinned potatoes, cut into 1-inch chunks
¼ cup olive oil
1 teaspoon paprika
½ teaspoon onion powder
1 teaspoon garlic powder
1 teaspoon black pepper
½ teaspoon cayenne pepper
1 teaspoon dried thyme
1 teaspoon dried oregano

1. Preheat the oven to 400°F.

2. Toss the potatoes with the olive oil in a large roasting pan.

3. In a separate bowl, combine the paprika, onion powder, garlic powder, black pepper, cayenne pepper, thyme, and oregano and mix well.

4. Sprinkle the potatoes generously with the spice mix.

5. Roast for 45 to 60 minutes, turning and mixing the potatoes every 15 minutes until done. Serve piping hot.

6 to 8 portions

SEAFOOD FARE

Sautéed
Soft-Shell Crabs
· · ·
Cajun-Spiced
Roasted Potatoes
· · ·
Coleslaw♦
· · ·
Deep-Dish Blueberry-
Nectarine Pie

**INTIMATE
DINNER PARTY**

Peking Salmon◆
· · ·
Asparagus with
Balsamic Butter
· · ·
Potatoes Germaine
· · ·
Ice Cream
· · ·
Chocolate Truffles
Cabernet

POTATOES GERMAINE

Layers of thinly sliced potatoes are baked with a sweet, pungent ginger-peach chutney glaze. The chutney may be prepared up to 1 week in advance and stored in the refrigerator. It also doubles as a tantalizing relish for chicken and a sparkling topping for baked brie.

Chutney:
³/₄ cup ginger preserves
2 large peaches, peeled, pitted, and cut into ¹/₂-inch chunks
2 large cloves garlic, crushed
¹/₃ cup diced red pepper
¹/₄ cup diced red onion
¹/₄ cup red wine vinegar

3 large Idaho potatoes with their skins, cut into ¹/₈-inch thick slices
salt and pepper to taste
2 tablespoons butter, melted

1. Prepare the chutney. In a large saucepan, combine the ginger preserves, peaches, garlic, red pepper, red onion, and vinegar. Bring to a boil, reduce the heat, and simmer for about 1 hour until thick, stirring occasionally. Transfer to a covered container and store in the refrigerator until needed.

2. Preheat the oven to 400°F. Grease a 9-inch deep-dish pie pan.

3. Arrange layers of potatoes in the pan, seasoning each layer with salt and pepper. Drizzle the melted butter over the top.

4. Spread the chutney over the potatoes. Bake for 50 minutes. Cover the potatoes if they are getting too brown; return to the oven and bake 10 minutes more. Serve piping hot.

1 generous cup of chutney; 6 portions

GARLIC AND HERB MASHED POTATOES

Mashed potatoes are an old-fashioned favorite. In this updated savory and wholesome version, garlic and herbs are mixed into mashed red-skinned potatoes. I like my mashed potatoes chunky, not smooth and creamy, so I hand mash the vegetable, skin and all!

2 pounds red-skinned potatoes, cut into 1-inch chunks
6 tablespoons butter
1/3 cup milk
2 large cloves garlic, crushed
1 1/2 teaspoons dried rosemary
1 teaspoon dried thyme
salt to taste
1 teaspoon coarsely ground black pepper

1. Boil the potatoes for 10 minutes until tender. Drain well and then mash them with their skins.

2. Add the butter, milk, garlic, rosemary, thyme, salt, and pepper and mix well. Serve at once. (This can be refrigerated for later use; reheat in a microwave to serve.)

6 hearty portions

STEAK AND POTATOES MENU

Grilled Steak with Tomato Chutney
. . .
Zucchini Mandoline◆
. . .
Garlic and Herb Mashed Potatoes
. . .
Shredded Romaine with Caraway Vinaigrette
. . .
Chocolate Chip Cookies

**FORMAL DINNER
PARTY FOR 6**

Apple-Butternut
Squash Soup
. . .
Hoisin-Glazed Rack
of Lamb
. . .
Chèvre Mashed
Potatoes
. . .
Oven-Roasted
Asparagus
. . .
Asian Pear Tart

CHÈVRE MASHED POTATOES

The humble potato is elevated to gastronomic heights, lavished with goat cheese and chives.

2 pounds red-skinned potatoes, cut into 1-inch chunks
¹/₂ cup buttermilk
6 ounces goat cheese
¹/₄ cup snipped chives
1 teaspoon salt
1 teaspoon coarsely ground black pepper

1. Boil the potatoes for 10 minutes until tender. Drain well and mash to a chunky consistency with their skins.

2. Add the buttermilk, goat cheese, chives, salt, and pepper, and mix well. Serve at once. (This may be made 6 to 8 hours in advance and reheated in a microwave to serve.)

6 portions

DELUXE MASHED POTATOES

Mashed Idahos team up with mashed sweet potatoes for a dynamic combination, lavished with a balsamic butter. This is real comfort food.

2 large Idaho potatoes, peeled and cut into 1-inch chunks
2 large sweet potatoes, peeled and cut into 1-inch chunks
6 tablespoons butter
1/4 cup balsamic vinegar
salt and freshly ground pepper to taste

1. Boil the potatoes for 10 minutes until tender. Drain well and mash them.

2. Add the butter and vinegar and season with salt and pepper. Mix well and serve. (This may be prepared up to 24 hours in advance and refrigerated; reheat in a microwave to serve.)

6 to 8 portions

SUNDAY NIGHT SUPPER

Chicken Stuffed with Spinach and Chèvre
. . .
Deluxe Mashed Potatoes
. . .
Slow-Roasted Tomatoes
. . .
Chocolate-Almond Pound Cake◆

DINNER MENU

Pork Chops with
Blueberry Sauce
. . .
Sweet Potatoes and
Red Onions
. . .
Parsnip Chips
. . .
Chocolate Cake

SWEET POTATOES AND RED ONIONS

In addition to their delicious taste, sweet potatoes are also highly nutritious, loaded with vitamin A, potassium, and calcium. The bright orange-fleshed tuber is set against the deep purple of the red onion for a vibrant effect, both colorful and savory.

2 pounds sweet potatoes, peeled and cut into 1¹/₂-inch chunks
2 medium-size red onions, sliced into ¹/₄-inch thick rounds
¹/₃ cup olive oil
¹/₂ cup dry red wine
1¹/₂ teaspoons dried thyme
1 teaspoon dried sage
salt and pepper to taste

1. Preheat the oven to 400°F.

2. Arrange the potatoes and onions in a large casserole dish.

3. In a small bowl, combine the olive oil, wine, thyme, sage, salt, and pepper. Pour the vinaigrette over the vegetables and toss well to coat evenly.

4. Bake for 1 hour, stirring every 15 minutes. Serve hot.

8 portions

PICKLED RED ONIONS

Red onion rings are steeped in a light sweet-sour pickling mixture and left to marinate overnight. These make a tasty relish for roasted meats, poultry, and burgers. Try adding them to salads and sandwiches, too!

> 1½ cups cider vinegar
> 1 cup sugar
> ½ cup water
> 1 tablespoon mustard seeds
> 6 whole juniper berries, crushed
> salt to taste
> 1½ pounds red onions, sliced into ¼-inch thick rings

1. In a large saucepan, combine the vinegar, sugar, water, mustard seeds, juniper berries, and salt. Bring the mixture to a boil.

2. Add the onion rings and stir well. When the mixture returns to a boil, turn off the heat and let cool completely. Transfer the onions and pickling juice to a jar or container. Cover and refrigerate for 6 to 24 hours. (These will keep up to 2 weeks in the refrigerator.)

4 cups; 8 portions

TROPICAL TASTES

Jamaican-Spiced
Pork Loin
· · ·
Rice with Apple-
Pear Chutney
· · ·
Pickled Red Onions
· · ·
Coconut Cake

SPINACH ROMANO

This is a typically Italian presentation of the green, leafy vegetable. Spinach is quickly sautéed in garlic and olive oil and embellished with raisins and a hint of nutmeg.

2 tablespoons olive oil
2 large cloves garlic, minced
1 pound fresh spinach, cleaned and tough stems removed
1/4 cup raisins
generous pinch nutmeg
salt and pepper to taste

1. Heat the olive oil in a large skillet. Add the garlic and sauté until lightly golden.

2. Add the spinach and raisins. Season with nutmeg, salt and pepper. Stir through, cover, and cook over low heat for about 2 minutes until the spinach is tender. Serve hot, warm, or at room temperature—whatever your preference.

4 portions

SESAME SUGAR SNAP PEAS

Sweet sugar snaps are daubed with a snappy Oriental sesame-flavored sauce. These make great buffet food and picnic fare.

1¹/₂ pounds sugar snap or snow peas (or a combination of both), stems removed
1 small clove garlic, minced
1 tablespoon Dijon mustard
1 tablespoon soy sauce
1¹/₂ tablespoons red wine vinegar
1 tablespoon Oriental sesame oil
¹/₄ cup olive oil
freshly ground pepper to taste
2 tablespoons sesame seeds, toasted

1. Blanch the sugar snap peas for 30 seconds in boiling water. Drain well and arrange them in a serving bowl.

2. In a small bowl, whisk together the garlic, Dijon, soy sauce, vinegar, sesame oil, olive oil, pepper, and sesame seeds. Pour the vinaigrette over the pea pods and mix well. Serve at room temperature. (These may be left to marinate in the refrigerator overnight; return to room temperature to serve.)

6 portions

ORIENTAL FARE

Oriental-Glazed
Cornish Hens
· · ·
Kung Pao Shrimp
and Noodles
· · ·
Sesame Sugar
Snap Peas
· · ·
Fresh Pineapple
· · ·
Fortune Cookies

SIMPLE SUPPER

Tuna au Poivre
· · ·
Linguine with Red
Onion Relish
· · ·
Mixed Green Salad
with Herb-Dried
Cherry Tomatoes
· · ·
Lemon Sorbet

HERB-DRIED CHERRY TOMATOES

For an aromatic touch to the rich flavor of sun-dried tomatoes, try adding your favorite herb. Some good choices are basil, thyme, oregano, dill, mint, and rosemary.

*1 pint cherry tomatoes, cut in half
coarse salt and freshly ground black pepper to taste
your choice of dried herb (My favorites are basil and thyme.)*

1. Preheat the oven to 200°F. Line baking sheets with wire racks.

2. Place the tomatoes, cut side up on the racks. Sprinkle lightly with coarse salt, ground pepper, and dried herbs.

3. Dry (bake) in the oven for 7 to 9 hours until the tomatoes are shriveled, deep red, leathery, and dry. Remove the tomatoes as they are ready and cool for 30 minutes.*

4. Store the tomatoes in an airtight jar or container in the refrigerator for up to 2 months.

*The tomatoes will dry at varying rates, depending on their size and their moisture content. After 7 hours, check them every 30 minutes thereafter, removing those that are done.

SLOW-ROASTED TOMATOES

The rich flavor of tomatoes lavished with basil is brought out by the slow-roasting method. Any garden variety of tomato is suitable, but my special preference is for plum tomatoes.

3 large, ripe tomatoes, cut in half across the middle
1 tablespoon extra-virgin olive oil
salt and pepper to taste
1 teaspoon dried basil

1. Preheat the oven to 300°F.

2. Place the tomatoes on a baking sheet, cut side up. Drizzle with the olive oil and season with salt and pepper. Sprinkle with the basil.

3. Roast in the oven for 2 hours. Serve warm or at room temperature. (These may be made up to 24 hours in advance and refrigerated until needed; return to room temperature before reheating.)

4 to 6 portions

ITALIAN DINNER PARTY

Shredded Greens with Strawberry Vinaigrette
· · ·
Chicken Rustica
· · ·
Slow-Roasted Tomatoes
· · ·
Italian Noodle Bake
· · ·
Lemon Ice❖
· · ·
Assorted Cookies

TURNIPS ANNA

Akin to the glorious French dish, potatoes Anna, this layered torte of thinly sliced turnips is sweet and simple to prepare. It makes a wonderful addition to the Thanksgiving table.

2 pounds young white turnips, peeled and thinly sliced
5 to 6 tablespoons butter, melted
salt and pepper to taste

1. Preheat the oven to 425°F. Grease a 9-inch deep-dish pie pan.

2. Arrange a layer of overlapping turnip slices in the pan. Brush the layer with melted butter and season with salt and pepper. Repeat with the remaining ingredients. When the layering is complete, cover the dish tightly with silver foil. Place another pie pan or oven-proof weight on top of the turnips and press down.

3. Bake the turnips with the weight for 30 minutes. Remove the weight, uncover, press the turnips down with a spatula, and bake for 30 minutes more until crisp and browned. Slice into pie-shaped wedges and serve at once.

6 portions

MOROCCAN GRILLED VEGETABLES

Grilled vegetables are certainly the rage! The flavors of North African cuisine—cumin, garlic, ginger, turmeric, paprika, and cinnamon—dominate this vegetable medley that is grilled to a turn. This dish makes a most satisfying companion for grilled and roasted meats, poultry, or fish.

MOROCCAN-INSPIRED MENU

Spice-Roasted
Chick Peas
. . .
Curried Chicken
Tenders with
Mango Chutney
. . .
Couscous
. . .
Moroccan Grilled
Vegetables
. . .
Fresh Fruit

2 Asian eggplants, halved lengthwise
1 medium-size zucchini, quartered lengthwise
1 large red pepper, quartered lengthwise
2 large carrots, halved lengthwise
1 medium-size Spanish onion, sliced into 1/2-inch thick rounds
2 large cloves garlic, crushed
1 teaspoon ground cumin
1 teaspoon ground ginger
1/4 teaspoon ground turmeric
1 teaspoon paprika
1/4 teaspoon cinnamon
salt and pepper to taste
2 tablespoons lemon juice
1/4 cup extra-virgin olive oil

1. Arrange the vegetables on a large dish or platter.

2. In a small bowl, mix together the garlic, cumin, ginger, turmeric, paprika, cinnamon, salt, pepper, lemon juice, and olive oil. Paint the vegetables with the spice blend, and let marinate for 30 minutes, or as much as 6 hours.

3. Grill over hot coals, 4 inches from the heat source, about 12 to 15 minutes, until lightly charred on all sides. Serve hot, warm, or at room temperature.

4 portions

RIBBONS OF ZUCCHINI AND SUMMER SQUASH

Gold and green ribbons of squash are delicately sautéed in garlic butter and finished with finely chopped walnuts and a generous sprinkling of Parmesan cheese. By slicing the vegetables in this manner, it turns even the most apathetic eater into a squash fan.

2 medium-size zucchini
2 medium-size summer squash
4 tablespoons butter
1 medium-size clove garlic, crushed
1/2 cup finely chopped walnuts
salt and pepper to taste
1/2 cup freshly grated Parmesan cheese

1. Using a vegetable peeler, cut long ribbons of the zucchini and summer squash, reserving the seed core for another use.

2. Heat the butter in a large skillet. Add the garlic, squash ribbons, and nuts. Season with salt and pepper and stir-fry over high heat for 2 to 3 minutes until the vegetables are tender-crisp.

3. Sprinkle with the Parmesan. Stir well, remove from the heat, and serve.

4 to 6 portions

GREAT GRAINS AND BEANS

Bean cuisine is definitely "in." It used to be true that grains and dried beans or legumes were strictly for vegetarians or for those on limited budgets. The 90s has seen a gastronomic awakening, as beans and grains have found a most prominent place in haute cuisine. Beans and grains are trendy. Restaurateurs, gourmet chefs, and home cooks have taken to serving up all types of legumes—red, navy, kidney, ceci, great Northern—and grains—rice, couscous, bulgur, barley, corn—in both traditional and innovative ways. For so long beans were neglected because they were considered dull and bland. Their importance as a high fiber, low fat source of protein has been recognized. Both beans and grains have become most sophisticated and fashionable foods.

HOW TO COOK DRIED BEANS

All dried beans, with the exception of lentils and split peas, need to be rehydrated by soaking before cooking. During the soaking period, the beans absorb water, which increases their bulk, softens the legumes, and thereby reduces the cooking time. Dried beans generally triple in volume after soaking and cooking, so that 1 cup of dried beans will measure 3 cups of cooked beans. (Beans may be cooked 2 to 3 days in advance and refrigerated.) There are two soaking methods from which to choose. Before selecting a soaking method, it is necessary to pick over the beans to remove any stones or grit.

1. The overnight soak method. This is easy and always effective, but requires advance planning. Place the dried beans in a large bowl and cover with 3 times the volume of cold water. Soak for 10 to 12 hours or overnight. Drain and set aside until ready to cook.

2. The quick-soak method. This method works well if you are in a hurry. Place the dried beans in a large saucepan and cover them with 2 inches of water. Place over high heat and boil for 1 minute, then cover the pot and let sit for 1 hour. Drain the beans and proceed.

OLD-FASHIONED BAKED BEANS

This dish is a wholesome and gustatory combination of all the best in baked bean presentations. Navy pea beans are infused with a rich, savory brown sugar and hickory-flavor sauce. It's great buffet food, and makes ordinary grilled burgers and hot dogs extraordinary. Actually, this dish improves with time and is better if made in advance.

1 pound dry navy pea beans, pre-soaked (see page 319,
    How to Cook Dried Beans)
2 tablespoons vegetable oil
2 cups chopped yellow onions
3 large cloves garlic, minced
28-ounce can tomatoes, crushed with their juice
1 cup ketchup
$^1/_4$ pound bacon, cooked until crisp and coarsely chopped
$^1/_4$ cup molasses
1 cup packed dark brown sugar
2 tablespoons Worcestershire sauce
2 teaspoons dry mustard
$^1/_2$ teaspoon salt
lots of freshly ground pepper

1. Rinse the soaked beans and place them in a large saucepan. Cover with water and bring to a boil. Reduce the heat and simmer for 1$^1/_4$ hours until the beans are tender. Drain well. (Up to this point may be done 1 to 2 days in advance and refrigerated.)

2. Preheat the oven to 350°F.

3. Heat the oil in a large casserole or Dutch oven. Add the onions and garlic and cook over medium heat until the onions are soft, about 10 minutes.

4. Add the tomatoes, ketchup, bacon, molasses, brown sugar, Worcestershire, mustard, salt, pepper, and pre-cooked beans and mix well.

5. Remove the casserole from the heat. Cover and bake in the oven for 1 hour. Then uncover and bake for 1 hour longer, stirring occasionally until thick and syrupy. Serve piping hot.

10 to 12 portions

Note—This dish reheats well in the microwave.

WHITE BEAN STEW

ITALIAN MEAL

Veal Chops with
Tomato Relish
· · ·
White Bean Stew
· · ·
Sautéed Zucchini
Rounds
· · ·
Chocolate-Almond
Biscotti

Great Northern beans star in this humble bean dish, lavished with onion, garlic, and carrot, and scented with thyme. It makes a refreshing alternative to potato or rice, and is actually better if made in advance, allowing the flavors to mellow.

1 cup dry Great Northern beans, pre-soaked (see page 319,
*   How to Cook Dried Beans)*
2 tablespoons olive oil
1 large Vidalia, Maui, or Spanish onion, chopped
1 large carrot, chopped
2 large cloves garlic, minced
1 bay leaf
1/4 teaspoon dried thyme
salt and pepper to taste
2 to 2 1/2 cups chicken broth

1. Heat the olive oil in a large saucepan. Add the onion, carrot, and garlic and sauté over medium-high heat until the onion is lightly golden.

2. Add the beans, bay leaf, thyme, salt, pepper, and 2 cups broth. Bring to a boil and simmer for 1 1/2 to 2 hours until the beans are tender, adding more broth if the liquid evaporates. Cover and let sit for 10 minutes. Serve warm. (You may choose to refrigerate the beans at this point; return to room temperature before reheating.)

4 to 6 portions

WHITE BEANS AND SHRIMP

The peasant white bean is elevated to gastronomic heights when paired with shrimp and covered with a lemon-parsley pesto. This Italian-inspired dish is filling and satisfying.

1 cup dry Great Northern beans, pre-soaked (see page 319, How to Cook Dried Beans)
4 cups water
1 large clove garlic, cut in half
1 teaspoon salt
freshly ground pepper to taste
¹/₂ pound small-size shrimp, poached

Parsley Pesto:
1 cup firmly packed Italian parsley, stems removed
1 large clove garlic, minced
¹/₄ cup pine nuts, toasted
1¹/₂ teaspoons finely grated lemon zest
¹/₂ cup extra-virgin olive oil

1. In a large stockpot, combine the beans, water, garlic, salt, and pepper. Bring to a boil, lower the heat, and simmer for 45 minutes until the beans are barely tender. Drain well.

2. While the beans are cooking, prepare the pesto. Place the parsley, garlic, pine nuts, and lemon zest in the bowl of a food processor and process until the mixture forms a paste. With the motor running, add the olive oil in a slow, steady stream until all the oil is incorporated. (The pesto may be made 2 to 3 days in advance and refrigerated.)

3. Combine the cooked beans with the pesto and mix well. Gently stir in the shrimp and adjust the seasonings if necessary. Serve at room temperature.

4 portions

SUMMER LUNCHEON

White Beans
and Shrimp
. . .
Mixed Greens with
Chèvre Vinaigrette
. . .
Grilled Fruits

FAMILY DINNER

Chicken with
Tomato Salsa
. . .
Barley-Corn Pilaf
. . .
Roasted Broccoli
. . .
Blondies◆

BARLEY-CORN PILAF

Barley, the soft-textured cereal, is combined with corn and vegetables for a magical double-grain pilaf. Serve it with your favorite
poultry.

2 tablespoons olive oil
1 medium-size yellow onion, chopped
1 medium-size red pepper, chopped
1 cup pearl barley
1 teaspoon dried thyme
2¹/₂ cups chicken broth
²/₃ cup chopped scallions
1¹/₂ cups corn kernels, fresh or frozen
salt and pepper to taste

1. Heat the olive oil in a 3-quart saucepan. Add the onion and
pepper and sauté over medium heat until tender, about 5 minutes.

2. Add the barley and stir constantly until all the barley kernels are
coated with oil. Stir in the thyme and chicken broth and mix well.
Bring to a boil, cover, lower the heat, and simmer for 40 minutes until
the barley is tender and all the liquid is absorbed.

3. Add the scallions, corn, salt, and pepper, stirring until evenly
mixed. Heat through and serve.

6 portions

BULGUR PILAF

Cracked wheat lends a change of pace from the classic rice version. The bulgur is offset by a variety of flavors and textures—scallions, currants, and almonds—in this glorious and nutritious grain dish.

> 2 tablespoons olive oil
> 2 cups chopped scallions
> 1/2 cup slivered almonds
> 1/4 cup currants
> 1 1/2 cups bulgur
> 3 cups chicken broth
> salt to taste

1. Heat the olive oil in a large saucepan. Add the scallions and almonds and sauté for 1 minute over medium heat.

2. Add the rest of the ingredients and stir well. Bring to a boil, cover, reduce the heat to low, and simmer gently for 20 minutes. Fluff with a fork and serve.

6 portions

HOT WEATHER COOLER

Green Gazpacho
· · ·
Grilled Swordfish
· · ·
Bulgur Pilaf
· · ·
Mango and Red Pepper Salad
· · ·
Pear Ice

DINNER PARTY
MENU

Shredded Greens with
Strawberry Vinaigrette
• • •
Chicken Breasts
St. Michelle
• • •
Bulgur with
Walnut Gremolata
• • •
Asparagus with
Mustard Butter◆
• • •
Grand Dame Cake◆

BULGUR WITH WALNUT GREMOLATA

This presentation is akin to tabbouli with an interesting twist. Cracked wheat is lush with gremolata—chopped parsley, garlic, and lemon—and heady with the mellow nuttiness of toasted walnuts. The dish makes a grand statement on the buffet table, totes well to picnics, and is divine for dining al fresco.

1 cup bulgur
boiling water
1¹/₂ cups toasted walnuts, ground
1¹/₂ cups finely chopped fresh parsley
2 large cloves garlic, minced
1 tablespoon grated lemon zest
¹/₄ cup lemon juice
salt and pepper to taste
6 tablespoons olive oil

1. Place the cracked wheat in a 2-quart mixing bowl and add enough boiling water to come 2 inches above the bulgur. Allow to stand for 1 hour, or until the bulgur is light and fluffy. Toss with a fork and squeeze out any excess water.

2. In a small bowl, combine the walnuts, parsley, garlic, lemon zest, lemon juice, salt, pepper, and olive oil and mix well.

3. Add the walnut gremolata to the bulgur and stir until evenly blended. Serve at room temperature.

6 to 8 portions

BASIC COUSCOUS

Couscous is the cereal-like grain of North African origin, made from semolina and prized for its soft, fluffy texture. Classically it serves as a background for various meats and vegetable toppings. It cooks instantly and provides a refreshing alternative to rice.

1¹/₃ *cups chicken broth*
¹/₂ *teaspoon salt*
1 *tablespoon butter*
1 *cup couscous*

1. In a 2-quart saucepan, bring the chicken broth, salt, and butter to a boil.

2. Stir in the couscous, cover, and remove from the heat. Let stand for 5 minutes, then fluff with a fork. Serve warm or at room temperature.

4 portions

**MOROCCAN-
INSPIRED MENU**

Spice-Roasted
Chick Peas
· · ·
Curried Chicken
Tenders with
Mango Chutney
· · ·
Couscous
· · ·
Moroccan Grilled
Vegetables
· · ·
Fresh Fruit

COUSCOUS WITH DRIED FRUITS

The delicate cereal grain is embellished with the roasted, nutty flavor of walnuts, the tartness of dried apricots, and the rich, sweet taste of dates.

1¹/₃ cups chicken broth
¹/₂ teaspoon salt
2 tablespoons butter
1 cup couscous
¹/₂ cup coarsely chopped walnuts, toasted
¹/₂ cup coarsely chopped dried apricots
¹/₂ cup coarsely chopped dates

1. In a 2-quart saucepan, bring the chicken broth, salt, and butter to a boil. Stir in the couscous, cover, and remove from the heat. Let stand for 5 minutes, then fluff with a fork.

2. Mix in the chopped nuts and dried fruits. Serve warm or at room temperature.

4 to 6 portions

MEDITERRANEAN COUSCOUS

Common to Mediterranean cuisine, couscous is liberally seasoned with mint and dotted with raisins in this distinctive dish. It makes a savory accompaniment to grilled or roasted lamb and poultry.

1¹/₃ cups water
¹/₂ teaspoon salt
2 tablespoons virgin olive oil
1 cup couscous
¹/₃ cup raisins
2 teaspoons dried mint
2 tablespoons snipped chives

1. In a 2-quart saucepan, bring the water, salt, and olive oil to a boil. Stir in the couscous and raisins, cover, and remove from the heat. Let stand for 5 minutes, then fluff with a fork.

2. Add the mint and chives and mix well. Serve hot or at room temperature. (This reheats well in a microwave.)

4 to 6 portions

MIDDLE EASTERN MENU

Feta-Spinach Dip
. . .
Grilled Shrimp
. . .
Middle Eastern Chick Peas and Tomatoes
. . .
Mediterranean Couscous
. . .
Apricot Bon Bons

COUSCOUS NIÇOISE

Couscous takes on Niçoise flavors with pine nuts, capers, basil, black olives, and sun-dried tomatoes. It's easy to fix and makes great buffet or picnic food.

1¹/₃ cups water
¹/₂ teaspoon salt
1 cup couscous
3 tablespoons pine nuts, toasted
¹/₃ cup chopped sun-dried tomatoes
1 tablespoon capers
12 imported black olives
2 tablespoons finely chopped fresh basil
2 tablespoons olive oil

1. In a 2-quart saucepan, bring the water and salt to a boil. Stir in the couscous, cover, and remove from the heat. Let stand for 5 minutes, then fluff with a fork.

2. Add the remaining ingredients and mix well. Serve hot or at room temperature.

4 portions

COUSCOUS WITH TOMATO-MINT SAUCE

The semolina grain is featured with a Greek-inspired tomato sauce punctuated with garlic and almonds and redolent with mint.

> 3 tablespoons olive oil
> 1 large yellow onion, chopped
> 2 large cloves garlic, minced
> 2 large, ripe tomatoes, chopped
> 3 tablespoons slivered almonds, toasted
> 2 teaspoons dried mint
> 1¹/₃ cups chicken broth
> ¹/₂ teaspoon salt
> 1 cup couscous

1. Prepare the tomato sauce. Heat the olive oil in a 1¹/₂-quart saucepan. Add the onion and garlic and sauté over medium-high heat for 5 minutes until soft.

2. Add the tomatoes, almonds, and mint, and simmer for 10 minutes.

3. Prepare the couscous while the sauce simmers. In a 2-quart saucepan, bring the chicken broth and salt to a boil. Stir in the couscous, cover, and remove from the heat. Let stand for 5 minutes, then fluff with a fork.

4. When the sauce is finished, mix it into the cooked couscous and serve.

4 to 6 portions

MIDDLE EASTERN DINNER

Stuffed Grape Leaves
. . .
Grilled Lamb Chops
. . .
Couscous with Tomato-Mint Sauce

Green Beans
. . .
Dates Almondine

COUSCOUS COMBINATIONS

For an interesting and tasty alternative to a rice dish, try any one of the following mixtures combined with basic couscous:

- Embellished with herbs—parsley, sage, rosemary, and thyme.
- Swirled with sun-dried tomato pesto.
- Tossed with freshly grated Parmesan cheese and butter.
- Topped with grilled lamb and onions.
- Mixed with poached fruits of the sea—shrimp, scallops, mussels, and clams—with garlic and olive oil.
- Combined with sautéed spinach, raisins, and pine nuts for a Catalan influence.
- Woven with stir-fried red and yellow peppers, peapods, and mushrooms, and seasoned with soy sauce and ginger for an Oriental flair.
- Mixed with sautéed mushrooms and Romano cheese.
- Textured with sautéed broccoli, red pepper, asparagus, zucchini, and leeks and laced with cream as a primavera.
- Spiced with Southwestern flavors—chili powder, cumin, paprika, and oregano.
- Finished with sautéed onion, bacon, and a dusting of freshly shaved Parmesan cheese.
- Dotted with roasted garlic.

KASHA

This updated rendition of the hearty, peasant dish is reminiscent of what my grandma used to prepare. Kasha, the nutty, roasted buckwheat groat, is paired with sautéed onion and the woodsy flavor of wild mushrooms, lending a distinctive earthy taste to the dish. It is important to sauté the kasha with an egg wash first, which helps to keep the grains separate and crisp during further cooking.

1 cup whole or coarse-ground kasha
1 large egg, lightly beaten
3 tablespoons butter
1 large red onion, chopped
1 pound assorted wild mushrooms (portobello, crimini, and shiitake), coarsely chopped
2 large cloves garlic, minced
2 cups beef broth
$^1/_2$ teaspoon dried thyme
salt and pepper to taste

1. Stir the kasha with the egg in a medium-size bowl until evenly combined.

2. Transfer the kasha to a medium-size skillet and place over medium heat. Stir the kasha constantly with a fork until it is dry and the grains separate, about 3 minutes. Set aside.

3. Melt the butter in a large saucepan over medium-high heat. Add the onion, mushrooms, and garlic and sauté, stirring occasionally, until the mushrooms release their liquid and are browned, about 10 to 15 minutes.

4. Add the kasha, broth, thyme, salt, and pepper. Bring to a boil, cover, reduce the heat, and simmer for 15 minutes. Stir the kasha and let stand, covered, for 10 minutes before serving.

6 portions

FAMILY DINNER

Berber-Spiced
Game Hens
· · ·
Kasha
· · ·
Roasted Broccoli
· · ·
Peanut Butter-
Mascarpone Pie

CHILI-SPICED LENTILS

Chili fans take heed! Lentils take on a Southwestern mode in this hearty side dish that doubles as an entree. Lentils are immersed in a chili-flavored tomato sauce that will knock off your socks.

COMFORT FOOD

Slow-Roasted
Texas Brisket
. . .
Chili-Spiced Lentils
. . .
Carrots and
Turnips Gilbert
. . .
Rum-Raisin
Rice Pudding

1 cup brown lentils
6 cups water
1 tablespoon olive oil
1 large yellow onion, chopped
28-ounce can tomatoes, broken up into chunks with their juice
2 large cloves garlic, minced
1 bay leaf, crushed
1½ tablespoons chili powder
1 teaspoon dried oregano
¼ cup chopped fresh parsley
1 teaspoon salt
freshly ground pepper to taste

1. Combine the lentils and water in a large saucepan. Bring to a boil, lower the heat, and simmer partially covered for 20 minutes. Drain well.

2. While the lentils cook, prepare the chili sauce. Heat the olive oil in a separate large saucepan. Add the onion and sauté over medium heat until lightly golden, about 10 minutes.

3. Add the tomatoes, garlic, bay leaf, chili powder, oregano, parsley, salt, and pepper and mix well.

4. Stir in the partially cooked lentils. Simmer over low heat, partially covered for 20 minutes more until the lentils are barely tender. Serve at once.

6 to 8 side portions; 3 to 4 main-dish portions

LENTILS AND BULGUR

This double-grain treat pairs the nutty flavor and soft-texture of cracked wheat with the mild, yet distinctive taste of button-shaped lentils. Punctuated with garlic, ginger, and dried cranberries, this is a complex, yet satisfying marriage of flavors.

1 cup brown lentils
6 cups water
2 tablespoons olive oil
1 medium-size red onion, chopped
2 large cloves garlic, minced
1 tablespoon minced gingerroot
$1/2$ cup dried cranberries
1 cup bulgur
salt and pepper to taste
3 cups chicken broth

1. Combine the lentils and water in a large saucepan. Bring to a boil, lower the heat, and simmer partially covered for 10 minutes. Drain well and set aside.

2. Heat the olive oil in the large saucepan. Add the onion, garlic, and ginger and sauté for 10 minutes over medium heat until the onion is soft.

3. Add the cranberries, bulgur, lentils, salt, pepper, and chicken broth.

4. Cover the saucepan, bring to a boil, reduce the heat to low, and cook until all the liquid is absorbed, about 20 minutes. Fluff with a fork and serve.

6 portions

**MEDITERRANEAN
FARE**

Warm Tomato and
Goat Cheese Salad
. . .
Sicilian-Roasted
Swordfish
. . .
Polenta
. . .
Sautéed Zucchini
. . .
Fresh Melon

POLENTA

Polenta is the starchy cornmeal staple that is the basis of Northern Italian cooking. This is a smooth, creamy version finished with a dusting of Parmesan cheese. You may choose to eat it warm when freshly made, or chilled, then sliced and reheated until lightly browned. You may also top the polenta with various grilled or sautéed meats, fish, and vegetables.

1¹/₂ cups cornmeal
5 cups water
¹/₂ teaspoon salt
2 tablespoons butter
³/₄ cup freshly grated Parmesan cheese

1. In a bowl, mix the cornmeal with 1 cup water until evenly blended.

2. In a saucepan, bring 4 cups water and salt to a boil. Add the cornmeal mixture, stirring constantly with a wooden spoon until smooth. Lower the heat to a simmer, and continue to cook, stirring for 10 minutes until thick.

3. Add the butter and ¹/₄ cup Parmesan cheese and mix well.* Serve at once sprinkled with the remaining ¹/₂ cup Parmesan.

8 portions

*As an alternative to a smooth and creamy polenta, you may choose to turn the polenta into a greased 9 x 5-inch loaf pan. Cool to room temperature, then cover and refrigerate until firm, about 2 hours, or as much as overnight. Unmold the chilled polenta and cut into 1-inch thick slices. Lay the slices in a baking dish and sprinkle with the remaining ¹/₂ cup Parmesan cheese. Reheat in a preheated 375°F oven for 15 to 20 minutes until the cheese is lightly browned. Serve hot.

POLENTA COMBINATIONS

For a quick, nutritious meal, top freshly made polenta with any one of the following mixtures:

- Sliced, roasted red and yellow peppers splashed with balsamic vinegar and olive oil.
- Poached shrimp tossed with pesto.
- Crumbled goat cheese and chopped plum tomatoes.
- Ratatouille.
- Sautéed sausages and assorted hot and sweet peppers.
- Sautéed assorted wild mushrooms—shiitake, cremini, and oyster—in garlic and olive oil.
- Grated fontina cheese and caramelized onions.
- Grated mozzarella cheese and chopped sun-dried tomatoes.
- Sun-dried peppers and thinly sliced prosciutto drizzled with a garlic-infused olive oil.
- Poached asparagus and chunks of crabmeat covered with Hollandaise sauce.
- Sliced smoked salmon with sautéed snow peas in dill butter.
- Marinara sauce.

RISOTTO WITH ASPARAGUS AND SMOKED SALMON

Risotto is the heavenly rice dish indigenous to Northern Italy. The distinctive short-grained Arborio rice requires slow simmering and constant stirring as it gradually absorbs its cooking liquid to achieve its characteristic creamy texture. This risotto is outrageous and colorful, enriched with mascarpone cheese, asparagus, and strips of smoked salmon.

> 2 tablespoons butter
> 1 small yellow onion, diced
> 1 cup raw Arborio rice
> 1/3 cup dry white wine
> 2 1/2 to 3 cups simmering chicken broth
> 4 ounces mascarpone cheese
> 1/4 pound asparagus (preferably thin ones), poached and
>   cut into 2-inch lengths
> 3 ounces sliced Nova Scotia lox, cut into 1/2-inch wide strips

1. Melt the butter in a large non-stick pot. Add the onion and sauté over medium heat for 5 minutes until soft and lightly golden.

2. Stir in the rice and mix well until all the grains are evenly coated with the butter and onions.

3. Add the wine and 1/2 cup broth, and continue cooking, stirring constantly, until the liquid is absorbed. Continue adding the remaining hot liquid, 1/2 cup at a time, stirring constantly, until the rice is creamy and tender, about 25 to 30 minutes.

4. Remove the risotto from the heat. Stir in the mascarpone cheese and asparagus, mixing well. Gently stir in the lox, being careful that it does not break up into bit pieces. Serve immediately.

6 side portions; 4 main-course portions

PILAF WITH POPPED WILD RICE

Rice pilaf has become a great American favorite. Here it is combined with the light and crispy kernels of popped wild rice lending a nutty, popcorn flavor to the dish.

vegetable oil for shallow-frying
2 tablespoons raw wild rice
2 tablespoons butter
1 medium-size yellow onion, chopped
2 cups chicken broth
1 cup raw long-grain rice

1. Prepare the popped wild rice. Heat ½-inch of oil in a wok or fry pan over high heat until hot. Add the wild rice and fry until the rice is puffed, which takes about 10 seconds. Scoop out the popped rice with a strainer and drain on paper towels. Set aside until needed. (Up to this point may be done several hours in advance.)

2. Heat the butter in a 2-quart saucepan. Add the onion and sauté over medium heat until golden.

3. Add the chicken broth and bring to a boil. Stir in the rice.

4. Cover the saucepan, reduce the heat, and simmer for 20 minutes until all the liquid is absorbed. Fluff with a fork.

5. To serve, mix the popped rice into the pilaf and present.

6 portions

**DINNER PARTY
FOR 6**

Chèvre Turnovers
. . .
Salmon Olivada
. . .
Asparagus with
Balsamic Butter
. . .
Pilaf with
Popped Wild Rice
. . .
Fruit Tart

VEGETABLE RICE PILAF

A medley of finely chopped, sautéed vegetables pairs up with rice in this delicate, herb-flavored pilaf.

1/4 cup olive oil
2 medium-size carrots, diced
2 stalks celery, diced
3 medium-size leeks, chopped (white part only)
2 large cloves garlic, minced
1 teaspoon dried mint
2 tablespoons finely chopped fresh cilantro
salt and freshly ground pepper to taste
2 cups chicken broth
1 cup raw long-grain rice

1. Heat the olive oil in a 3-quart casserole. Add the vegetables and garlic and sauté over medium-high heat for 10 minutes.

2. Add the seasonings and chicken broth. Bring the mixture to a boil and stir in the rice.

3. Cover the casserole, reduce the heat to low, and simmer undisturbed for 20 minutes or until all the liquid is absorbed. Fluff with a fork and serve at once.

6 portions

RICE WITH APPLE-PEAR CHUTNEY

Rice is rippled with the assertive, somewhat spicy, sweet, and fruity flavors of apple-pear chutney. The chutney also makes a tasty hors d'oeuvre with cream cheese and crackers and a tantalizing relish for grilled pork or chicken. It actually improves with time and is therefore best made up to a week in advance and kept refrigerated.

Apple-Pear Chutney:
2 large Granny Smith apples, peeled, cored, and diced
2 large ripe pears, peeled, cored, and diced
1 medium-size yellow onion, chopped
1 medium-size red pepper, chopped
1 jalapeño pepper, seeded and finely diced
1 tablespoon grated gingerroot
$^{1}/_{4}$ cup white vinegar
$^{3}/_{4}$ cup packed light brown sugar
salt and pepper to taste

Rice:
2 cups water
salt to taste
1 cup raw long-grain rice

1. Prepare the chutney. In a large saucepan, combine all of the chutney ingredients. Bring to a boil, lower the heat, and simmer for 1 hour, stirring occasionally until thick. Pack into a sterilized jar and store in the refrigerator until needed. (The chutney will keep for 1 month under refrigeration.)

2. Prepare the rice. In a large saucepan, bring the water and salt to a boil. Stir in the rice and cover the pot. Lower the heat to a simmer, and cook the rice undisturbed for 20 minutes until all the liquid is absorbed. Remove the pan from the heat and fluff with a fork.

3. Stir 1$^{1}/_{2}$ cups chutney into the cooked rice and serve.

3 cups of chutney; 6 portions

TROPICAL TASTES

Jamaican-Spiced Pork Loin
. . .
Rice with Apple-Pear Chutney
. . .
Pickled Red Onions
. . .
Coconut Cake

BAYOU RICE AND CORN

Featuring flavors from the heart of the Deep South, this spicy rice is textured with corn kernels for added sparkle.

BAYOU-STYLE SUPPER

Baked Catfish with
Cornbread Crumbs
. . .
Bayou Rice and Corn
. . .
Coleslaw♦
. . .
Pecan Pie

3 tablespoons butter
1 medium-size yellow onion, chopped
1/2 teaspoon ground cumin
1/2 teaspoon chili powder
1/4 teaspoon cayenne pepper
1/4 teaspoon black pepper
1/2 teaspoon garlic powder
1/2 teaspoon dried oregano
1/2 teaspoon salt
2 cups chicken broth
1 cup raw long-grain rice
1 1/2 cups corn kernels (fresh or frozen), blanched

1. Heat the butter in a large saucepan. Add the onion and sauté over medium heat until lightly golden.

2. Stir in the seasonings and cook for 1 more minute.

3. Add the chicken broth. Bring the mixture to a boil and stir in the rice. Cover the saucepan, lower the heat, and simmer gently for 20 minutes. Fluff with a fork. Stir in the corn and serve.

6 portions

RED BEANS AND RICE

Red beans and rice is a typical Southern dish, particular to the Louisiana area. Dazzling flavors highlight this bean, rice, sausage, and vegetable medley. It can be served as an entree for luncheon or supper, or as a delicious wintertime accompaniment to roasted meats or poultry.

1 cup dried red kidney beans, pre-soaked (see page 319,
    How to Cook Dried Beans)
1 quart water
1/4 pound pork sausage, sliced into 1-inch thick rounds
1 small yellow onion, finely chopped
1 large stalk celery, finely chopped
1/2 cup diced red pepper
2 large cloves garlic, minced
1 bay leaf
1/2 teaspoon dried thyme
1/4 teaspoon Tabasco sauce
1 tablespoon Worcestershire sauce
salt and pepper to taste
3 cups cooked white rice

1. In a large saucepan, combine the pre-soaked beans, water, sausage, onion, celery, red pepper, garlic, bay leaf, thyme, Tabasco, Worcestershire, salt, and pepper.

2. Simmer partially covered for 1 1/2 hours until the beans are soft and the liquid has thickened. (Up to this point may be prepared 1 to 2 days in advance and refrigerated. Return to room temperature before reheating.)

3. Serve over the rice.

6 side portions; 4 main-course portions

LOUISIANA-STYLE MENU

Cajun-Spiced
Grilled Shrimp
. . .
Red Beans and Rice
. . .
Cornbread
. . .
Coconut Cake

CHINESE DINNER

Grilled Hunan Beef
. . .
Fried Wild Rice
. . .
Sesame Sugar
Snap Peas
. . .
Fresh Pineapple
Wedges

FRIED WILD RICE

This is an "East meets West" interpretation of the classic Oriental fried rice. The nutty flavor of wild rice is fused with stir-fried red and yellow peppers, scallions, and slivered almonds in a soy and molasses-flavored sauce. Try it as an accompaniment to poultry, fish, or meat.

I prefer my wild rice firm and slightly chewy, rather than soft in texture. Once you sample it this way, I think you'll agree.

1 cup raw wild rice
3 cups water
salt to taste
1 tablespoon soy sauce
1 tablespoon molasses
2 tablespoons vegetable oil
1 large clove garlic, minced
1 teaspoon grated gingerroot
1 small red pepper, cut into julienne slices
1 small yellow pepper, cut into julienne slices
3/4 cup coarsely chopped scallions
1/3 cup slivered almonds

1. Rinse the rice well under cold water and drain. In a large saucepan, bring 3 cups water and salt to a boil. Add the rice, return to a boil, reduce the heat to a simmer, cover, and cook for 35 to 40 minutes. Drain the rice well and set aside until needed.

2. In a small bowl, mix the soy sauce and molasses together and set aside.

3. In a wok or large skillet, heat the oil over high heat. Add the garlic and gingerroot and stir-fry for 1 minute. Add the peppers, scallions, and nuts and continue to stir-fry for 3 minutes more.

4. Stir in the cooked rice, mixing well.

5. Add the soy mixture and stir-fry for 2 minutes more. Serve at once.

4 to 5 portions

WILD RICE STUFFING

This stuffing showcases the glorious grain, wild rice. Wild rice is not a rice at all as its name implies, but is actually the seed of a tall grass that is harvested by the Native American Indians of Minnesota. This savory stuffing is heightened by the addition of sautéed vegetables, currants, pecans, and Canadian bacon. It makes a delicious accompaniment to roasted poultry and meats.

WINTER DINNER

Roast Chicken
. . .
Wild Rice Stuffing
. . .
Roasted Winter
Vegetables
. . .
Apple Crisp

1 cup raw wild rice
3 cups water
salt to taste
4 tablespoons butter
1 large yellow onion, chopped
1 large clove garlic, minced
1 medium-size red pepper, chopped
2 large stalks celery, chopped
1 teaspoon dried marjoram
pepper to taste
$1/3$ cup currants
$1/4$ pound Canadian bacon, cut into $1/4$-inch pieces
$1/2$ cup toasted pecans, coarsely chopped
$1/4$ cup cream sherry

1. Rinse the rice well under cold water and drain. In a large saucepan, bring 3 cups water and salt to a boil. Add the rice, cover, lower the heat, and simmer gently for 35 to 40 minutes. Drain well.

2. Heat the butter in a large skillet. Add the onion, garlic, pepper, celery, marjoram, salt, and pepper. Sauté over medium heat until the vegetables are soft, about 10 minutes.

3. Transfer the sautéed vegetables to a 3-quart casserole. Add the cooked rice, currants, bacon, pecans, and sherry and mix well. (Up to this point may be done as much as 24 hours in advance and refrigerated. Return to room temperature before continuing.)

4. Cover and bake in a preheated 325°F oven for 30 minutes. Serve at once.

6 to 8 portions

SUPER SALADS

Salads hold a place of importance in American cuisine. The days of iceberg lettuce are past. We are no longer bound to the garden salad offering only lettuce, tomato, and cucumber with a bottled dressing. Salads of today have a far-reaching, more expansive definition. They offer a variety of tastes and textures, combining an unusual array of flavorful and colorful ingredients—sun-dried tomatoes, black olives, pine nuts, chick peas, artichoke hearts, anchovies, prosciutto, grated cheeses, fresh and dried fruits, nuts, and croutons. We have dazzling dressings that feature Parmesan, goat cheese, herbs, mustards, and assorted vinegars and oils.

Salads should be seductive, sparkling and crisp, embracing the freshest of ingredients. They no longer only begin a meal or follow the main course, but may be the featured attraction. Our salad repertoire has been expanded by a cornucopia of ingredients from around the globe. I have created some unusual and wholesome combinations with Asian, French, Mediterranean, Middle Eastern, South-of-the-Border, and North African influences.

Garden salads take advantage of seasonal produce—a variety of mixed greens with an array of vegetable, fruit, and nut garnishes. Heartier salads showcase grains, legumes, seafood, poultry, meats, and pastas.

Creating a unique salad reflects an appreciation for the composite ingredients. Keep in mind the marriage of ingredients. Do they complement one another? Does each component add to the whole and not overpower any other ingredient, masking its identity? Do the ingredients create a visually colorful experience?

Salad making is an art in itself.

Note—Unless a salad is intended to be marinated, always dress the salad just before serving to ensure crisp, flavorful results.

GARDEN VARIETIES

LIGHT SUMMER REPAST

Chicken with
White Bean Purée
. . .
Onion Crostini
. . .
Salad Aromatica
. . .
Sliced Tomatoes
. . .
Assorted Melons

SALAD AROMATICA

Leaves of red leaf lettuce are tossed in a delicate raspberry-scented vinaigrette and adorned with honey-glazed pecans.

1/2 cup coarsely chopped pecans
1 1/2 tablespoons honey
1 large head red leaf lettuce, torn into bite-size pieces

Raspberry Vinaigrette:
salt and pepper to taste
1/2 teaspoon dry mustard
2 tablespoons raspberry vinegar
1/3 cup virgin olive oil

1. Prepare the glazed nuts. Preheat the oven to 350°F. Grease a cookie sheet. In a bowl, mix the pecans and honey together and spread out in a single layer on the prepared pan. Bake for 10 minutes. Remove the nuts and any glaze to a clean, greased cookie sheet and let cool. If the nuts seem sticky after cooling, put them in the freezer for 10 minutes, then proceed. Break up into pieces. (These may be made up to 1 week in advance and stored in an air-tight container.)

2. Heap the lettuce in a large bowl.

3. In a separate bowl, whisk together the salt, pepper, mustard, vinegar, and olive oil.

4. Pour the dressing over the greens and toss well. Garnish with the glazed nuts and serve at once.

4 to 6 portions

SALAD ASIAGO

Asiago cheese is touted as the Italian cheddar, being sharp and nutty. This hard cheese is harmoniously coupled with a trio of toasted nuts over leaves of romaine with a creamy vinaigrette.

1 large head romaine, torn into bite-size pieces
1 endive, thinly sliced
1/4 cup walnuts, toasted
1/4 cup pecans, toasted
1/4 cup slivered almonds, toasted
1/2 cup freshly grated Asiago cheese

Creamy Dressing:
1 medium-size clove garlic, crushed
salt to taste
1/4 teaspoon freshly ground black pepper
1 teaspoon Dijon mustard
1 tablespoon lemon juice
1 tablespoon red wine vinegar
1 tablespoon mayonnaise
1/3 cup virgin olive oil

1. Heap the romaine and endive in a large bowl. Adorn the greens with the walnuts, pecans, almonds, and grated cheese.

2. In a separate bowl, whisk together the garlic, salt, pepper, Dijon, lemon juice, vinegar, mayonnaise, and olive oil until thick and creamy.

3. Pour the dressing over the salad, toss well, and serve.

4 to 6 portions

ITALIAN-INSPIRED MEAL

Salad Asiago
. . .
Chicken Marsala
. . .
Pasta with Pesto
. . .
Romano-Crusted Eggplant
. . .
Melon Wedges

AUTUMN SALAD

A bed of Boston lettuce provides a background for ruby-red grapefruit and avocado slices. All is dressed in a savory vinaigrette bespeckled with the bittersweet, juicy seeds of the pomegranate. Yes, you can eat the seeds from this most prized fruit!

1 large or 2 small heads Boston lettuce, torn into bite-size pieces
2 endive, sliced into thin julienne pieces
2 pink or red grapefruit, peeled, sectioned, and membranes removed
1 ripe Haas avocado, peeled, pitted, and cut into 1/2-inch thick slices

Pomegranate Vinaigrette:
1 shallot, minced
salt and pepper to taste
2 tablespoons balsamic vinegar
1/2 cup virgin olive oil
1/2 cup pomegranate seeds

1. Heap the lettuce and endive in a large bowl. Add the grapefruit and avocado slices.

2. In a separate bowl, whisk together the shallot, salt, pepper, vinegar, olive oil, and pomegranate seeds.

3. Pour the vinaigrette over the salad. Toss very gently so as not to break up the grapefruit and avocado. Serve at once.

6 portions

BACON AND ORANGE SALAD

Orange slices and hickory-flavored bacon are set against a background of Boston lettuce, dressed in an orange marmalade vinaigrette, and garnished with sugar-glazed walnuts.

2 tablespoons sugar
1/2 teaspoon water
1/3 cup chopped walnuts
1 large head Boston lettuce, torn into bite-size pieces
2 medium-size oranges, peeled and cut into 1/4-inch thick slices
4 slices bacon, cooked and cut into 1-inch pieces

Orange Vinaigrette:
1 tablespoon finely diced shallot
black pepper to taste
1 1/2 tablespoons orange marmalade
1 tablespoon orange juice
2 tablespoons lemon juice
1/3 cup vegetable oil

1. Make the sugar-glazed walnuts. Grease a cookie sheet. Heat the sugar and water in a small saucepan over low heat until the sugar melts and turns a light caramel color. Stir in the walnuts and immediately pour the mixture onto the prepared pan and let cool. Break into pieces. (These may be made 2 to 3 days in advance and stored in an airtight container.)

2. Heap the lettuce in a large bowl. Top with the orange slices and bacon.

3. In a separate bowl, whisk together the shallot, pepper, orange marmalade, orange juice, lemon juice, and oil.

4. Pour the vinaigrette over the salad and toss well. Garnish with the glazed walnuts and serve.

4 portions

**LUNCHEON
MENU**

Bacon and
Orange Salad
· · ·
Country Bread
· · ·
Scallop Chowder
· · ·
Strawberry Bread

**SIMPLE GRILLED
DINNER**

Jerk-Style Bluefish
· · ·
Belmont Salad
· · ·
Rice
· · ·
Grilled Fruits
· · ·
Lemon Ice◆

BELMONT SALAD

Rich with autumn flavors, tender leaves of Boston lettuce sport apple chunks and a Honey-Walnut Vinaigrette.

2 medium-size heads Boston lettuce, torn into bite-size pieces
1 large Granny Smith apple, chopped

Honey-Walnut Vinaigrette:
$1^{1}/_{2}$ tablespoons diced shallot
1 tablespoon honey
1 teaspoon Dijon mustard
salt and pepper to taste
1 tablespoon lemon juice
$^{1}/_{4}$ cup apple cider
$^{1}/_{3}$ cup vegetable oil
$^{1}/_{4}$ cup finely chopped walnuts, toasted

1. Heap the lettuce in a large bowl. Top with the chopped apple.

2. In a separate bowl, whisk together the shallot, honey, Dijon, salt, pepper, lemon juice, apple cider, oil, and walnuts.

3. Pour the vinaigrette over the salad, toss well, and serve at once.

6 portions

BLUE CHEESE CAESAR SALAD

This new wave rendition of the classic Caesar struts a leafy spinach base napped with a creamy dressing rippled with Parmesan, and the distinctive tang of blue cheese. Toasted walnuts provide a nutty, crunchy garnish. For a delicious winter treat, add sliced pears to the salad.

10 ounces fresh spinach, stems removed
^{1}/2 cup coarsely chopped walnuts, toasted

Blue Cheese Dressing:
1 large clove garlic, minced
^{1}/4 teaspoon salt
^{1}/4 teaspoon freshly ground pepper
2 tablespoons lemon juice
6 tablespoons virgin olive oil
^{1}/2 cup crumbled blue cheese
3 tablespoons Parmesan cheese

1. Heap the spinach in a large bowl. Garnish with the toasted walnuts.

2. In a separate bowl, whisk together the garlic, salt, pepper, lemon juice, olive oil, blue cheese, and Parmesan until thick and creamy.

3. Pour the dressing over the salad, toss well, and serve.

4 portions

BACKYARD BARBECUE

Blue Cheese
Caesar Salad
. . .
Burgers with Vidalia
Onion Marmalade
. . .
Roasted Homestyle
Potatoes
. . .
Gingerbread

RISOTTO FARE

Bruschetta Provençal
. . .
Risotto with Asparagus
and Smoked Salmon
. . .
Boston Lettuce and
Grapefruit Salad
. . .
Frozen Yogurt

BOSTON LETTUCE AND GRAPEFRUIT SALAD

Leaves of Boston lettuce are lavished with succulent pink grapefruit sections and dressed in a raspberry-poppy seed vinaigrette.

1 large head Boston lettuce, torn into bite-size pieces
1 ruby red grapefruit, peeled

Poppy Seed Dressing:
1/2 tablespoon honey
1 tablespoon poppy seeds
salt and pepper to taste
2 tablespoons raspberry vinegar
1/3 cup virgin olive oil

1. Place the lettuce in a serving bowl.

2. Separate the grapefruit into sections. Remove the membrane from each section, then cut each section in half. Add the grapefruit to the lettuce.

3. In a separate bowl, whisk together the honey, poppy seeds, salt, pepper, vinegar, and olive oil.

4. Pour the Poppy Seed Dressing over the salad and toss gently until evenly coated. Serve at once.

4 portions

CARIBBEAN MELON SALAD

A colorful trio of melons—honeydew, cantaloupe, and watermelon—sport a delicate Honey-Lime Vinaigrette spiked with cilantro and chives. It's a refreshing salad and also works well as a relish for grilled chicken or fish.

2 cups watermelon, cut into 1-inch chunks, seeds removed
2 cups honeydew melon, cut into 1-inch chunks
2 cups cantaloupe, cut into 1-inch chunks

Honey-Lime Vinaigrette:
1 teaspoon finely grated lime zest
3 tablespoons lime juice
1 tablespoon honey
3 tablespoons diced red onion
2 tablespoons snipped chives
1 tablespoon finely chopped fresh cilantro
freshly ground pepper to taste

1. Heap the melons in a serving bowl.

2. In a separate small bowl, combine the lime zest, lime juice, honey, red onion, chives, cilantro, and pepper. Mix well and pour over the fruit. Toss until evenly coated. Serve chilled.

4 portions

TROPICAL ISLAND DINNER

Piña Colada Soup
. . .
Shrimp Margarita
. . .
Caribbean
Melon Salad
. . .
Grilled Corn
on the Cob
. . .
Assorted Sherbets

**ASIAN SALAD
DAYS FOR 12**

Marinated Shiitake
Mushrooms
. . .
Cucumber and
Crab Salad
. . .
Oriental Shrimp Salad
. . .
Oriental Black
Bean Salad
. . .
Indonesian
Lo Mein Salad

CUCUMBER AND CRAB SALAD

This salad is Oriental in design. Light and delicately flavored, crab teams up with cucumber and is accented by water chestnuts, scallions, and toasted sesame seeds in a soy vinaigrette.

1 large English cucumber, thinly sliced
1/2 pound fresh lump crabmeat, cartilage removed
8-ounce can water chestnuts, drained and sliced
2 scallions, thinly sliced
1 tablespoon sesame seeds, toasted

Soy Vinaigrette:
3 tablespoons soy sauce
freshly ground pepper to taste
1 1/2 teaspoons sugar
1 tablespoon grated gingerroot
2 tablespoons rice vinegar
2 tablespoons vegetable oil

1. Arrange the cucumber, chunks of crab, water chestnuts, and scallions on a platter.

2. In a small bowl, whisk together the soy sauce, pepper, sugar, gingerroot, vinegar, and oil.

3. Drizzle the vinaigrette over the salad. Sprinkle with the sesame seeds and serve.

4 portions

FENNEL SALAD

The anise flavor of the illustrious fennel bulb is featured along with the rich, lusty taste of roasted red peppers in this refreshing salad.

2 large fennel bulbs, top fronds removed, sliced wafer thin
2 large red peppers, roasted and cut into 1/2-inch pieces
1/2 cup thinly sliced scallions

Dijon-Soy Vinaigrette:
1 tablespoon Dijon mustard
1 tablespoon soy sauce
freshly ground pepper to taste
2 tablespoons balsamic vinegar
1/4 cup virgin olive oil

1. Place the fennel, roasted peppers, and scallions in a large serving bowl.

2. In a separate bowl, whisk together the Dijon, soy sauce, pepper, vinegar, and olive oil.

3. Pour the dressing over the salad, toss well, and serve.

4 to 6 portions

CHICKEN DINNER

Roast Chicken
· · ·
Lentils and Bulgur
· · ·
Fennel Salad
· · ·
Orange Sunshine Cake

GREENS WITH WALNUT VINAIGRETTE

A riot of mixed greens are dotted with toasted walnuts and dried cherries, and dressed in a walnut oil-based vinaigrette. Toasting the walnuts brings out their nutty essence, adding an extra dimension to this delightful salad.

*12 to 14 cups mixed greens—endive, radicchio, escarole, watercress,
    red leaf lettuce, arugula, and frisée—torn into bite-size pieces*
1/2 cup walnuts, toasted and coarsely chopped
1/3 cup dried cherries

Walnut Vinaigrette:
1 teaspoon Dijon mustard
salt and pepper to taste
2 tablespoons lemon juice
6 tablespoons walnut oil

1. Heap the salad greens in a large serving bowl. Garnish with the toasted walnuts and dried cherries.

2. In a separate bowl, whisk together the Dijon, salt, pepper, lemon juice, and walnut oil. Pour the dressing over the greens, toss well, and serve at once.

6 portions

HUNTER'S SALAD

This salad boasts the buttery taste of pears coupled with chunks of creamy Brie cheese, golden raisins, toasted pecans, and diced red onion. Pears and Brie have a curious affinity, making this a savory combination.

1/2 cup golden raisins
2 tablespoons balsamic vinegar
3 ripe pears, cut into 1/2-inch cubes
3/4 pound Brie cheese, white rind removed, cut into 1/2-inch cubes
3/4 cup toasted pecan meats, coarsely chopped
1/3 cup diced red onion
salt and pepper to taste
1/2 cup mayonnaise

1. Plump the raisins in balsamic vinegar for 15 minutes.

2. In a large bowl, combine the pears, Brie, raisins with the vinegar, pecans, and red onion.

3. Season with salt and pepper. Add the mayonnaise, mix well, and serve.

6 portions

COLD WEATHER COMFORT FOOD

Hunter's Salad
. . .
Sourdough Bread
. . .
Tuscan White
Bean Soup
. . .
Apple Crisp

JICAMA SLAW

Jicama is a rather large, bulbous root vegetable indigenous to Mexico. It has a sweet, nutty flavor and white crunchy flesh. It makes an excellent salad, retaining its crisp, water chestnut texture, enhanced here with a mustard mayonnaise. This slaw is marvelous for buffets, for toting to picnics, and for casual dining.

5 cups jicama, peeled and cut into 1/4 x 1/4 x 3-inch matchstick pieces
2 cups carrots, cut into 1/4 x 1/4 x 3-inch matchstick pieces
1 medium-size red pepper, cut into matchstick pieces

Mustard Mayonnaise:
1/4 cup Dijon mustard
1/3 cup mayonnaise
3 tablespoons cider vinegar
1 teaspoon sugar
salt to taste
1/4 teaspoon black pepper

1. Combine the jicama, carrots, and red pepper in a large bowl.

2. In a separate bowl, mix together the mustard and mayonnaise. Stir in the vinegar, sugar, salt, and pepper.

3. Pour the mustard mayonnaise over the salad, toss well, and serve. (This salad may be made 3 to 4 hours in advance and chilled; when ready to serve, return to room temperature, mix well, and present.)

6 to 8 portions

SALAD LUCIA

A simple lettuce, tomato, and cucumber salad is turned into the extraordinary, daubed with a snappy, creamy basil and Parmesan dressing.

1 large head romaine, torn into bite-size pieces
1 small head radicchio, torn into bite-size pieces
2 ripe tomatoes, cut into chunks
1 pickling cucumber, sliced
1 small green pepper, sliced

Basil-Parmesan Dressing:
1 medium-size clove garlic, crushed
salt and freshly ground pepper to taste
1 teaspoon dried basil
1 teaspoon capers
2 tablespoons light cream
2 tablespoons red wine vinegar
1/3 cup extra-virgin olive oil
1/3 cup Parmesan cheese

1. Heap the romaine and radicchio in a large salad bowl. Top with the tomatoes, cucumber, and green pepper.

2. In a separate bowl, whisk together the garlic, salt, pepper, capers, cream, vinegar, olive oil, and Parmesan until thick and creamy.

3. Pour the dressing over the salad, toss well, and serve.

6 portions

SIMPLE SUPPER

Pasta Marino
. . .
Salad Lucia
. . .
Garlic Bread
. . .
Pot de Crème◆

SUMMER
SOLSTICE MENU

Beet Gazpacho
. . .
Raspberry-Glazed
Chicken
. . .
Mango and
Red Pepper Salad
. . .
Pilaf with
Popped Wild Rice
. . .
Down East
Blueberry Cake

MANGO AND RED PEPPER SALAD

Mango has complex flavors that are spicy, sweet, and acidic. The exotic, fragrant flesh of mangoes blends with red pepper and scallions for a fruity and colorful summer salad. Also try it as a relish for grilled chicken or fish.

2 ripe mangoes, peeled, pitted, and coarsely chopped
1 large red pepper, coarsely chopped
1/2 cup thinly sliced scallions
1/4 cup pine nuts, toasted
salt and pepper to taste
1 tablespoon honey
2 tablespoons balsamic vinegar
2 tablespoons virgin olive oil

1. Place the mangoes, red pepper, scallions, and pine nuts in a serving bowl.

2. In a separate bowl, whisk together the salt, pepper, honey, vinegar, and olive oil.

3. Pour the dressing over the fruits and toss well. Serve at once or let marinate for 1 to 2 hours and then present.

4 portions

VERMONT MAPLE-WALNUT SALAD

This green leaf salad is adorned with the sweet, rich flavor of chopped dates and toasted walnuts and dressed with a Mustard-Maple Vinaigrette. Use only pure maple syrup for flavor-packed results. It's a must for maple-walnut fans!

1 large or 2 small heads green leaf lettuce, torn into bite-size pieces
3/4 cup coarsely chopped dates
2/3 cup coarsely chopped walnuts, toasted

Mustard-Maple Vinaigrette:
1 tablespoon Dijon mustard
salt and pepper to taste
2 tablespoons snipped chives
2 1/2 tablespoons pure maple syrup
2 tablespoons red wine vinegar
1/3 cup olive oil

1. Heap the lettuce in a large bowl. Garnish with the chopped dates and walnuts.

2. In a separate bowl, whisk together the Dijon, salt, pepper, chives, maple syrup, vinegar, and olive oil.

3. Pour the vinaigrette over the salad, toss well, and serve.

6 portions

**ROAST BEEF
DINNER**

Vermont Maple-
Walnut Salad
· · ·
Roast Beef
· · ·
Onion Pudding
· · ·
Brussels Sprouts
Genovese
· · ·
Chocolate Mousse◆

MESCLUN SALAD WITH PANSIES

Pansies in a salad? Believe it or not, pansies are edible flowers. They add excitement and color to the table and are readily available in the home garden. This is a seasonal salad that is light and delicate, sporting a Chive Vinaigrette. If pansies are unavailable, substitute any other edible flower—violas, jonny jump-ups, or impatiens.

14 cups mesclun—mixed baby greens
$1/2$ cup pecans, toasted
18 pansies—try to use different colors for a more vibrant effect

Chive Vinaigrette:
1 small clove garlic, minced
salt and freshly ground pepper to taste
$1/4$ cup snipped chives
2 tablespoons balsamic vinegar
$1/3$ cup extra-virgin olive oil

1. Heap the mesclun in a large bowl. Add the pecans.

2. In a separate bowl, whisk together the garlic, salt, pepper, chives, vinegar, and olive oil.

3. Pour the vinaigrette over the greens and toss until evenly mixed. Garnish the salad with the pansies and serve.

6 portions

MEXICAN CAESAR SALAD

The classic Caesar theme is expanded to include South-of-the-Border ingredients—tomato, avocado, black olives, and tortilla chips—with a lively dressing.

1 large head romaine, torn into bite-size pieces
1 medium-size tomato, chopped
1/2 cup sliced ripe black olives
1 ripe Haas avocado, peeled, pitted, and chopped
1 cup tortilla chips, coarsely broken

Zesty Dressing:
2 medium-size cloves garlic, minced
1 teaspoon Dijon mustard
salt to taste
1/4 teaspoon black pepper
1/2 teaspoon crushed red pepper flakes
2 tablespoons lime juice
1/2 cup virgin olive oil
1/3 cup Parmesan cheese

1. Heap the romaine in a large bowl. Top with the tomato, black olives, and avocado.

2. In a separate bowl, mix the garlic, Dijon, salt, black pepper, red pepper flakes, and lime juice. Whisk in the olive oil until it is completely incorporated. Stir in the Parmesan.

3. Pour the dressing over the salad. Add the tortilla chips, toss well, and serve at once.

6 portions

MEXICAN MENU

Chili-Cheese Puffs
. . .
Mexican Caesar Salad
. . .
Mexican-Flavored
Shrimp
. . .
White Rice
. . .
Orange Freeze◆

**LIGHT
LUNCHEON**

Rhubarb Soup
. . .
Mixed Greens
with Chèvre
Vinaigrette
. . .
French Bread
. . .
Poppy Seed
Butter Cookies

MIXED GREENS WITH CHÈVRE VINAIGRETTE

This salad boasts a distinguished, creamy dressing heady with goat cheese and accented with a potpourri of herbs.

12 to 14 cups mixed salad greens—red leaf lettuce, radicchio, water-cress, Boston lettuce, and frisée—torn into bite-size pieces
6 slices of French bread, cut ¹/₂-inch thick

Chèvre Vinaigrette:
2 ounces Chèvre
1 teaspoon dried basil
¹/₂ teaspoon dried thyme
¹/₂ teaspoon dried marjoram
1 tablespoon chopped fresh parsley
1 tablespoon snipped chives
salt to taste
¹/₄ teaspoon black pepper
2 tablespoons balsamic vinegar
³/₄ cup extra-virgin olive oil

1. Preheat the oven to 350°F.

2. Heap the greenery in a large serving bowl.

3. Prepare the croutons. Cut the French bread slices into ¹/₂-inch chunks. Place on a baking sheet and bake for 5 minutes. Turn the croutons over and bake for 5 minutes more until golden brown on all sides. Remove from the oven and let cool completely. (This may be done 1 to 2 days in advance and stored in an airtight container.)

4. Put the chèvre, basil, thyme, marjoram, parsley, chives, salt, pepper, vinegar, and olive oil in the bowl of a food processor. Puree until smooth.

5. Garnish the salad with the croutons. Pour the dressing over the greens, toss well, and serve at once.

6 portions

NECTARINES AND TOMATOES

Lush tomatoes are coupled with fragrantly sweet nectarines, dotted with slivered almonds, and finished in a Raspberry Vinaigrette. This also makes a refreshing relish for grilled steak, burgers, or pork.

2 large, ripe tomatoes, cut into wedges
4 medium-size nectarines, pitted and cut into wedges
1/2 small red onion, thinly sliced
1/4 cup slivered almonds, toasted

Raspberry Vinaigrette:
1 small clove garlic, crushed
1 tablespoon raspberry preserves
salt and pepper to taste
2 tablespoons raspberry vinegar
1/3 cup virgin olive oil

1. Place the tomatoes, nectarines, onion, and almonds in a serving bowl.

2. In a separate bowl, whisk together the garlic, raspberry preserves, salt, pepper, vinegar, and olive oil.

3. Pour the Raspberry Vinaigrette over the fruits and toss well. Serve at once or let marinate for 1 to 2 hours and then present.

4 portions

SIMPLE DINNER

Swordfish Rum Rickey
· · ·
White Rice
· · ·
Nectarines and
Tomatoes
· · ·
Grilled Fruits

ORANGES AND RED ONION

This colorful and refreshing combination is typically Italian. Rounds of sliced oranges, red onion, and fennel are marinated in an Orange-Raspberry Vinaigrette scented with rosemary, and punctuated with black olives.

6 navel oranges, peeled and sliced into $1/4$-inch thick rounds
1 large red onion, thinly sliced into rings
1 large fennel bulb, top fronds removed, thinly sliced
$1/2$ cup Greek black or brine-cured black olives

Orange-Raspberry Vinaigrette:
1 teaspoon Dijon mustard
1 teaspoon dried rosemary
freshly ground pepper to taste
$1/2$ cup orange juice
$1/4$ cup raspberry vinegar
$3/4$ cup extra-virgin olive oil

1. In a large glass bowl, combine the oranges, red onion, fennel, and olives.

2. In a separate bowl, whisk together the Dijon, rosemary, pepper, orange juice, vinegar, and olive oil.

3. Pour the vinaigrette over the salad and toss gently. Cover and marinate for 3 to 4 hours before serving. (If marinating for a longer period of time, refrigerate; return to room temperature to serve.)

6 to 8 portions

RED CABBAGE SLAW

This slaw is colorful and dramatic. The eggplant-hued shredded cabbage is set against the bright orange of grated carrot, dotted with raisins, and coated with a sweet-sour dressing spiked with cumin. The sweet taste of the raisins and the honey vinaigrette complement the pungency of the cumin. The vinaigrette is oil-free—a boon to those on restricted diets!

4 cups shredded red cabbage
4 cups coarsely grated carrots
1/2 cup raisins

Honey Vinaigrette:
1 tablespoon Dijon mustard
salt and freshly ground pepper to taste
1 1/2 teaspoons ground cumin
1/3 cup honey
1/2 cup white vinegar

1. Combine the cabbage, carrots, and raisins in a large serving bowl.

2. In a separate bowl, whisk together the Dijon, salt, pepper, cumin, honey, and vinegar.

3. Pour the vinaigrette over the slaw, toss well, and serve. (This may be made 5 to 6 hours in advance and chilled; return to room temperature to serve.)

6 portions

**MEXICAN-
INSPIRED PICNIC**

Guacamole
· · ·
South-of-the-Border
Chicken
· · ·
Southwestern
Corn Salad
· · ·
Red Cabbage Slaw
· · ·
Chocolate-Chocolate
Chip Wafers

ROASTED PEPPER SALAD

The complex flavors in this composition are both intriguing and savory—rich roasted red peppers, sweet raisins, freshly shaved Parmesan, and a balsamic vinaigrette. It also works well as an appetizer.

1/2 cup raisins
2 tablespoons balsamic vinegar
6 large red peppers, roasted and cut into quarters
1/2 cup freshly shaved Parmesan cheese (use a vegetable peeler)

Vinaigrette:
salt and freshly ground pepper to taste
1/2 teaspoon dried oregano
1/4 teaspoon crushed red pepper flakes
6 tablespoons extra-virgin olive oil

1. Place the raisins in a small bowl. Pour the balsamic vinegar over them and let macerate for 30 minutes.

2. Arrange the roasted peppers in a serving dish.

3. Add the salt, pepper, oregano, red pepper flakes, and olive oil to the macerated raisins and mix well.

4. Pour the vinaigrette over the peppers. Sprinkle with the Parmesan and serve. (This may be prepared several hours in advance and chilled; return to room temperature to serve.)

6 to 8 portions

ROMAINE WITH SOY VINAIGRETTE

Asian ingredients—soy sauce, scallions, almonds, and water chestnuts—fuse with romaine and sun-dried tomatoes in this Oriental-inspired salad.

1 large head romaine, torn into bite-size pieces
¹/₂ cup coarsely chopped sun-dried tomatoes
¹/₃ cup thinly sliced scallions
8-ounce can water chestnuts, drained and sliced
¹/₂ cup slivered almonds, toasted

Soy Vinaigrette:
1 large clove garlic, crushed
¹/₄ teaspoon freshly ground black pepper
2 tablespoons soy sauce
¹/₂ teaspoon sugar
2 tablespoons lemon juice
¹/₂ cup extra-virgin olive oil

1. Heap the romaine in a large bowl. Top with the sun-dried tomatoes, scallions, water chestnuts, and almonds.

2. In a separate bowl, whisk together the garlic, pepper, soy sauce, sugar, lemon juice, and olive oil.

3. Pour the vinaigrette over the salad, toss well, and serve.

6 portions

DINNER WITH
ASIAN FLAIR

Barbecued
Leg of Lamb
· · ·
Romaine with
Soy Vinaigrette
· · ·
Sushi-Style Rice
· · ·
Ginger Ice Cream

**STEAK AND
POTATOES MENU**

Grilled Steak with
Tomato Chutney
· · ·
Zucchini Mandoline♦
· · ·
Garlic and Herb
Mashed Potatoes
· · ·
Shredded Romaine
with Caraway
Vinaigrette
· · ·
Chocolate Chip
Cookies

SHREDDED ROMAINE WITH CARAWAY VINAIGRETTE

Thin strips of romaine lettuce are napped in a vinaigrette teeming with the assertive flavor of Romano cheese and the sweet, sharp anise-like taste of caraway seeds. The dressing gives new dimension to the dark brown seeds we frequently associate with baked goods.

1 large head romaine, cut into 1/2-inch wide strips

Caraway Vinaigrette:
1 large clove garlic, smashed
salt and freshly ground pepper to taste
1 teaspoon Dijon mustard
1 teaspoon caraway seeds
2 tablespoons lemon juice
1/2 cup virgin olive oil
1/4 cup freshly shredded Romano cheese

1. Heap the shredded romaine in a large bowl.

2. In a separate bowl, mix together the garlic, salt, pepper, Dijon, caraway seeds, and lemon juice. Whisk in the olive oil until it is completely incorporated. Stir in the Romano cheese.

3. Pour the vinaigrette over the salad, toss well, and serve.

6 portions

SANTA FE SALAD

Southwestern flavors prevail in this Mexican-style salad. Lettuce is dappled with tomatoes, corn, cheddar cheese, and red onion and coated with a buttermilk-based cilantro dressing. Try adding grilled chicken for a more hearty repast.

1 head iceberg lettuce, torn into bite-size pieces
1 cup fresh or frozen corn kernels, blanched
2 ripe plum tomatoes, chopped
1 cup grated sharp cheddar cheese
¹/₂ cup thinly sliced red onion

Cilantro-Buttermilk Dressing:
³/₄ cup mayonnaise
1¹/₂ teaspoons tomato paste
1 teaspoon sugar
¹/₂ cup buttermilk
3 tablespoons lime juice
1 large clove garlic, minced
¹/₂ teaspoon paprika
¹/₄ teaspoon cayenne pepper
salt and freshly ground pepper to taste
3 tablespoons coarsely chopped fresh cilantro

1. Heap the lettuce in a large bowl. Add the corn, tomatoes, cheddar cheese, and red onion.

2. In a separate bowl, mix together the mayonnaise, tomato paste, sugar, buttermilk, and lime juice. Stir in the garlic, paprika, cayenne, salt, pepper, and cilantro until evenly blended.

3. Add only enough dressing to the salad to lightly coat the ingredients. Any extra dressing may be saved in a covered container in the refrigerator for 1 week. Try it as a fanciful dip for crudites!

6 portions; 1¹/₃ cups of dressing

A TASTE OF THE SOUTHWEST

Chili-Roasted Salmon
. . .
Cornbread
. . .
Santa Fe Salad
. . .
Chocolate Bundles

SOUTHWESTERN-STYLE HEARTS OF PALM SALAD

This is a colorful medley of julienned vegetables—hearts of palm, red and yellow peppers, zucchini, and red onion—in a chili-infused vinaigrette. It makes great buffet fare.

14-ounce can hearts of palm, drained and cut into ¹/₄-inch thick
*   julienne pieces*
1 medium-size red pepper, cut into julienne strips
1 medium-size yellow pepper, cut into julienne strips
1 medium-size zucchini, cut into ¹/₈ x 2-inch matchstick pieces
1 small red onion, cut into ¹/₈-inch thick strips

Southwestern Vinaigrette:
1 large clove garlic, minced
salt and pepper to taste
1 teaspoon chili powder
2 tablespoons orange juice
2 tablespoons red wine vinegar
¹/₃ cup virgin olive oil

1. Combine the hearts of palm, red and yellow peppers, zucchini, and red onion in a large bowl.

2. In a separate bowl, whisk together the garlic, salt, pepper, chili powder, orange juice, vinegar, and olive oil.

3. Pour the vinaigrette over the vegetables and mix well. Let marinate for 1 to 2 hours. Toss again before serving.

4 to 6 portions

SHREDDED GREENS WITH STRAWBERRY VINAIGRETTE

The tangy, bitter, and peppery, magenta, white, and green-hued greens—radicchio, endive, and arugula—are complemented by a sweet and fruity strawberry dressing. It's a vision to behold!

6 cups shredded radicchio
2 cups thinly sliced endive
2 cups shredded arugula

Strawberry Vinaigrette:
1 medium-size clove garlic, smashed
salt and freshly ground pepper to taste
1 tablespoon diced shallot
2 tablespoons strawberry preserves
2 tablespoons red wine vinegar
½ cup virgin olive oil

1. Heap the radicchio, endive, and arugula in a large bowl.

2. In a separate bowl, mix together the garlic, salt, pepper, shallot, strawberry preserves, and vinegar. Whisk in the olive oil until it is completely incorporated.

3. Pour the vinaigrette over the greens, toss well, and serve at once.

4 to 6 portions

ITALIAN DINNER PARTY

Shredded Greens with Strawberry Vinaigrette
· · ·
Chicken Rustica
· · ·
Slow-Roasted Tomatoes
· · ·
Italian Noodle Bake
· · ·
Lemon Ice◆
· · ·
Assorted Cookies

SPINACH AND SMOKED OYSTERS WITH CRANBERRY VINAIGRETTE

Vibrant green spinach leaves team up with the smoky flavor of oysters for a dynamic combination. The salad is napped in a slightly sweet, whole Cranberry Vinaigrette accented with candied ginger. I like to serve this salad at Thanksgiving.

10 ounces fresh spinach, heavy stems removed
3^1/$_2$ ounce can smoked oysters, rinsed and drained

Cranberry Vinaigrette:
^{1}/$_2$ cup whole berry cranberry sauce (homemade is preferable)
1 heaping tablespoon finely chopped crystallized candied ginger
1 tablespoon diced shallot
1 tablespoon soy sauce
2 tablespoons red wine vinegar
^{1}/$_2$ cup vegetable oil

1. Heap the spinach in a large bowl. Garnish with the smoked oysters.

2. In a separate bowl, whisk together the cranberry sauce, candied ginger, shallot, soy sauce, vinegar, and oil.

3. Pour the vinaigrette over the salad, toss gently, and serve.

4 portions

SPINACH, SMOKED SALMON, AND GOAT CHEESE SALAD

This salad offers a wonderful balance of colors—green, white, and pink—and flavors—the heady, earthy flavor of chèvre, the slightly smoky taste of salmon, and the aromatic, subtle anise flavor of a Dill Vinaigrette.

12 ounces fresh spinach, stems removed
1/4 pound sliced smoked salmon, cut into 1/2-inch wide strips
6 ounces chèvre, crumbled
1/2 cup thinly sliced scallions

Dill Vinaigrette:
1 small clove garlic, smashed
salt to taste
1/4 teaspoon black pepper
1 teaspoon Dijon mustard
2 tablespoons chopped fresh dillweed
2 tablespoons lemon juice
1/3 cup virgin olive oil

1. Heap the spinach in a large bowl. Add the smoked salmon, goat cheese, and scallions.

2. In a separate bowl, whisk together the garlic, salt, pepper, Dijon, dillweed, lemon juice, and olive oil.

3. Pour the vinaigrette over the salad, toss well, and serve.

4 to 6 portions

HOT WEATHER FARE

Pickled Grapes
. . .
Grilled Shrimp and Artichoke Hearts with Cumin Mayonnaise
. . .
Spinach, Smoked-Salmon, and Goat Cheese Salad
. . .
Focaccia
. . .
Ginger-White Chocolate Chunk Cookies
. . .
Strawberries

SUMI SALAD

**ASIAN-INSPIRED
MENU**

Avocado and Smoked
Salmon with
Wasabi Vinaigrette
. . .
Sumi Salad
. . .
Korean Sesame
Grilled Tuna
. . .
White Rice
. . .
Orange Wedges

This Oriental slaw is addictive—one mouthful just doesn't suffice. It makes an important addition to the buffet table and totes well to picnics.

1 medium-size head cabbage, shredded
2 large carrots, coarsely grated
1 English cucumber, thinly sliced
1 cup thinly sliced scallions
4 cups bean sprouts
8-ounce can water chestnuts, drained and sliced

Soy Vinaigrette:
1/4 cup sugar
salt to taste
1 teaspoon black pepper
1/2 cup soy sauce
6 tablespoons rice vinegar
1 cup vegetable oil

Garnishes:
2 tablespoons sesame seeds, toasted
1/2 cup slivered almonds, toasted

1. Heap the cabbage, carrots, cucumber, scallions, bean sprouts, and water chestnuts in a large bowl.

2. In a separate small bowl, whisk together the sugar, salt, pepper, soy sauce, vinegar, and oil.

3. Pour the vinaigrette over the salad and toss well. Cover and refrigerate, allowing the salad to marinate for at least 2 hours, or as much as 6 hours.

4. To serve, garnish with the sesame seeds and almonds, mix well, and present.

8 to 10 portions

SWEET POTATO SALAD

Chunky, mashed sweet potatoes are dotted with diced pineapple, red pepper, and red onion in a slightly sweet Lime Vinaigrette. It's a great companion for picnics and barbecues.

2 pounds sweet potatoes, peeled and cut into 1-inch chunks
1 cup diced pineapple (fresh or canned)
³/₄ cup diced red pepper
¹/₂ cup diced red onion

Lime Vinaigrette:
1 medium-size clove garlic, minced
salt and pepper to taste
1 teaspoon dry mustard
2 tablespoons ketchup
¹/₂ teaspoon finely grated lime zest
3 tablespoons lime juice
²/₃ cup olive oil

1. Boil the sweet potatoes in water for 10 to 15 minutes until very tender. Transfer to a strainer and let sit for 20 minutes to drain completely.

2. Remove the potatoes to a large bowl and mash to a chunky consistency. Add the pineapple, red pepper, and red onion.

3. In a separate bowl, whisk together the garlic, salt, pepper, mustard, ketchup, lime zest, lime juice, and olive oil.

4. Pour the vinaigrette over the vegetables, mix well, and let marinate for 1 to 2 hours. (This may be made up to 24 hours in advance and refrigerated; return to room temperature to serve.) Stir thoroughly and present.

6 portions

BACKYARD BARBECUE

Grilled Burgers
· · ·
Crusty Bread
· · ·
Sweet Potato Salad
· · ·
Red Cabbage Slaw
· · ·
Cream Cheese Brownies◆
· · ·
Watermelon

PERSIAN VEGETABLE SALAD

Typical of Middle Eastern cuisine, this chopped vegetable salad features diced cucumbers, tomatoes, celery, and red onion in a yogurt sauce redolent with mint.

2 cucumbers, diced
3 medium-size tomatoes, diced
2 large stalks celery, diced
1/2 cup diced red onion
1 tablespoon dried mint
salt and pepper to taste
1 cup plain yogurt

1. Put the cucumbers, tomatoes, celery, and red onion in a serving bowl. Sprinkle with the mint and season with salt and pepper.

2. Add the yogurt and mix well until evenly blended. Serve at once atop lettuce-lined plates.

6 to 8 portions

THAI VEGETABLE SALAD

A Thai-style peanut dressing adorns greenery and an array of vegetables for a taste of the Far East. The dressing is also tasty over linguine with assorted vegetables.

1 large head Boston lettuce, torn into bite-size pieces
1 large carrot, cut into thin julienne pieces
1/4 pound snow peas, blanched and sliced in half on the diagonal
1 pickling cucumber, thinly sliced

Peanut Dressing:
1 tablespoon creamy peanut butter
1 small clove garlic, smashed
1 tablespoon soy sauce
1 teaspoon dark brown sugar
1/8 teaspoon cayenne pepper
1/4 teaspoon black pepper
2 tablespoons rice vinegar
1/2 cup vegetable oil

1. Heap the lettuce in a large bowl. Add the carrot, snow peas, and cucumber.

2. In a separate bowl, mix together the peanut butter, garlic, soy sauce, brown sugar, cayenne pepper, black pepper, and vinegar. Slowly whisk in the oil until it is completely incorporated and the dressing is smooth and creamy.

3. Pour the Peanut Dressing over the salad, toss well, and serve.

6 portions

ASIAN DELIGHT

Oriental-Glazed
Cornish Hens
· · ·
Thai Vegetable Salad
· · ·
Fried Wild Rice
· · ·
Sautéed Bananas

TOMATOES AND PINE NUTS

Simple ingredients—lusty tomatoes, fragrant parsley, and toasted pine nuts—provide a colorful trio of tastes and textures.

4 large, ripe tomatoes, chopped
2 cups coarsely chopped Italian parsley
1/2 cup pine nuts, toasted
1/4 cup extra-virgin olive oil
1 tablespoon balsamic vinegar
salt and freshly ground pepper to taste

1. Combine the tomatoes, parsley, and pine nuts in a large serving bowl.

2. In a separate small bowl, whisk together the olive oil, vinegar, salt, and pepper. Pour the dressing over the vegetables. Toss until evenly mixed and serve. (This actually improves with time, so it can be prepared several hours in advance.)

6 portions

WARM TOMATO AND GOAT CHEESE SALAD

The rich flavor of tomatoes marries well with the heady taste of goat cheese in this divine dish. Herbed plum tomatoes are warmed in a garlic-infused olive oil, crowned with crumbled goat cheese, and garnished with French bread croutons. I will be forever grateful to my friend, Joe Charter, for sharing this heaven-sent dish.

MEDITERRANEAN
FARE

Warm Tomato and
Goat Cheese Salad
· · ·
Sicilian-Roasted
Swordfish
· · ·
Polenta
· · ·
Sautéed Zucchini
· · ·
Fresh Melon

1/4 cup extra-virgin olive oil
2 large cloves garlic, minced
2 1/4 pounds ripe plum tomatoes, coarsely chopped
1 1/2 teaspoons dried basil
1/2 teaspoon dried rosemary
salt and pepper to taste
6 ounces goat cheese, crumbled
4 cups fresh French bread croutons, cut into 1/2-inch cubes

1. Heat the olive oil and garlic in a large skillet. Add the tomatoes. Sprinkle with the basil and rosemary and season with salt and pepper.

2. Cook the tomatoes over high heat for 3 minutes. Remove to a platter with any accumulated pan juices.

3. Sprinkle with the crumbled goat cheese and garnish with the chunks of bread. Serve at once. (The goat cheese will melt from the warmth of the cooked tomatoes, which makes for delicious eating.)

4 to 6 portions

**HEARTY
ITALIAN DINNER**

Bruschetta with
Roasted Garlic
· · ·
Tuscan Salad
· · ·
Chicken with
Three Cheese Melt
· · ·
Pasta with Green
Olive Tapenade
· · ·
Rhubarb Crisp

TUSCAN SALAD

Italian in design, this salad incorporates prosciutto, artichoke hearts, and dried cherries with a tangy, creamy Romano Dressing atop Boston lettuce.

1 large head Boston lettuce, torn into bite-size pieces
14-ounce can artichoke hearts, drained and cut in half
1/8 pound thinly sliced prosciutto
1/3 cup dried cherries, plumped in warm water for 1 minute
*   and drained*

Romano Dressing:
1 large clove garlic, crushed
salt to taste
1/8 teaspoon black pepper
1/2 teaspoon dried oregano
1 teaspoon capers
2 tablespoons mayonnaise
1 tablespoon red wine vinegar
1 tablespoon balsamic vinegar
1/3 cup virgin olive oil
3 tablespoons freshly grated Romano cheese

1. Heap the lettuce in a large bowl. Top with the artichoke hearts, prosciutto, and dried cherries.

2. In a separate bowl, whisk together the garlic, salt, pepper, oregano, capers, mayonnaise, vinegars, olive oil, and Romano cheese until thick and creamy.

3. Pour the dressing over the salad, toss well, and serve at once.

6 portions

WALDORF SALAD

This is not your typical apple-celery-nut trio. Chopped apple, sliced fennel, celery, and toasted walnuts are covered in a creamy Blue Cheese Dressing. The dressing also doubles as a tasty topping for baked potatoes.

> 1 large Red Delicious apple, cored and coarsely chopped
> 1 cup thinly sliced fennel
> 2 large stalks celery, sliced into $1/2$-inch thick pieces
> $1/4$ cup walnuts, toasted
>
> **Blue-Cheese Dressing:**
> $1/2$ cup sour cream
> 1 tablespoon white wine vinegar
> 1 teaspoon sugar
> salt and freshly ground pepper to taste
> $1/4$ cup crumbled Saga Blue cheese

1. Combine the apple, fennel, celery, and walnuts in a large bowl.

2. In a separate bowl, mix together the sour cream, vinegar, sugar, salt, pepper, and blue cheese.

3. Pour the dressing over the salad, toss well, and serve atop leaves of lettuce.

3 to 4 portions

FALL LUNCH

Waldorf Salad
. . .
French Bread
. . .
Split Pea Soup
. . .
Fresh Pears

WATERCRESS AND STRAWBERRIES

The sweet, succulent, ruby-red berry complements the peppery taste of the dark green sprigs. It's both a vibrant and refreshing treat.

1 pint ripe strawberries, hulled and sliced
1 tablespoon sugar
3 bunches watercress, heavy stems removed
salt and pepper to taste
1 tablespoon balsamic vinegar
¼ cup virgin olive oil

1. Place the strawberries in a bowl and sprinkle with the sugar. Let sit for 30 minutes.

2. Heap the watercress in a salad bowl. Adorn the greens with the berries and any accumulated juices.

3. In a separate bowl, whisk together the salt, pepper, vinegar, and olive oil.

4. Pour the dressing over the salad, toss well, and serve.

4 portions

WINTER SALAD WITH WALNUT PESTO

Toasted walnuts, Italian parsley, and garlic all come together in this readily available winter version of the fragrant Italian pesto sauce we have come to adore. Try the Walnut Pesto on pasta, atop grilled fish or chicken, mixed with steamed vegetables, or stirred into rice.

1 large or 2 small heads Boston lettuce, torn into bite-size pieces
1 endive, thinly sliced
1 large fennel bulb, top fronds removed, and thinly sliced
1/4 cup coarsely chopped walnuts, toasted

Walnut Pesto:
1 large clove garlic
1/2 cup packed Italian parsley
1/4 cup walnuts, toasted
salt and pepper to taste
2 tablespoons white wine vinegar
1/2 cup extra-virgin olive oil

1. Heap the Boston lettuce, endive, and fennel in a large bowl. Garnish with the chopped walnuts.

2. Make the pesto. In the bowl of a food processor, place the garlic, parsley, walnuts, salt, pepper, and vinegar. Grind to a fine paste. With the motor running, add the olive oil in a slow, steady stream until it is completely incorporated. (The pesto may be made up to 1 week in advance and stored in the refrigerator; return to room temperature to use.)

3. Spoon the pesto over the salad greens, toss well, and serve at once.

6 portions

**SUNDAY NITE
WINTER SUPPER**

Winter Salad with
Walnut Pesto
. . .
Beef Carbonnade
. . .
Buttered Noodles
. . .
Chocolate-Banana
Bread Pudding

GRAIN AND LEGUME SALADS

ORIENTAL BLACK BEAN SALAD

Black beans, yellow peppers, scallions, and sun-dried tomatoes are embraced by an Oriental Sesame Vinaigrette for an "East meets West" sensation.

1 pound dried black turtle beans, pre-soaked (see page 319,
    How to Cook Dried Beans)
6 cups water
1 teaspoon salt
1 medium-size yellow pepper, diced
1/2 cup diced sun-dried tomatoes
1 cup thinly sliced scallions

Sesame Vinaigrette:
1/2 teaspoon freshly ground black pepper
2 tablespoons finely grated gingerroot
1/4 cup soy sauce
3 tablespoons rice vinegar
1/4 cup Oriental sesame oil
2 tablespoons vegetable oil

1. Put the beans, water, and salt in a large pot. Bring to a boil, reduce the heat, and simmer for 45 minutes until the beans are barely tender. Drain well and transfer the beans to a large bowl.

2. Add the yellow pepper, sun-dried tomatoes, and scallions.

3. In a separate bowl, whisk together the pepper, gingerroot, soy sauce, vinegar, sesame and vegetable oils.

4. Pour the vinaigrette over the warm beans and mix well. Allow to marinate for 1 to 2 hours and serve. (This may be prepared 24 hours in advance and refrigerated; return to room temperature to serve.)

8 portions

WHITE BEAN SALAD

Cannelli beans are presented in typical Tuscan fashion with sage, olive oil, and prosciutto, the distinctive salt-cured Italian ham.

2 cups dried Great Northern beans, pre-soaked (see page 319,
How to Cook Dried Beans)
8 cups water
2 teaspoons salt
1/4 teaspoon black pepper
2 whole fresh sage leaves
1/2 cup diced red onion
1/8 pound prosciutto, sliced 1/8-inch thick, and diced

Sage Vinaigrette:
salt and pepper to taste
2 tablespoons finely minced fresh sage
3 tablespoons lemon juice
3/4 cup extra-virgin olive oil

1. Put the beans, water, salt, pepper, and sage leaves in a large pot. Bring to a boil, reduce the heat, and simmer for 45 minutes until the beans are barely tender. Drain well and discard the sage leaves. Transfer the beans to a large bowl.

2. Add the onion and prosciutto.

3. In a separate bowl, whisk together the salt, pepper, minced sage, lemon juice, and olive oil.

4. Pour the dressing over the warm beans and toss until well mixed. Serve warm, or chill and let marinate for 4 to 6 hours. Return to room temperature to serve.

8 to 10 portions

**ANTIPASTO
PARTY FOR 24**

Spiced Mediterranean
Olives
. . .
Cherry Tomatoes
and Mozzarella
. . .
Oranges and
Red Onion
. . .
Green Beans Olivada
. . .
Bruschetta with
Artichoke Pesto
. . .
Marinated
Mushrooms✦
. . .
Roasted Pepper Salad
. . .
Melon Wrapped
with Prosciutto
. . .
White Bean Salad
. . .
Italian Pasta Salad✦
. . .
Focaccia and
Bread Sticks

THREE BEAN SALAD

Red kidney, white cannelli, and black turtle beans team up with tomatoes and black olives, spiked with a Chili Vinaigrette for a South-of-the-Border palate pleaser.

$^1/_2$ cup dried red kidney beans, pre-soaked*
$^1/_2$ cup dried Great Northern beans, pre-soaked*
$^1/_2$ cup dried black turtle beans, pre-soaked*
$4^1/_2$ cups water
1 teaspoon salt
1 large clove garlic
$^1/_2$ cup sliced ripe black olives
2 ripe plum tomatoes, chopped
$^1/_3$ cup thinly sliced scallions

Chili Vinaigrette:
salt and pepper to taste
1 large clove garlic, crushed
1 tablespoon chili powder
$^1/_2$ teaspoon ground cumin
$^1/_4$ teaspoon cayenne pepper
$^1/_4$ cup coarsely chopped fresh cilantro
3 tablespoons lime juice
$^2/_3$ cup virgin olive oil

1. Put the beans, water, salt, and clove of garlic in a large pot. Bring to a boil, reduce the heat, and simmer for 45 minutes until the beans are barely tender. Drain well and discard the garlic. Transfer the beans to a large bowl.

2. Add the olives, tomatoes, and scallions.

3. In a separate bowl, whisk together the salt, pepper, garlic, chili powder, cumin, cayenne pepper, cilantro, lime juice, and olive oil.

4. Pour the vinaigrette over the warm beans and mix well. Serve warm, or chill and let marinate for 4 to 6 hours. Return to room temperature to serve.

4 to 6 portions

*See page 319, How to Cook Dried Beans.

LENTIL SALAD

Healthy, nutritious, and delicious are apt words to describe this salad, which combines legumes, walnuts, tomatoes, and currants in a Walnut Oil Vinaigrette.

1 cup dried lentils, rinsed
salt
4 ripe plum tomatoes, diced
1/2 cup coarsely chopped walnuts, toasted
1/4 cup currants
1 cup coarsely chopped Italian parsley
1/2 cup snipped chives

Walnut Oil Vinaigrette:
3/4 teaspoon salt
freshly ground black pepper to taste
1 tablespoon Dijon mustard
2 tablespoons red wine vinegar
2 tablespoons walnut oil
1/4 cup extra-virgin olive oil

1. Cook the lentils in boiling salted water until tender-crisp, about 30 minutes. Drain well and transfer the lentils to a large bowl.

2. Add the tomatoes, walnuts, currants, parsley, and chives.

3. In a separate bowl, whisk together the salt, pepper, Dijon, vinegar, and walnut and olive oils until thick and creamy.

4. Pour the vinaigrette over the lentil mixture and toss well. Let marinate for 1 to 2 hours for flavors to mellow.

6 to 8 portions

LIGHT SUMMER DINNER

Grilled Swordfish
. . .
Lentil Salad
. . .
Asparagus with Mustard Butter♦
. . .
Citrus Angel Food Cake

**MEXICAN-
INSPIRED PICNIC**

Guacamole
. . .
South-of-the-Border
Chicken
. . .
Southwestern
Corn Salad
. . .
Red Cabbage Slaw
. . .
Chocolate-Chocolate
Chip Wafers

SOUTHWESTERN CORN SALAD

A medley of corn and assorted peppers are highlighted by a Mexican-inspired Cilantro Vinaigrette. It's a colorful, refreshing dish for picnics and buffets! For a heartier salad, try adding cooked black beans for a truly delicious, prize-winning, South-of-the-Border combination.

8 cups corn kernels (fresh or frozen), blanched
1 large red pepper, diced
1 large orange pepper, diced
1/2 cup thinly sliced scallions

Cilantro Vinaigrette:
1 medium-size clove garlic, smashed
salt to taste
1/4 teaspoon black pepper
heaping 1/4 teaspoon ground cumin
generous pinch cayenne pepper
3 tablespoons chopped fresh cilantro
1/2 cup chopped Italian parsley
1/4 cup orange juice
1/2 cup virgin olive oil

1. Combine the corn, red and orange peppers, and scallions in a large bowl.

2. In a separate bowl, whisk together the garlic, salt, pepper, cumin, cayenne pepper, cilantro, parsley, orange juice, and olive oil.

3. Pour the vinaigrette over the salad, toss well, and serve. (This may be made up to 24 hours in advance and refrigerated; return to room temperature to serve.)

8 portions

CORNBREAD SALAD

This is a Mexican variation of the classic Italian bread salad, panzanella. Cornbread croutons form the base for chopped vegetables and all is laced with a Cilantro-Lime Vinaigrette. Cornbread lovers will certainly appreciate this salad.

4½ cups cornbread croutons, cut from cornbread or muffins into
¾-inch cubes
1 medium-size red pepper, coarsely chopped
1 medium-size yellow pepper, coarsely chopped
½ cup thinly sliced red onion

Cilantro-Lime Vinaigrette:
1 medium-size clove garlic, minced
salt and pepper to taste
⅛ teaspoon cayenne pepper
1 tablespoon finely chopped fresh cilantro
1 teaspoon finely grated lime zest
2 tablespoons lime juice
⅓ cup extra-virgin olive oil

1. Preheat the oven to 400°F. Place the croutons on a cookie sheet and bake for 10 minutes. Turn them over and bake for 3 to 5 minutes more until golden. Remove from the oven and let cool completely. (This may be done 1 to 2 days in advance and stored in an airtight container.)

2. Combine the croutons, red and yellow peppers, and onion in a large bowl.

3. In a separate bowl, whisk together the garlic, salt, pepper, cayenne pepper, cilantro, lime zest, lime juice, and olive oil.

4. Pour the vinaigrette over the salad, toss well, and serve at once.

4 portions

CASUAL DINNER

Grilled Shrimp with
Orange-Tomato Relish
. . .
Cornbread Salad
. . .
Sautéed Zucchini
Rounds
. . .
Assorted Cookies

MIDDLE EASTERN CHICK PEAS AND TOMATOES

Chick peas, tomatoes, and red onion join forces with a tahini sauce, reminiscent of the taste of hoomis. Tahini is a thick paste of ground, hulled sesame seeds bearing a distinctive nutty flavor.

19-ounce can chick peas, rinsed and drained
4 large, ripe plum tomatoes, chopped
1/2 cup diced red onion

Tahini Vinaigrette:
1 large clove garlic, crushed
salt and pepper to taste
1/4 cup chopped fresh parsley
1/4 cup tahini
2 tablespoons lemon juice
2 tablespoons olive oil

1. Combine the chick peas, tomatoes, and onion in a large bowl.

2. In a separate bowl, whisk together the garlic, salt, pepper, parsley, tahini, lemon juice, and olive oil until thick and creamy.

3. Pour the dressing over the vegetables, toss well, and serve.

6 portions

GREEN BEANS AND ROASTED CHICK PEAS

This salad teems with poached green beans, roasted red peppers, and roasted chick peas, dressed in a Mint Vinaigrette. Roasting the chick peas gives them a nutty, crunchy quality. The roasted chick peas are also delicious as a snack for eating out of hand.

BROWN-BAG LUNCH

Fez's Pasta with
Fresh Tomato Sauce
. . .
Green Beans and
Roasted Chick Peas
. . .
Pecan Shortbreads

19-ounce can chick peas, rinsed and drained
1 1/2 tablespoons olive oil
1 pound green beans, poached 5 minutes
2 large red peppers, roasted and cut into 1/4-inch thick slices

Mint Vinaigrette:
1 large clove garlic, smashed
salt and pepper to taste
1 teaspoon dried mint
1 1/2 tablespoons lemon juice
1/4 cup virgin olive oil

1. Make the roasted chick peas. Preheat the oven to 400°F. Mix together the chick peas and 1 1/2 tablespoons olive oil. Spread the mixture out in a single layer on a baking sheet. Roast for 50 to 55 minutes until golden and crunchy, shaking the pan after 30 minutes to stir up the legumes. Remove from the oven and let cool. Set aside or store in an airtight container until needed. (These will keep for 2 weeks.)

2. Mix the roasted chick peas, green beans, and roasted peppers in a large bowl.

3. In a separate bowl, whisk together the garlic, salt, pepper, mint, lemon juice, and olive oil.

4. Pour the vinaigrette over the vegetables, toss well, and serve. (This may be made 24 hours in advance and refrigerated; return to room temperature to serve.)

4 to 6 portions

CHOPPED VEGETABLE SALAD WITH TAHINI DRESSING

A medley of chopped vegetables is cloaked in a thick hoomis-tahini sauce, particular to Middle Eastern cuisine.

1 cucumber, peeled and diced into $1/2$-inch pieces
2 large stalks celery, diced into $1/2$-inch pieces
1 medium-size red pepper, diced into $1/2$-inch pieces
1 medium-size green pepper, diced into $1/2$-inch pieces
1 cup diced radishes
$1/2$ cup thinly sliced scallions

Hoomis-Tahini Dressing:
1 cup canned chick peas, rinsed and drained
2 large cloves garlic, crushed
$1/2$ teaspoon salt
freshly ground pepper to taste
$1/3$ cup tahini
2 teaspoons finely grated lemon zest
2 tablespoons lemon juice
2 tablespoons olive oil

1. Mix the cucumber, celery, red pepper, green pepper, radishes, and scallions in a large bowl.

2. Place the chick peas, garlic, salt, pepper, tahini, lemon zest, lemon juice, and olive oil in the bowl of a food processor. Purée until thick and smooth.

3. Pour the dressing over the vegetables and mix well. Let marinate for 1 to 2 hours. Serve at room temperature.

6 portions

CRACKED WHEAT AND OLIVE SALAD

Bulgur makes a grand statement with a medley of diced vegetables and green olives in this tantalizing dish. The slight tang and piquancy of the olives adds life to this cracked wheat presentation.

1 cup bulgur
boiling water
2/3 cup finely diced red pepper
2/3 cup finely diced yellow or orange pepper
1/2 cup finely diced red onion
3/4 cup diced pimiento-stuffed green olives
1/2 cup toasted walnuts, finely chopped
2/3 cup chopped Italian parsley

Lemon Vinaigrette:
1 large clove garlic, minced
freshly ground pepper to taste
1/4 cup lemon juice
1/4 cup extra-virgin olive oil

1. Place the bulgur in a 2-quart mixing bowl and add enough boiling water to come 2 inches above the cracked wheat. Allow this to stand for 1 hour. Toss with a fork, and squeeze out any excess water.

2. Combine the bulgur, red pepper, yellow pepper, red onion, green olives, walnuts, and parsley in a large serving bowl.

3. In a separate bowl, whisk together the garlic, pepper, lemon juice, and olive oil.

4. Pour the dressing over the salad and mix well. Cover and chill for 3 to 4 hours or as much as overnight. Return to room temperature to serve.

6 to 8 portions

MIDDLE EASTERN DINNER

Middle Eastern
Eggplant Spread
· · ·
Roast Lamb with
Mint Pesto
· · ·
Cracked Wheat
and Olive Salad
· · ·
Baklava

**HOT WEATHER
FARE**

Melon with Prosciutto
. . .
Venetian-Style Sole
. . .
Herbed Rice Salad
. . .
Slow-Roasted
Tomatoes
. . .
Berries and Cream

HERBED RICE SALAD

Long grain rice explodes with the intriguing flavors of a melange of herbs, capers, and Parmesan cheese. This makes great barbecue fare and totes well to picnics.

2 cups water
1 cup raw long-grain rice
salt and pepper to taste
1 cup coarsely chopped Italian parsley
1 teaspoon dried sage
1 teaspoon dried rosemary
1 teaspoon dried thyme
2 tablespoons capers
3 tablespoons Parmesan cheese
3 tablespoons balsamic vinegar
3 tablespoons extra-virgin olive oil

1. Bring the water to a boil in a 2-quart saucepan. Stir in the rice, cover, lower the heat, and simmer for 20 minutes until all the water is absorbed. Fluff with a fork.

2. In a small bowl, whisk together the salt, pepper, herbs, capers, Parmesan, vinegar, and olive oil.

3. Add the vinaigrette to the cooked rice and stir until evenly mixed. Serve warm or at room temperature.

6 portions

SUSHI-STYLE RICE

Sushi ingredients—soy sauce, wasabi, rice vinegar, and ginger—join forces for a Japanese-style rice salad, embellished with cucumber, avocado and baby shrimp. Wasabi is the bold-tasting, Japanese horseradish powder that gives sushi its blast of flavor.

2 cups water
salt to taste
1 cup raw long-grain rice
3 tablespoons rice vinegar
2 tablespoons soy sauce
1 tablespoon wasabi powder* mixed with 2 teaspoons of water
    to make a paste
1 tablespoon grated gingerroot
1/2 cup thinly sliced scallions
1 cup peeled and diced English (seedless) cucumber
1 Haas avocado, peeled, pitted, and diced
5 ounces cooked baby shrimp

1. Bring the water and salt to a boil in a saucepan. Add the rice, cover, lower the heat, and simmer for 20 minutes until all the water is absorbed. Fluff with a fork and let sit for 5 minutes.

2. In a small bowl, mix together the vinegar, soy sauce, wasabi, gingerroot, and scallions.

3. Transfer the rice to a large bowl. Add the soy mixture to the rice along with the cucumber, avocado, and shrimp. Toss well to combine. Serve at room temperature.

6 side portions; 4 main-course portions

*Available in Oriental markets.

DINNER WITH ASIAN FLAIR

Barbecued
Leg of Lamb
· · ·
Romaine with
Soy Vinaigrette
· · ·
Sushi-Style Rice
· · ·
Ginger Ice Cream

ORANGE WILD RICE SALAD

The exotic grain wild rice, basks in the glory of this orange-scented salad. The composition of wild rice, dried cherries, toasted pine nuts, scallions, and mandarin oranges is flavorful, colorful, and delicious. Try it with grilled or roasted poultry or fish.

**BUFFET PARTY
FOR 12**

Cucumbers and
Caviar
· · ·
Crab Rangoon
· · ·
Poached Salmon◆
· · ·
Orange Wild
Rice Salad
· · ·
Springtime Asparagus
Salad◆
· · ·
Maple-Pecan
Pound Cake

1 cup raw wild rice
3 cups water
salt to taste
11-ounce can mandarin oranges, drained
¼ cup pine nuts, toasted
⅓ cup thinly sliced scallions
⅓ cup dried cherries
⅓ cup orange juice
1 teaspoon finely grated orange peel
¾ cup coarsely chopped Italian parsley
2 tablespoons balsamic vinegar
2 tablespoons extra-virgin olive oil
pepper to taste

1. Rinse the rice well under cold water and drain. In a large saucepan, bring the water and salt to a boil. Add the rice, cover, lower the heat, and simmer gently for 35 to 40 minutes. Drain well and transfer the rice to a large bowl.

2. Add the oranges, pine nuts, and scallions to the rice.

3. In a small bowl, mix the cherries and orange juice and let sit for 5 minutes. Then whisk in the orange peel, parsley, vinegar, and olive oil. Season with salt and pepper.

4. Pour the dressing over the rice salad and mix gently so as not to break up the oranges. Serve at once or chill for later use. (This may be made 24 hours in advance and refrigerated; return to room temperature to serve.)

6 portions

WILD RICE AND CORN SALAD

This double-grain salad boasts a flavor-packed experience. It combines the nutty taste of wild rice, the succulence of corn, the hickory flavor of bacon, the piquancy of stuffed green olives, and the richness of sun-dried tomatoes.

1 cup raw wild rice
3 cups water
salt to taste
1 cup fresh or frozen corn kernels, blanched
4 slices bacon, cooked until crisp and coarsely chopped
1/2 cup chopped pimiento-stuffed green olives
1/2 cup coarsely chopped sun-dried tomatoes

Herbed Vinaigrette:
salt and pepper to taste
1/2 teaspoon dried thyme
1/2 teaspoon dried tarragon
3 tablespoons white wine vinegar
1/3 cup virgin olive oil

1. Rinse the rice well under cold water and drain. In a large saucepan, bring the water and salt to a boil. Add the rice, cover, lower the heat, and simmer gently for 35 to 40 minutes. Drain well and transfer the rice to a large bowl.

2. Add the corn, bacon, olives, and tomatoes.

3. In a separate bowl, whisk together the salt, pepper, thyme, tarragon, vinegar, and olive oil.

4. Pour the vinaigrette over the rice salad and mix well. Serve at once or chill for later use. (This may be made in advance and refrigerated; return to room temperature to serve.)

6 portions

EASTER DINNER

Sweet Potato
Vichyssoise
. . .
Baked Ham
. . .
Wild Rice and
Corn Salad
. . .
Oven-Roasted
Asparagus
. . .
Chocolate-
Strawberry Tart

HEARTY
SALADS

COBB SALAD

My version of the classic cobb features a composed salad of Boston lettuce topped with artichoke hearts, avocado, plum tomatoes, and crabmeat covered with a buttermilk-blue cheese dressing.

2 large heads Boston lettuce, separated into individual leaves
4 ripe plum tomatoes, sliced
1 ripe Haas avocado, peeled, pitted, and cut into 1/2-inch chunks
14-ounce can artichoke hearts, drained and cut in half
1/2 pound fresh lump crabmeat, cartilage removed

Blue Cheese Dressing:
3/4 cup sour cream
1/2 cup mayonnaise
1 large clove garlic, crushed
salt and pepper to taste
2/3 cup buttermilk
2 tablespoons red wine vinegar
4 ounces Saga Blue cheese, crumbled

1. Arrange the lettuce on a large platter or on 8 individual plates. Adorn the lettuce with the tomatoes, avocado, artichoke hearts, and crabmeat.

2. In a small bowl, mix the sour cream, mayonnaise, garlic, salt, pepper, buttermilk, vinegar, and blue cheese.

3. Spoon dollops of the dressing over the salad and serve. (Any extra dressing may be kept in the refrigerator for 3 to 4 days. It also makes a marvelous dip for crudités.)

8 portions; 2 cups of dressing

SMOKED CHICKEN SALAD WITH APRICOT-DATE CHUTNEY

A lovely, smoky flavor embraces chunks of chicken which are offset by the sweet-tart flavor of the dried fruit chutney. The chutney should actually be made in advance and refrigerated, allowing the flavors a chance to mellow. Try it mixed with cream cheese atop bagels for a breakfast or brunch treat!

4 large boneless, skinless chicken breasts, split in half (about 3 pounds)
1 tablespoon lemon juice
2 tablespoons dark brown sugar
¼ cup vegetable oil
1 tablespoon liquid smoke
½ cup mayonnaise
1⅓ cups Apricot-Date Chutney (see page 11)

1. Preheat the oven to 350°F.

2. Place the chicken breasts in a roasting pan.

3. In a separate bowl, mix together the lemon juice, brown sugar, oil, and liquid smoke. Pour the dressing over the chicken and marinate for 30 minutes.

4. Cover the chicken and bake for 25 minutes. Cut the chicken into 1-inch chunks and transfer to a bowl, reserving the pan juices.

5. In a separate bowl, mix together the chutney with the mayonnaise and reserved pan juices from the chicken.

6. Spoon the chutney dressing over the chicken and mix well. Serve atop leaves of radicchio lettuce.

PICNIC FARE

Strawberries Balsamic
· · ·
Smoked Chicken Salad with Apricot-Date Chutney
· · ·
Mixed Green Salad
· · ·
Orange Muffins

LIGHT SUPPER

Wild Mushroom Soup
· · ·
French Bread
· · ·
Grilled Chicken
Caesar Salad
· · ·
Frozen Yogurt

GRILLED CHICKEN CAESAR SALAD

The much beloved Caesar salad takes on a new complexion in this light repast. Romaine lettuce is crowned with grilled chicken tenders, dressed in a creamy Parmesan vinaigrette, and bespeckled with toasted walnuts.

1¹/₂ pounds chicken tenders
2 tablespoons olive oil
salt and pepper to taste
1 large head romaine, torn into bite-size pieces
¹/₂ cup coarsely chopped walnuts, toasted

Caesar Dressing:
1 large clove garlic, minced
salt and pepper to taste
dash of Worcestershire sauce
1 teaspoon Dijon mustard
1 tablespoon mayonnaise
3 tablespoons red wine vinegar
²/₃ cup extra-virgin olive oil
¹/₄ cup freshly grated Parmesan cheese

1. Drizzle the chicken with the 2 tablespoons olive oil and season with salt and pepper. Cook over a hot grill, 4 inches from the heat source, about 2 minutes per side.

2. Heap the romaine on a large platter. Top with the grilled chicken and garnish with the toasted walnuts.

3. In a small bowl, whisk together the garlic, salt, pepper, Worcestershire, Dijon, mayonnaise, vinegar, olive oil, and Parmesan until thick and creamy.

4. Pour the dressing over the salad, toss to mix, and serve.

5 to 6 portions

TARRAGON ROASTED CHICKEN WITH MIXED GREENS

SOUP 'N SALAD SUPPER

Succotash Chowder
. . .
Tarragon-Roasted
Chicken with
Mixed Greens
. . .
Sourdough Bread
. . .
Pound Cake with
Ice Cream

Roasted chicken slices are set atop mixed greens with plums and walnuts in a heavenly tarragon-walnut oil vinaigrette. The fresh fruits and nuts add dimension and flavor to this salad, turning it into the extraordinary!

3 to 4 pound whole broiler
1 tablespoon lemon juice
1 tablespoon walnut oil
salt and pepper to taste
1 teaspoon dried tarragon
10 to 12 cups mixed greens (radicchio, arugula, beet greens, red leaf
*   lettuce, endive, and watercress)*
1/2 cup sliced scallions
3 large, ripe plums, sliced into wedges
1/2 cup walnuts, toasted

Tarragon Vinaigrette:
1 small clove garlic, minced
salt to taste
1/4 teaspoon black pepper
1 1/2 teaspoons dried tarragon
3 tablespoons mayonnaise
3 tablespoons tarragon vinegar
1/3 cup walnut oil

1. Preheat the oven to 400°F.

2. Place the chicken in a roasting pan.

3. In a small bowl, combine the lemon juice, 1 tablespoon walnut oil, salt, pepper, and 1 teaspoon tarragon. Rub this mixture over all parts of the chicken.

4. Roast for 1 hour or until the juices run clear and the chicken is golden. Remove from the oven and let rest for 10 minutes. Then carve the roast into slices, leaving the wings intact. (Up to this point the chicken may be prepared 24 hours in advance and refrigerated. Return to room temperature to serve.)

5. Arrange the mixed greens on a large platter. Top with the roasted chicken. Adorn with the scallions, plums, and walnuts.

6. In a small bowl, whisk together the garlic, salt, pepper, tarragon, mayonnaise, vinegar, and walnut oil until thick and creamy.

7. Pour the vinaigrette over the salad and serve.

4 to 6 portions

INDONESIAN LO MEIN SALAD

When you crave a taste of the Orient, try this pasta primavera that boasts a curry sauce redolent with ginger and soy sauce. The dish totes well to picnics and makes a colorful addition to the buffet table.

¹/₄ cup vegetable oil
¹/₄ soy sauce
1 tablespoon grated gingerroot
1 large clove garlic, minced
2 tablespoons lemon juice
1 tablespoon honey
1¹/₂ teaspoons curry powder
freshly ground pepper to taste
8 ounces fresh fettuccine
1¹/₂ cups bean sprouts
2 large carrots, cut into spaghetti strands
1 medium-size red pepper, cut into julienne strips
2 scallions, cut into 2-inch lengths and julienned
¹/₃ cup slivered almonds, toasted

1. In a small bowl, combine the oil, soy sauce, ginger, garlic, lemon juice, honey, curry, and pepper and mix well.

2. Cook the pasta according to the package directions and drain well. Transfer the pasta to a large bowl.

3. Add the vegetables and sauce and toss well until evenly mixed. Garnish with the toasted almonds. Serve at room temperature.

6 to 8 side portions; 3 to 4 main-course portions

BRUNCH

Iced Strawberry Soup
. . .
Lobster and
Tortellini Salad
. . .
Mixed Green Salad◆
. . .
French and
Sourdough Breads
. . .
World's Best Sour
Cream Coffeecake

LOBSTER AND TORTELLINI SALAD

This star-spangled, colorful combination—lobster, corn, roasted red peppers, and tortellini—is the stuff of which dreams are made. Dressed in a lemon-dill vinaigrette, it's sublime. You may substitute poached shrimp for the lobster.

9-ounce package fresh cheese-filled egg tortellini
9-ounce package fresh cheese-filled spinach tortellini
3 medium-size red peppers, roasted and coarsely chopped
1¹/₂ cups fresh or frozen corn kernels, blanched
2 cups cooked lobster meat, cubed
¹/₃ cup thinly sliced scallions

Lemon-Dill Vinaigrette:
salt and freshly ground pepper to taste
1 teaspoon Dijon mustard
3 tablespoons chopped fresh dill
1 teaspoon finely grated lemon zest
3 tablespoons lemon juice
²/₃ cup extra-virgin olive oil

1. Cook the tortellini according to the package directions. Drain well and transfer the pasta to a large bowl.

2. Add the roasted peppers, corn, lobster, and scallions.

3. In a separate bowl, whisk together the salt, pepper, Dijon, dill, lemon zest, lemon juice, and olive oil.

4. Pour the vinaigrette over the salad, toss well, and serve. (This may be made 24 hours in advance and refrigerated; return to room temperature to serve.)

10 side portions; 6 to 8 main-course portions

MUSSELS, TOMATOES, AND ARUGULA

I love the subtle flavors and complex tastes in this glorious salad. The lushness of chopped tomatoes and the peppery tang of arugula mixed with a Mustard Vinaigrette add new dimension to the sweet mussels.

4 pounds mussels, scrubbed and debearded
2 cups dry white wine
2 bunches arugula
4 large, ripe tomatoes, chopped
2/3 cup sliced scallions

Mustard Vinaigrette:
salt and pepper to taste
1 tablespoon capers
3 tablespoons Dijon mustard
2/3 cup chopped parsley
1/4 cup white wine vinegar
3/4 cup extra-virgin olive oil

SUMMER LUNCHEON

Strawberry-Banana
Daiquiri Soup
. . .
Mussels, Tomatoes,
and Arugula
. . .
Assorted Rolls
. . .
Honeydew Freeze

1. Rinse the mussels under cold running water to make sure they are free of sand. Heap them in a large pot.

2. Add the wine. Cover, bring to a boil, and simmer gently just until the mussels open, about 5 minutes.

3. Transfer the mussels to a colander to drain, discarding any unopened ones. Remove the mussels from their shells.

4. Heap the arugula in a large bowl. Add the mussels, tomatoes, and scallions.

5. In a separate small bowl, whisk together the salt, pepper, capers, Dijon, parsley, vinegar, and olive oil until thick and creamy.

6. Pour the vinaigrette over the salad, toss well, and serve.

8 side portions; 4 main-course portions

ORIENTAL SHRIMP SALAD

Spinach leaves take on an Oriental flair with grilled shrimp, scallions, and toasted almonds, dressed in a soy and sesame vinaigrette. Oriental sesame oil has a toasted, nutty flavor, lending a distinctive taste to this refreshing salad.

1½ pounds raw large shrimp, shelled
¼ cup soy sauce
¼ cup Oriental sesame oil
1 tablespoon grated gingerroot
2 teaspoons sugar
¼ teaspoon black pepper
1 pound fresh spinach, stems removed
8-ounce can water chestnuts, drained and sliced
¾ cup chopped scallions
½ cup slivered almonds, toasted

1. Place the shrimp in a bowl.

2. In a separate small bowl, whisk together the soy sauce, sesame oil, gingerroot, sugar, and pepper.

3. Pour the dressing over the shrimp and marinate for 30 minutes.

4. Skewer the shrimp, reserving the marinade. Grill (or broil) the shrimp, 4 inches from the heat source, for 2 to 3 minutes per side.

5. Heap the spinach in a large bowl. Top with the grilled shrimp and any accumulated juices. Garnish with the water chestnuts, scallions, and almonds.

6. Pour the reserved marinade over the salad, toss well, and serve.

4 to 6 portions

GRILLED SQUID SALAD

Squid, or calamari, is a shellfish that sports long tentacles on an elongated body. Once considered a "poor man's" fish, squid has become quite fashionable. In this dish, squid and red onions are grilled, coated in a snappy Orange-Fennel Vinaigrette, and embellished with raisins, capers, and pine nuts, lending a Mediterranean touch. Try the salad over freshly cooked linguine for a stylish pasta pleaser.

SUMMER SPLENDOR

Grilled Squid Salad
. . .
Pasta with Garlic and Oil
. . .
Marinated Olives◆
. . .
Wild Berry
Pound Cake

2 pounds squid
2 medium-large size red onions, sliced into 1/4-inch thick rounds
1/4 cup olive oil
salt and pepper to taste
1/2 cup raisins
1/4 cup pine nuts, toasted
2 tablespoons capers

Orange-Fennel Vinaigrette:
1 large clove garlic, smashed
salt to taste
1/4 teaspoon black pepper
1 teaspoon dried orange peel
1 teaspoon fennel seeds
1/4 teaspoon crushed red pepper flakes
1 tablespoon orange juice
2 tablespoons red wine vinegar
1/2 cup virgin olive oil

1. Drizzle the 1/4 cup olive oil over the squid and onion slices. Season with salt and pepper. Grill over hot coals, 4 inches from the heat source, until cooked and browned. (Allow 2 to 3 minutes per side for the squid; 5 to 7 minutes per side for the onions.)

2. Slice the squid into 1/2-inch wide rings, leaving the tentacles whole. Separate the onions into individual rings.

3. In a large bowl, combine the squid, onions, raisins, pine nuts, and capers.

4. In a separate bowl, whisk together the garlic, salt, pepper, orange peel, fennel, red pepper flakes, orange juice, vinegar, and olive oil.

5. Pour the vinaigrette over the squid salad, toss well, and serve. (This may be made 4 to 6 hours in advance and refrigerated; return to room temperature to serve.)

6 portions

**HOT WEATHER
FARE**

Artichoke Heart
Roll-Ups
. . .
Grilled Sausage Salad
. . .
Focaccia
. . .
Melon and Sorbet

GRILLED SAUSAGE SALAD

This robust, Italian-influenced dish showcases grilled sausages, peppers, mushrooms, and onion atop mixed greens with a Mustard Vinaigrette.

1 large green pepper, cut into 2-inch wide strips
1 large red pepper, cut into 2-inch wide strips
1 Spanish onion, sliced into 1/4-inch thick rounds
3/4 pound fresh cultivated mushrooms
1/4 cup olive oil
salt and pepper to taste
1 1/4 pounds sweet or hot sausage (or a combination)
1 large head romaine, torn into bite-size pieces
1 head radicchio, torn into bite-size pieces

Mustard Vinaigrette:
1 large clove garlic, crushed
salt to taste
1/2 teaspoon black pepper
2 tablespoons Pommeroy mustard (grainy mustard)
2 tablespoons red wine vinegar
2/3 cup virgin olive oil

1. Heap the peppers, onion, and mushrooms in a large bowl. Drizzle with the 1/4 cup olive oil and season with salt and pepper.

2. Grill the sausages and vegetables over hot coals, 4 inches from the heat source, until cooked and browned. (Allow 10 minutes for the sausages; 10 to 15 minutes for the vegetables.)

3. Slice the cooked sausages into 1-inch chunks and the peppers into 1/2-inch wide strips. Separate the onion into individual rings.

4. Place the romaine and radicchio on a large platter. Arrange the grilled sausages and vegetables atop the greens.

5. In a small bowl, whisk together the garlic, salt, pepper, mustard, vinegar, and olive oil.

6. Pour the vinaigrette over the salad and serve.

4 to 5 portions

IRRESISTIBLES

Comforting conclusions, how sweet they are! They're the dramatic, grand finale to a meal. Whether you prefer a light fruit ice or a decadent chocolate torte, desserts are extraordinary. What can be said about sweets that hasn't already been said before? That they're luscious, heavenly, outrageous, devilishly exciting, delicious, tempting, seductive, sensational, and scrumptious? So, "Let them eat cake" and pies and cookies, and ices, etc.

Note—Always use extra-large eggs in baking unless otherwise specified. All cookies, pastries, and cakes freeze well with the exception of fruit pies which tend to break down.

FRUITS, ICES, AND PUDDINGS

APPLE CRISP

The ultimate dessert for apple lovers showcases sliced apples generously covered with a buttery, vanilla-scented crumb topping and baked until golden. It's delectable!

3 large Granny Smith apples, peeled and cut into 1/2-inch thick wedges
2 tablespoons sugar

Crumb Topping:
1 cup all-purpose flour
1/2 teaspoon baking powder
1 cup sugar
1 1/2 teaspoons vanilla
6 tablespoons butter, at room temperature

1. Preheat the oven to 350°F.

2. Toss the apple wedges with 2 tablespoons sugar. Place in a 9-inch pie pan.

3. Prepare the crumb topping. In a bowl, mix the flour, baking powder, sugar, vanilla, and butter until the texture of coarse meal. Cover the apples with the crumb mixture.

4. Bake for 40 minutes until golden. Serve warm.

6 to 8 portions

APRICOT BON BONS

The distinctive, tart flavor of apricots harmonizes well with the nutty taste of almonds in these dried fruit nuggets that are decorated with coconut.

1¼ cups dried apricots
½ cup slivered almonds, toasted
2 tablespoons light brown sugar
¼ cup apricot preserves
1 teaspoon almond extract
¾ cup sweetened, shredded coconut

1. Put the apricots, almonds, sugar, preserves, and extract in the bowl of a food processor. Pulse until the mixture comes together and forms a ball. Transfer the mixture to a bowl.

2. Stir in ½ cup coconut. Chill the ground fruit mixture for 30 minutes.

3. Using 1 tablespoon of ground fruit, form into balls. Roll the bon bons in the remaining ¼ cup coconut. Store in an airtight container.

24 bon bons

MIDDLE EASTERN MENU

Feta-Spinach Dip
. . .
Grilled Shrimp
. . .
Middle Eastern Chick Peas and Tomatoes
. . .
Mediterranean Couscous
. . .
Apricot Bon Bons

DATES ALMONDINE

Dates are an ancient food native to the Middle East. They're prized for their cloyingly sweet flesh that is more than 50% sugar. This dried fruit is also an excellent source of protein and iron. Stuffed with almond paste and rolled in sugar, these are the perfect confection.

60 pitted dates
7-ounce tube almond paste
1/2 cup sugar
1 teaspoon cinnamon

1. Stuff each date with 1/2 teaspoon of almond paste and press shut.

2. Combine the cinnamon and sugar, stirring until evenly mixed.

3. Roll the dates in sugar, coating completely. Store the confection in an airtight container.

60 stuffed dates

PETER'S SUGAR PLUMS

I will be forever grateful to Peter Riley for sharing this wonderful holiday confection. Reminiscent of miniature fruit cakes, the sugar plums are balls of ground dried fruits and nuts, laced with liqueur, and rolled in sugar. The longer these sit, the better they are!

1 1/2 *cups chopped dried figs*
1 1/2 *cups well-packed chopped, pitted dates*
2/3 *cup dried cherries*
2/3 *cup blanched almonds*
2 tablespoons chopped crystallized candied ginger
1 teaspoon grated orange peel
2 tablespoons Grand Marnier
granulated sugar

1. Put the figs, dates, cherries, almonds, candied ginger, orange peel, and Grand Marnier in the bowl of a food processor. Process until the fruits are ground and the mixture comes together, forming a ball.

2. Using a heaping teaspoonful of ground fruit mixture, form into balls. Roll the sugar plums in granulated sugar to coat completely. Let sit for 1 to 2 weeks in an airtight container for the flavors to mellow. Re-roll in sugar and serve.

4 dozen sugar plums

AFTERNOON TEA FOR 12

Lemon Tea Bread
. . .
Raspberry Muffins
. . .
Cream Cheese
. . .
Chocolate-Almond Biscotti
. . .
Peter's Sugar Plums
. . .
Heavenly Strawberries Adorned◆
. . .
Assorted Teas

**SUNDAY BRUNCH
FOR 12**

Cinnamon-Raisin Loaf
. . .
Coconut Muffins
. . .
Bagels
. . .
Cream Cheese
. . .
Bluefish Gravalax

Apricot Noodle
Pudding
. . .
Mimosas
. . .
Grapes with
Maple Cream

GRAPES WITH MAPLE CREAM

Red and green grapes are blanketed with a maple-infused sour cream and sprinkled with chopped pecans. Fruits and nuts make the perfect companions in this light dessert or summer luncheon fare.

4 cups red and green seedless grapes
1/2 cup sour cream
2 tablespoons pure maple syrup
1/4 cup finely chopped toasted pecans

1. Put the grapes in a large glass bowl.

2. In a separate small bowl, combine the sour cream, maple syrup, and pecans and mix well.

3. Pour the sauce over the grapes, toss well, and serve.

4 to 6 portions

CANDIED ORANGE PEEL

These savory tidbits are no-fat, no-cholesterol confections. They make marvelous gifts for the holidays and are divine for eating out of hand. For a real decadent treat, try dipping the candied peel in melted semi-sweet chocolate.

3 thick-skinned oranges, quartered and flesh removed
1¹/₂ cups sugar
¹/₂ cup water
2 tablespoons light corn syrup

1. Cut the orange peel into ¹/₄-inch wide strips. Put the peel in a 3-quart saucepan and cover with cold water. Bring to a full boil; then boil for 5 minutes. Drain. Repeat 2 more times. Let the peel drain in a colander. Boiling the peel repeatedly in fresh water helps to remove the bitterness from the white pith.

2. In the same saucepan, combine 1 cup sugar, ¹/₂ cup water, and corn syrup. Heat over low until the sugar dissolves. Add the peel and boil gently for 45 minutes, stirring occasionally, until almost all of the syrup is absorbed. Drain in a colander for 30 minutes.

3. Roll the peel in ¹/₂ cup sugar. Spread the peel out on sheets of waxed paper to dry. Let sit for 2 days, then store in an airtight container. It will keep up to 1 month, or you may choose to freeze it for a longer period of time.

About ¹/₂ pound of candied orange peel

DESSERT PARTY FOR 20

Cranberry-Glazed Brie
. . .
Candied Orange Peel
. . .
Spiced Walnuts◆
. . .
Chocolate-Almond Pound Cake◆
. . .
Lemon Cake Roll
. . .
Tiramisu Cake
. . .
Fruits in Midori◆
. . .
Truffle Brownies
. . .
Oatmeal Foggies

RHUBARB CRISP

The vibrant cherry red stalks of the perennial rhubarb plant are prized for their characteristic tart taste. Although treated as a fruit, botanically, it is a springtime vegetable. This maple-flavored sweet-tart crisp is crowned with a pecan-brown sugar topping.

When rhubarb is in season, I purchase extra stalks, cut them into pieces, and freeze them for later use.

6 cups rhubarb, cut into 1-inch pieces
1/2 cup granulated sugar
3 tablespoons all-purpose flour
1/4 cup pure maple syrup
1/4 cup finely diced crystallized candied ginger

Crumb Topping:
2/3 cup all-purpose flour
6 tablespoons butter
2/3 cup light brown sugar
1/2 cup chopped pecans

1. Preheat the oven to 350°F.

2. Combine the rhubarb, granulated sugar, 3 tablespoons flour, maple syrup, and candied ginger and mix well. Turn the mixture into a 2-quart casserole.

3. In a separate bowl, make the crumb topping. Mix the flour, butter, brown sugar, and pecans until crumbly. Cover the rhubarb with the mixture.

4. Bake for 50 minutes until golden. Serve warm.

8 portions

HEARTY ITALIAN FARE

Bruschetta with Roasted Garlic
· · ·
Tuscan Salad
· · ·
Chicken with Three Cheese Melt
· · ·
Pasta with Green Olive Tapenade
· · ·
Rhubarb Crisp

CHOCOLATE SORBET

Smooth, creamy, intensely chocolaty, and laced with a whisper of almond flavor, this sorbet is absolutely fat free!

½ cup unsweetened cocoa
1 cup strong coffee
1 cup water
1 cup light corn syrup
1 teaspoon almond extract

1. Combine all of the ingredients in a large bowl and mix well.

2. Process the mixture in an ice cream maker according to the manufacturer's directions.

3. Serve at once or store in the freezer for later use. If frozen, let thaw for 15 minutes before serving.

6 portions

FAMILY DINNER

Chicken with
Piccolini Sauce
. . .
Ribbons of Zucchini
and Summer Squash
. . .
Deluxe Mashed
Potatoes
. . .
Chocolate Sorbet

COFFEE ICE

Conceived with true coffee lovers in mind, this smooth, velvety, and richly coffee-infused sorbet is laced with Amaretto for a blast of coffee-almond flavor.

2 cups very strong black coffee
1 cup light corn syrup
¹/₄ cup Amaretto

1. Combine all of the ingredients and mix well.
2. Process the mixture in an ice cream maker according to the manufacturer's directions.
3. Serve at once or store in the freezer for later use.

6 portions

HONEYDEW FREEZE

This velvety, refreshing honeydew ice is made with puréed melon and splashed with Midori and lime juice. Its creamy texture makes you think you're eating sherbet.

2 cups puréed ripe honeydew melon
1 cup light corn syrup
1 teaspoon finely grated lime zest
1/4 cup Midori (honeydew melon liqueur)
2 tablespoons lime juice

1. Mix all of the ingredients together.
2. Process the mixture in an ice cream maker according to the manufacturer's directions.
3. Serve at once or store in the freezer for later use.

4 portions

SUMMER LUNCHEON

Strawberry-Banana
Daiquiri Soup
· · ·
Mussels, Tomatoes,
and Arugula
· · ·
Assorted Rolls
· · ·
Honeydew Freeze

**HOT WEATHER
COOLER**

Green Gazpacho
· · ·
Grilled Swordfish
· · ·
Bulgur Pilaf
· · ·
Mango and
Red Pepper Salad
· · ·
Pear Ice

PEAR ICE

The lush, buttery perfume of pears distinguishes this creamy sorbet that's dotted with candied ginger.

3 ripe pears, peeled, cored, and puréed
1 cup light corn syrup
1 tablespoon lemon juice
2 tablespoons minced crystallized candied ginger

1. Combine all of the ingredients and mix well.

2. Process the mixture in an ice cream maker according to the manufacturer's directions.

3. Serve at once or store in the freezer for later use.

4 portions

PINEAPPLE FREEZE

The tropical flavor of pineapple is embracing in this refreshing sorbet that's flecked with pineapple tidbits.

2 cups unsweetened pineapple juice
8-ounce can unsweetened crushed pineapple, well drained
1 cup light corn syrup
1 teaspoon vanilla
1 tablespoon lemon juice

1. Combine all of the ingredients and mix well.

2. Process the mixture in an ice cream maker according to the manufacturer's directions.

3. Serve at once or store in the freezer for later use.

6 portions

MEXICAN DINNER

Black Bean Soup
. . .
Chicken Fajitas
. . .
Pineapple Freeze

**SUNDAY NITE
WINTER SUPPER**

Winter Salad with
Walnut Pesto
. . .
Beef Carbonnade
. . .
Buttered Noodles
. . .
Chocolate-Banana
Bread Pudding

CHOCOLATE-BANANA BREAD PUDDING

All bread puddings have the same basic ingredients—bread, milk, eggs, and sugar. This new wave version is also rich with chunks of banana and dappled with chocolate chips for a sinfully delicious experience.

3/4 pound day-old Italian bread, broken into 1-inch chunks
1 quart milk
4 eggs, beaten
1 1/4 cups sugar
1 tablespoon vanilla
4 tablespoons butter, melted
1/8 teaspoon salt
3 large, ripe bananas, cut into 1/2-inch thick rounds
1 1/3 cups semi-sweet chocolate chips

1. Preheat the oven to 350°F. Grease a 9 x 13-inch baking dish.

2. Place the bread chunks in a large bowl. In a separate bowl, whisk together the milk, eggs, 1 cup sugar, vanilla, butter, and salt. Pour the custard over the bread chunks and let sit for 10 to 15 minutes so the bread can absorb the liquid.

3. Stir in the bananas and chocolate chips. Turn into the prepared pan. Sprinkle the top with 1/4 cup sugar.

4. Bake for 45 to 50 minutes until firm. Serve the pudding warm or at room temperature.

12 or more portions

Note—This reheats well in the microwave.

RUM-RAISIN RICE PUDDING

Rice pudding, an old-fashioned favorite, is distinguished by new-fashioned flair. The simplest of ingredients—rice, milk, sugar, and raisins plumped in rum—come together for real comfort food. The long, slow cooking allows the rice to cook and the pudding to thicken.

²/₃ cup raw long-grain rice
1 quart whole milk
²/₃ cup sugar
¹/₄ teaspoon salt
1 teaspoon vanilla
¹/₂ cup raisins
¹/₄ cup light rum

1. Preheat the oven to 300°F. Grease a 2-quart casserole.

2. In a bowl, combine the rice, milk, sugar, salt, and vanilla. Mix well and pour into the prepared casserole. Bake for 2 hours, stirring every 30 minutes.

3. While the pudding is baking, pour the rum over the raisins and let macerate for 30 minutes.

4. Add the plumped raisins with the rum to the partially cooked pudding, mixing well. Bake for 45 minutes more undisturbed. Run a knife around the edge of the pan to release the skin that has formed. Serve warm, room temperature, or chilled.

6 portions

WINTER SOUP PARTY

Mixed Green
Salad with
Balsamic Vinaigrette◆
. . .
Oriental Manhattan
Clam Chowder
. . .
Southwestern
Corn Chowder
. . .
Assorted Breads
. . .
Rum-Raisin
Rice Pudding

COOKIES AND PASTRIES

CHOCOLATE-ALMOND BISCOTTI

Biscotti are the Italian cookies that have become quite fashionable for dunking into coffee. Biscotti actually means twice-baked, which results in the characteristic hard, dry, and crunchy biscuits Americans have come to love. These are dappled with toasted almonds and laced with orange essence and ground chocolate.

1/2 cup butter
3/4 cup sugar
2 eggs
2 cups all-purpose flour
1 1/2 teaspoons baking powder
1/4 teaspoon salt
1/2 teaspoon cinnamon
2 teaspoons finely grated orange peel
1 cup slivered almonds, toasted and coarsely chopped
1 cup semi-sweet chocolate chips, finely ground in a food processor

1. Preheat the oven to 325°F. Grease and flour two cookie sheets.

2. In a large mixing bowl, cream the butter and sugar. Beat in the eggs.

3. Add the flour, baking powder, salt, cinnamon, and orange peel and mix well.

4. Stir in the almonds and chocolate chips.

5. Divide the dough in half and form into two logs, 2 1/2 inches wide and 13 inches long. Place on the prepared baking sheets.

6. Bake for 35 minutes. With a serrated knife, carefully slice the logs into 3/4-inch wide pieces. Place each slice on its side on the baking sheets. Return to the oven for 5 minutes; turn the slices over and bake for 5 minutes more. Transfer the biscotti to racks to cool completely.

30 biscotti

BUTTERSCOTCH MERINGUES

These cloud-like confections are light, crispy, and chock full of pecans.

2 egg whites, from extra-large eggs
1 teaspoon vanilla
³/₄ cup packed light brown sugar
²/₃ cup coarsely chopped pecans

1. Preheat the oven to 225°F. Generously grease two cookie sheets.

2. In the bowl of an electric mixer, beat the egg whites and vanilla to form stiff peaks. Gradually add the brown sugar. Continue to beat on high until the whites are stiff and glossy, about 5 minutes.

3. Gently fold in the pecans.

4. Drop the dough by rounded teaspoonfuls onto the prepared baking sheets, 2 inches apart.

5. Bake for 1¹/₂ hours. Remove the meringues to racks to cool completely.

3 dozen meringues

OLD-FASHIONED GOODNESS

Tomato Bisque◆
· · ·
Pasta Fontina
· · ·
Green Salad
· · ·
Butterscotch
Meringues

TEA AND . . .

Persimmon Muffins
. . .
Vanilla Tea Cookies
. . .
Chocolate Meringues
. . .
Strawberries with
Sour Cream and
Brown Sugar

CHOCOLATE MERINGUES

These melt-in-the-mouth chocolate clouds are amazingly cholesterol and fat free. Watch them disappear!

3 egg whites, from extra-large eggs
³/₄ cup granulated sugar
¹/₄ cup unsweetened cocoa
¹/₂ cup confectioners' sugar

1. Preheat the oven to 225°F. Grease two large cookie sheets.

2. In the bowl of an electric mixer, beat the egg whites until frothy. Gradually add the granulated sugar. Continue to beat on high until the whites are stiff and glossy, about 7 to 8 minutes.

3. Sift together the cocoa and confectioners' sugar. Add to the beaten egg whites and beat until evenly incorporated.

4. Using a heaping tablespoon of batter, spoon the meringues into 1¹/₂-inch mounds, 2 inches apart, on the prepared cookie sheets.

5. Bake for 1 hour. Leave the meringues on the baking sheets for 1 minute; then transfer them to racks to cool.

3 dozen meringues

TRIPLE CHOCOLATE CHUNK COOKIES

These chewy cookies are a chocolate lover's dream come true. They're punctuated with a trio of chocolate chunks—semi-sweet, white, and milk chocolate—making them rich and outrageous!

1 cup butter
3/4 cup granulated sugar
1/4 cup lightly packed light brown sugar
1 teaspoon vanilla
2 cups all-purpose flour
1/2 cup semi-sweet chocolate chunks
1/2 cup white chocolate chunks
1/2 cup milk chocolate chunks

1. In a large mixing bowl, cream the butter and sugars until fluffy. Add the vanilla and flour and mix well.

2. Stir in the chocolate chunks. Chill the dough for 1 hour.

3. Preheat the oven to 350°F. Grease two cookie sheets.

4. Using a heaping tablespoon of dough, form into mounds. Place on the cookie sheets 2 inches apart.

5. Bake for 15 minutes. Let cookies sit on the baking sheets for 2 to 3 minutes before removing to racks to cool completely. Keep the extra dough in the refrigerator while the first batch is in the oven.

32 cookies

TEXAS BARBECUE

Sam's Memphis-
Style Ribs
. . .
Cornbread
. . .
Baked Beans
. . .
Jicama Slaw
. . .
Watermelon
. . .
Triple Chocolate
Chunk Cookies

LEMON SUGAR COOKIES

WINTER LUNCH

Chicken Noodle Soup
. . .
Toasted Cheese and
Prosciutto Sandwiches
. . .
Lemon Sugar Cookies

Old-fashioned goodness is packed into these large, crispy, chewy, lemon-flavored cookies.

1 cup butter
2 cups sugar
1 egg
1 tablespoon finely grated lemon zest
2 tablespoons lemon juice
2 1/2 cups all-purpose flour
2 teaspoons baking powder
1/4 teaspoon salt
extra sugar for dipping

1. In a large mixing bowl, cream the butter and sugar. Add the egg, lemon zest, and lemon juice and mix well.

2. Sift the flour, baking powder, and salt and add to the batter, stirring until evenly combined. Chill the dough well, at least 2 hours.

3. Preheat the oven to 375°F. Grease several cookie sheets.

4. With greased hands, using 1 tablespoon of dough, roll into balls. Flatten slightly and dip one side into sugar, coating generously. Place sugar side up on the prepared baking sheets.

5. Bake for 10 to 12 minutes until lightly browned at the edges. Let cookies sit on the baking sheets for 2 minutes; then transfer them to racks to cool completely.

4 dozen cookies

ORANGE THINS

These thin, orange-scented wafers are delicate, crispy, and laced with orange essence. This recipe may be doubled easily.

5 tablespoons butter
3 tablespoons sugar
3 tablespoons orange marmalade
1 cup all-purpose flour
1½ teaspoons finely grated orange peel

1. Put all of the ingredients in the bowl of a food processor. Pulse until the dough forms a ball. Form the dough into a log, 5 inches long. Chill at least 1 hour or as much as overnight.

2. Preheat the oven to 350°F. Grease two cookie sheets.

3. Slice the dough into ¼-inch thick rounds. Place 2 inches apart on the prepared baking sheets. Bake for 10 to 12 minutes until lightly golden. Transfer the cookies to racks to cool completely.

20 wafers

SALSA SASS

Grilled Chicken with
Pineapple, Mango,
and Papaya Salsa

· · ·

Pasta with Black Bean-
Corn Salsa

· · ·

Sliced Tomatoes

· · ·

Orange Thins

MEXICAN-
INSPIRED PICNIC

Guacamole
. . .
South-of-the-Border
Chicken
. . .
Southwestern
Corn Salad
. . .
Red Cabbage Slaw
. . .
Chocolate-Chocolate
Chip Wafers

CHOCOLATE-CHOCOLATE CHIP WAFERS

These rich, double chocolaty, crispy, and chewy wafers are a chocolate fancier's delight. The cocoa-based batter is scented with cinnamon and studded with chocolate chips.

1/2 cup butter
1/2 cup light brown sugar
1/2 cup granulated sugar
1 egg
1 teaspoon vanilla
2 tablespoons instant coffee powder
1 cup all-purpose flour
1/2 teaspoon baking soda
1/8 teaspoon salt
1/3 cup unsweetened cocoa
1/2 teaspoon cinnamon
1/4 teaspoon nutmeg
2/3 cup semi-sweet chocolate chips

1. Preheat the oven to 350°F. Grease several cookie sheets.

2. In a large mixing bowl, cream the butter and sugars. Add the egg, vanilla, and coffee powder.

3. Sift together the flour, baking soda, salt, cocoa, cinnamon, and nutmeg and add to the batter, stirring until well mixed.

4. Stir in the chocolate chips.

5. Using a tablespoon, drop the batter onto the prepared baking sheets 3 inches apart.

6. Bake for 10 to 12 minutes. Let cookies sit on the baking sheets for 1 minute; then remove the cookies to racks to cool completely.

3 dozen wafers

VANILLA TEA COOKIES

These delicate vanilla-infused wafers are slightly soft in the center and crunchy around the edges.

1/2 cup butter
3/4 cup confectioners' sugar
1 tablespoon vanilla
1 cup all-purpose flour
1/4 teaspoon salt

1. Preheat the oven to 350°F. Grease two cookie sheets.

2. In a large mixing bowl, cream the butter and sugar until light and fluffy. Add the vanilla. Stir in the flour and salt and mix well.

3. Chill the dough for 1 hour. Using 1 tablespoon of dough, roll into balls. Flatten and place on the prepared cookie sheets.

4. Bake for 15 minutes until lightly browned at the edges. Let the cookies cool on the baking sheets for 2 minutes before removing to racks to cool completely.

20 cookies

TEA AND . . .

Persimmon Muffins
· · ·
Vanilla Tea Cookies
· · ·
Chocolate Meringues
· · ·
Strawberries with
Sour Cream and
Brown Sugar

GINGER-WHITE CHOCOLATE CHUNK COOKIES

Crispy, chewy, redolent with ginger, and teeming with white chocolate chunks, these rival the infamous chocolate chip cookie!

³/₄ cup butter
1 cup packed light brown sugar
¹/₄ cup molasses
1 egg
2 cups all-purpose flour
2 teaspoons baking soda
¹/₄ teaspoon salt
2 teaspoons ground ginger
¹/₃ cup finely chopped crystallized candied ginger
8 ounces white chocolate, coarsely chopped

1. Preheat the oven to 350°F. Grease several cookie sheets.

2. In a large mixing bowl, cream the butter and sugar. Add the molasses and egg and mix well.

3. Sift together the flour, baking soda, salt, and ground ginger and add to the batter.

4. Mix in the candied ginger and white chocolate chunks.

5. Using a tablespoon, drop the batter, 3 inches apart, onto the prepared baking sheets. Bake for 10 to 12 minutes until browned. Leave the cookies on the baking sheets for 2 minutes; then remove them to racks to cool completely.

4¹/₂ dozen cookies

POPPY SEED BUTTER COOKIES

These butter cookies are crispy around the edges, chewy in the middle, and bespeckled with the nutty crunch of poppy seeds.

1 cup butter
1 cup sugar
1 egg
1 teaspoon vanilla
2 cups all-purpose flour
2 tablespoons poppy seeds

1. Preheat the oven to 375°F.

2. In a large mixing bowl, cream the butter and sugar. Add the egg and vanilla and mix well.

3. Stir in the flour and poppy seeds and mix thoroughly. Using a tablespoon of dough, roll into balls. Place on cookie sheets 2 inches apart.

4. Bake for 10 minutes until lightly browned at the edges. Let the cookies cool on the baking sheet for 2 minutes before removing to racks to cool completely.

4 dozen cookies

**LIGHT
LUNCHEON**

Rhubarb Soup
. . .
Mixed Greens with
Chèvre Vinaigrette
. . .
French Bread
. . .
Poppy Seed
Butter Cookies

PECAN SHORTBREADS

BROWN-BAG LUNCH

Fez's Pasta with
Fresh Tomato Sauce
. . .
Green Beans and
Roasted Chick Peas
. . .
Pecan Shortbreads

Pecan fanciers will appreciate these dainty, buttery, characteristic shortbreads rich with chopped pecans.

1 cup butter
³/4 cup packed light brown sugar
1 tablespoon vanilla
2 cups all-purpose flour
1 cup finely chopped pecans
48 whole pecans

1. Preheat the oven to 350°F.

2. In a large mixing bowl, cream the butter and sugar until fluffy. Add the vanilla.

3. Stir in the flour and chopped pecans and mix well.

4. Form the dough into 1-inch size balls. Place on ungreased cookie sheets 2 inches apart. Flatten the dough with the palm of your hand and press a pecan in the center of each cookie.

5. Bake for 10 minutes. Remove the cookies to racks to cool.

4 dozen cookies

OATMEAL FOGGIES

This is the quintessential oatmeal cookie—packed with oats, nuts, raisins, and coconut, laced with maple syrup, and baked until crispy.

1/2 cup butter, at room temperature
1/2 cup granulated sugar
1/2 cup packed dark brown sugar
3 tablespoons pure maple syrup
1 cup all-purpose flour
1 teaspoon baking soda
1/4 teaspoon salt
1 cup old-fashioned oats
1 cup chopped walnuts
1/2 cup raisins
1/2 cup sweetened, shredded coconut

1. Preheat the oven to 350°F.

2. In a large mixing bowl, cream the butter, sugars, and maple syrup until fluffy.

3. Add the flour, baking soda, and salt and mix well.

4. Add the oatmeal, nuts, raisins, and coconut and stir until evenly blended.

5. Form the dough into walnut-size balls. Place on ungreased cookie sheets and flatten with the palm of your hand.

6. Bake for 10 minutes. Leave the foggies on the baking sheets for 3 minutes; then transfer them to racks to cool completely.

32 cookies

DESSERT PARTY FOR 20

Cranberry-Glazed Brie
. . .
Candied Orange Peel
. . .
Spiced Walnuts◆
. . .
Chocolate-Almond
Pound Cake◆
. . .
Lemon Cake Roll
. . .
Tiramisu Cake
. . .
Fruits in Midori◆
. . .
Truffle Brownies
. . .
Oatmeal Foggies

SOUP'S ON

Split Pea Soup
. . .
Cobb Salad
. . .
Peasant Bread
. . .
Peanut Butter-
Chocolate Chip
Cookies

PEANUT BUTTER-CHOCOLATE CHIP COOKIES

The marriage of two all-American favorites, peanut butter and the chocolate chip cookie, results in a first-rate cookie, that's large, chewy, and peanutty!

1/2 cup butter, at room temperature
3/4 cup packed dark brown sugar
2 tablespoons light corn syrup
1 egg
1 1/2 teaspoons vanilla
1/2 cup chunky peanut butter
1 1/4 cups all-purpose flour
3/4 teaspoon baking soda
1/4 teaspoon salt
1 cup semi-sweet chocolate chips
1/2 cup dry roasted, unsalted peanuts, coarsely chopped

1. Preheat the oven to 375°F. Grease two cookie sheets.

2. In a large mixing bowl, cream the butter, brown sugar, and corn syrup. Add the egg, vanilla, and peanut butter and mix well.

3. Stir in the flour, baking soda, and salt.

4. Add the chocolate chips and peanuts and mix well.

5. Drop heaping tablespoonfuls of dough onto the prepared baking sheets 3 inches apart.

6. Bake for 7 to 8 minutes until lightly brown. Let cookies sit on the baking sheets for 3 minutes before removing to racks to cool completely.

30 cookies

PISTACHIO SHORTBREADS

Almond-flavored butter cookies are dipped in melted chocolate and encrusted with chopped pistachio nuts. This gets a 5-star rating in taste and eye appeal.

1 cup butter
¹/₂ cup confectioners' sugar
1 teaspoon almond extract
2 cups all-purpose flour
6 ounces semi-sweet chocolate (not chips)
³/₄ cup shelled, skinned, and finely chopped pistachio nuts

1. Preheat the oven to 350°F.

2. In a large mixing bowl, cream the butter and sugar. Add the almond extract and mix well.

3. Stir in the flour until evenly blended. Using 1 tablespoon of dough, roll into balls. Flatten the balls and place on ungreased cookie sheets 2 inches apart.

4. Bake for 10 to 12 minutes until lightly golden around the edges. Remove the cookies to racks to cool completely.

5. Melt the chocolate in the top of a double boiler. Dip the tops of the cookies in the melted chocolate and then into the chopped nuts to coat generously. Refrigerate for 30 minutes to set the chocolate.

32 cookies

**GIFTS FROM
THE HEARTH**

Olivada
. . .
Pecan Bread
. . .
Tomato Chutney
. . .
Vanilla Extract
. . .
Pistachio Shortbreads
. . .
Composed Butters

CHOCOLATE BUNDLES

Pillows of semi-sweet chocolate, pecans, and brown sugar are baked to a turn for a decadent indulgence.

> $^3/_4$ *cup mini semi-sweet chocolate chips*
> $^1/_2$ *cup finely chopped pecans*
> $^1/_4$ *cup packed dark brown sugar*
> *1 teaspoon cinnamon*
> *30 wonton wraps*
> *2 tablespoons butter, melted*
> *confectioners' sugar*

1. Preheat the oven to 350°F. Grease two cookie sheets.

2. Combine the chocolate chips, pecans, brown sugar, and cinnamon.

3. Place 2 teaspoons of the chocolate mixture in the middle of each wonton skin. Fold over in half to form a triangle. Dampen the outer edges slightly with cold water. Press the edges together to seal. Arrange on the prepared baking sheets.

4. Brush the tops of the pillows with melted butter. Bake for 10 minutes until lightly golden. Remove the bundles to racks to cool completely. Dust with confectioners' sugar and serve.

30 bundles

CHOCOLATE TRUFFLES CABERNET

Truffles are the ultimate chocolate experience—velvety, rich, and outrageous. Bittersweet chocolate and the famous red wine of distinction, Cabernet Sauvignon, share the limelight in these heavenly confections.

¹/₂ cup heavy cream
¹/₂ cup butter, at room temperature
1 pound bittersweet chocolate, broken up
6 tablespoons Cabernet Sauvignon wine
unsweetened cocoa powder

1. Bring the cream and butter to a boil in a 1-quart heavy saucepan. Reduce the heat to low and add the chocolate, whisking until the chocolate is melted and the mixture is smooth.

2. Remove the pan from the heat and whisk in the Cabernet Sauvignon. Pour the mixture into a shallow bowl and refrigerate until firm, about 1¹/₂ to 2 hours.

3. Scoop the chocolate up with a teaspoon and form into 1¹/₄ inch balls. Roll the truffles in unsweetened cocoa.

4. Cover and refrigerate until serving time. Allow the truffles to stand at room temperature for 30 minutes before enjoying.

3 dozen truffles

HONEY-NUT GRANOLA BARS

Why buy granola bars when you can make your own that are packed with flavor? These snack and dessert bars are woven with cinnamon, honey, and brown sugar.

2 cups old-fashioned oats
$1/2$ cup coarsely chopped pecans, toasted
1 teaspoon cinnamon
6 tablespoons butter
$1/3$ cup packed dark brown sugar
3 tablespoons honey
1 teaspoon vanilla

1. Preheat the oven to 350°F. Line a 9-inch square pan with foil, extending the foil over the ends of the pan. Grease the foil.

2. In a large bowl, mix the oats, pecans, and cinnamon.

3. In a small saucepan, combine the butter, brown sugar, honey, and vanilla. Stir over medium heat until the butter melts and mixture comes to a boil. Pour over the oats, stirring well until evenly coated.

4. Turn the mixture into the prepared pan. Using a spatula, press the granola firmly into the pan. Bake for 20 minutes until golden.

5. Using the foil overlap, lift the granola out of the pan to a rack to cool. When cooled completely, place the granola on a level surface or cutting board, and with a sharp knife, cut into squares. Don't worry if the bars tend to crumble slightly when cut—the chunks are great for nibbling out of hand or for toppings on ice cream and yogurt. Store in an airtight container.

16 squares

HERMITS

Hermits are a long-time American favorite, having its origins in Cape Cod during the days of the clipper ships. Actually they are the precursor to the brownie. This version of the raisin-infused bar is rich with brown sugar, molasses, and a medley of spices.

¹/₂ cup butter
1 cup packed light brown sugar
¹/₄ cup molasses
1 egg, lightly beaten
2 cups all-purpose flour
¹/₂ teaspoon baking soda
¹/₄ teaspoon salt
1 teaspoon cinnamon
¹/₂ teaspoon ground cloves
¹/₄ teaspoon nutmeg
³/₄ cup raisins
1 tablespoon granulated sugar

1. Preheat the oven to 350°F. Lightly grease a 9 x 13-inch pan.

2. In a large mixing bowl, cream the butter and brown sugar until fluffy. Mix in the molasses and egg.

3. Stir in the flour, baking soda, salt, cinnamon, cloves, and nutmeg until evenly blended. Add the raisins and mix well.

4. Turn into the prepared pan. Sprinkle the top with granulated sugar. Bake for 20 to 23 minutes until a toothpick inserted in the center comes out clean. Cool on a rack for 15 minutes before cutting.

24 hermits

**SUPER BOWL
SUNDAY BASH**

Jen's Salsa with Chips
. . .
Snake Bites
. . .
Turkey Chili
. . .
French Bread
. . .
Green Salad with
Ranch Dressing
. . .
Hermits

TRUFFLE BROWNIES

These are the ultimate chocolate bars, being a cross between a truffle and a brownie. They're sheer decadence, super moist, fudgy rich, and chock full of walnuts.

8 ounces semi-sweet chocolate (not chips)
½ cup butter
2 tablespoons light cream
2 eggs
¾ cup sugar
1 teaspoon vanilla
¼ cup all-purpose flour
¾ cup coarsely chopped walnuts

1. Preheat the oven to 375°F. Line an 8-inch square pan with heavy duty foil, extending the foil 2 inches beyond the edges of the pan. Grease the foil.

2. In a saucepan, heat the chocolate, butter, and cream over low heat, stirring until the chocolate is melted and smooth. Set aside to cool.

3. With an electric mixer, beat the eggs, sugar, and vanilla until thick and lemon colored. Add the cooled chocolate to the batter and mix well.

4. Stir in the flour and walnuts. Turn the batter into the prepared pan.

5. Bake for 35 minutes. Remove to a rack to cool completely, then refrigerate until firm, about 4 hours. Lift the foil out of the pan and cut the brownies into squares. Keep refrigerated until ready to serve.

16 brownies

BAKLAVA

Baklava is a typical Greek pastry composed of flaky, buttery, layers of phyllo dough and ground walnuts. Baked until golden and soaked in a honey-citrus syrup, it's absolutely heavenly!

MIDDLE EASTERN DINNER

Middle Eastern
Eggplant Spread
. . .
Roast Lamb with
Mint Pesto
. . .
Cracked Wheat
and Olive Salad
. . .
Baklava

Filling:
4 cups (1 pound) walnuts, ground
^{2}/$_3$ cup sugar
1 tablespoon cinnamon
^{1}/$_2$ teaspoon nutmeg

1 pound frozen phyllo dough, thawed and trimmed to 11 x 17 inches
1 cup sweet butter, melted

Syrup:
1^1/$_4$ cups water
1 cup sugar
1 cup honey
1 cinnamon stick
1 tablespoon lemon juice
1 teaspoon grated orange peel

1. Preheat the oven to 350°F.

2. Combine the walnuts, sugar, cinnamon, and nutmeg in a large bowl and mix well.

3. Brush an 11 x 17-inch jelly roll pan with melted butter. Place 10 sheets of phyllo dough in the pan, brushing each with butter.

4. Spread half of the nut filling evenly on the dough. Cover with 3 sheets of phyllo, brushing each with butter. Spread on the remainder of the nut mixture.

5. Cover with the remaining sheets of phyllo, brushing each with butter. Brush the top with any remaining butter and cut into squares.

6. Bake for 40 minutes until golden. Let cool.

7. While the baklava is cooling, put all of the syrup ingredients in a saucepan. Bring the mixture to a boil, then lower the heat, and simmer for 10 minutes. Remove the cinnamon stick.

8. Pour the syrup evenly over the baklava. Let sit for 1 to 2 hours before serving to allow the phyllo to completely soak up the syrup.

24 squares

Note—This does not freeze well.

CAKES
AND PIES

SUMMER TIME DINNER

Mango Soup
. . .
Grilled Trout
. . .
Pasta with Grilled
Vegetables◆
. . .
Chocolate Angel
Food Cake with
Assorted Berries

CHOCOLATE ANGEL FOOD CAKE

Angel food cake is the perfect light dessert that doesn't taste skinny!
This cloudlike chocolate cake is garnished with whipped cream and
succulent raspberries.

10 egg whites (from large eggs), at room temperature
1¼ teaspoons cream of tartar
¼ teaspoon salt
1 teaspoon vanilla
1¼ cups granulated sugar
1 cup cake flour
¼ cup unsweetened cocoa
2 tablespoons confectioners' sugar

Garnishes:
1 pint whipped cream
½ pint raspberries

1. Preheat the oven to 350°F

2. In a large bowl with an electric mixer, beat the egg whites,
cream of tartar, salt, and vanilla until the whites form soft peaks.
Gradually add the granulated sugar, beating until the whites are stiff
and shiny, but not dry.

3. Sift together the flour, cocoa, and confectioners' sugar. With a
spatula, gently fold the dry ingredients into the beaten whites until
evenly incorporated. Spoon the batter into an ungreased, non-stick
10-inch tube pan.

4. Bake for 40 minutes until a toothpick inserted in the cake comes
out clean. Invert the pan onto a rack to cool completely; then remove
the cake from the pan onto a platter. Serve with whipped cream and
fresh raspberries.

12 portions

CITRUS ANGEL FOOD CAKE

This feather-light cake is a boon to those concerned about cholesterol and fat. It's delicate with the sparkling flavors of lemon and orange.

10 egg whites (from large eggs), at room temperature
1 teaspoon cream of tartar
¹/₄ teaspoon salt
1 tablespoon finely grated orange zest
1 tablespoon finely grated lemon zest
2 tablespoons orange juice
1 tablespoon lemon juice
1 teaspoon vanilla
1¹/₄ cups sugar
1 cup cake flour, sifted

1. Preheat the oven to 350°F.

2. In a large mixing bowl, with an electric mixer, beat the egg whites, cream of tartar, and salt, until soft peaks form. Add the orange zest, lemon zest, orange juice, lemon juice, and vanilla. Gradually add the sugar, beating until the whites become stiff and glossy.

3. With a spatula, gently fold the flour into the beaten whites.

4. Spoon the batter into an ungreased 10-inch tube pan. Bake for 40 minutes, or until a cake tester inserted in the center comes out clean. Invert the pan onto a rack to cool completely. When cooled, run a knife around the pan to loosen the cake. Carefully remove the cake to a platter.

12 portions

FAMILY DINNER

Baked Bluefish with
Walnut Gremolata
· · ·
Corn Sauté
· · ·
Herb-Baked Red-
Skinned Potatoes◆
· · ·
Citrus Angel
Food Cake

DOWN EAST BLUEBERRY CAKE

This blueberry cake, with its fluffy texture, is laden with fruit and generously dusted with a cinnamon-sugar topping. Try it for breakfast or brunch, for dessert, or as a snack, for a taste of Down East.

1/2 cup butter
1 cup sugar
2 eggs
1 1/2 teaspoons vanilla
2 cups plus 2 tablespoons all-purpose flour
2 teaspoons baking powder
1/2 teaspoon salt
1/2 cup buttermilk
2 cups blueberries

Topping:
1/4 cup sugar
1 teaspoon cinnamon

1. Preheat the oven to 350°F. Grease a 9-inch square baking pan.

2. In a large bowl, cream the butter and sugar until fluffy. Add the eggs and vanilla and mix well.

3. Wash the blueberries, then dust the wet berries with 2 tablespoons flour.

4. Sift together the 2 cups flour, baking powder, and salt. Add the dry ingredients alternately with the buttermilk to the batter.

5. Gently fold the fruit into the batter. Turn the batter into the prepared pan.

6. Mix the topping ingredients until evenly combined. Sprinkle over the top of the cake.

7. Bake for 45 to 50 minutes until a toothpick inserted in the center comes out clean. Remove to a rack to cool completely.

9 portions

WILD BERRY POUND CAKE

Moist, dense, and lavishly studded with big blues and delicate raspberries, this cake is reminiscent of home-made goodness.

1 cup sour cream
1¹/₂ teaspoons baking soda
1 cup butter, melted
2¹/₂ cups sugar
6 eggs
1 tablespoon vanilla
3 cups plus 1 tablespoon all-purpose flour
1 cup blueberries
³/₄ cup raspberries
confectioners' sugar

SUMMER MENU

Grilled Squid Salad
· · ·
Pasta with
Garlic and Oil
· · ·
Marinated Olives◆
· · ·
Wild Berry
Pound Cake

1. Combine the sour cream and baking soda and let stand at room temperature for 30 minutes.

2. Preheat the oven to 325°F. Grease a 10-inch bundt pan.

3. In the bowl of an electric mixer, cream the butter and sugar until light and fluffy. Add the eggs and vanilla and beat until the mixture is thick and pale yellow.

4. Add 3 cups flour alternately with the sour cream to the batter.

5. Combine the berries and dust with 1 tablespoon flour. Gently fold them into the batter. Turn the batter into the prepared pan.

6. Bake for 1 hour and 15 minutes. Remove to a rack to cool for 30 minutes; then remove the cake from the pan to the rack to cool completely. Dust with confectioners' sugar and serve.

12 or more servings

GINGERBREAD

Old-fashioned goodness is packed into this rich, dark, spice cake that's topped with a candied ginger whipped cream.

1/2 cup butter
1/2 cup packed dark brown sugar
2 eggs
1/4 cup molasses
1 1/2 cups all-purpose flour
1 teaspoon baking soda
1/2 teaspoon salt
1 teaspoon cinnamon
1 1/2 teaspoons ground ginger
1/4 teaspoon ground cloves
2/3 cup buttermilk
Ginger Whipped Cream (recipe follows)

1. Preheat the oven to 325°F. Grease an 8-inch square pan.

2. In a large bowl, cream the butter and brown sugar. Add the eggs and molasses and mix well.

3. Sift together the flour, baking soda, salt, cinnamon, ginger, and cloves. Add the dry ingredients alternately with the buttermilk to the batter.

4. Pour the batter into the prepared pan and bake for 40 minutes, or until a toothpick inserted in the center comes out clean. Let the cake cool completely. Cut into squares and serve with a dollop of Ginger Whipped Cream.

9 portions

Ginger Whipped Cream:
1 cup heavy cream
1/4 cup confectioners' sugar
2 to 3 tablespoons chopped crystallized candied ginger

With an electric mixer, whip the cream and sugar until stiff. Gently fold in the candied ginger. Refrigerate until needed.

COCONUT CAKE

Macaroon flavors of almond and coconut dominate this moist, dense cake that's finished with a sliced almond-butter cream frosting.

TROPICAL TASTES

Jamaican-Spiced
Pork Loin
· · ·
Rice with
Apple-Pear Chutney
· · ·
Pickled Red Onions
· · ·
Coconut Cake

1/2 cup butter
1 cup sugar
4 eggs
1 teaspoon almond extract
2 cups all-purpose flour
2 teaspoons baking powder
1/2 teaspoon salt
1 cup milk
1 1/4 cups sweetened, flaked coconut
Almond-Butter Cream (recipe follows)

1. Preheat the oven to 350°F. Grease a 9-inch tube pan.

2. In the bowl of an electric mixer, cream the butter and sugar. Add the eggs and almond extract and beat until the mixture is light and fluffy.

3. Sift together the flour, baking powder, and salt. Add the sifted dry ingredients alternately with the milk to the batter. Mix in the coconut.

4. Turn the batter into the prepared pan. Bake for 40 to 45 minutes, until a toothpick inserted in the center comes out clean. Let the cake cool in the pan for 20 minutes; then remove the cake to a rack to cool completely. Frost the top and sides of the cake with the Almond-Butter Cream. Refrigerate for 1 to 2 hours until the frosting is set; return to room temperature to serve.

8 to 10 portions

Almond-Butter Cream:
1/3 cup butter
1 cup confectioners' sugar
1 tablespoon milk
1/4 cup sliced almonds, toasted

With an electric mixer, cream the butter, sugar, and milk until smooth. Stir in the nuts.

Enough to frost one cake

ORANGE SUNSHINE CAKE

CASUAL DINNER

Crab-Corn Chowder
· · ·
Grilled Chicken with
Plum Coulis
· · ·
Zucchini Mandoline◆
· · ·
Couscous with
Dried Fruits
· · ·
Orange Sunshine Cake

Light and spongy with a refreshing citrus accent, this cake is delicate and satisfying without being cloyingly sweet.

3 eggs, separated
1¹/₂ cups sugar
6 tablespoons butter
1 tablespoon grated orange peel
1¹/₂ cups all-purpose flour
2 teaspoons baking powder
¹/₄ teaspoon salt
¹/₂ cup milk
¹/₄ cup orange juice
confectioners' sugar

1. Preheat the oven to 325°F. Grease a 10-inch tube pan.

2. With an electric mixer, beat the egg whites to soft peaks. Gradually add ¹/₂ cup sugar and continue beating until the whites are stiff and glossy, about 3 to 4 minutes. Set aside.

3. In a separate bowl, with the electric mixer, cream the butter and 1 cup sugar until fluffy. Add the egg yolks and orange peel and beat until thick.

4. Sift together the flour, baking powder, and salt. In a separate bowl, combine the milk and orange juice. Add the dry ingredients alternately with the milk mixture to the batter.

5. With a spatula, gently fold the beaten egg whites into the batter, mixing until there are no traces of white. Turn the batter into the prepared pan.

6. Bake in the lower third of the oven for 45 to 50 minutes or until a toothpick inserted in the cake come out clean. Remove to a rack to cool for 1 hour. Run a knife around the edge of the pan. Invert the pan, removing the cake to a plate. Using another plate, turn the cake right side up. Dust with confectioners' sugar and serve.

10 to 12 portions

LEMON CAKE ROLL

Feathery light, lusciously lemon, and very delicate describe this elegant cake roll.

6 eggs, separated
1 cup sugar
1 tablespoon lemon juice
1 tablespoon finely grated lemon zest
³/₄ cup cake flour
1 teaspoon baking powder
¹/₂ teaspoon salt
Vanilla Cream (recipe follows)
confectioners' sugar

1. Preheat the oven to 350°F. Grease a 10 x 15-inch jelly-roll pan. Line the pan with waxed paper and grease the paper.

2. In the bowl of an electric mixer, beat the egg yolks and sugar together until the mixture is thick and lemon colored. Add the lemon juice and lemon zest.

3. Sift together the flour, baking powder, and salt. Add the dry ingredients to the batter.

4. In a separate bowl, beat the egg whites until stiff. Gently fold them into the batter.

5. Pour the batter into the prepared pan. Bake for 20 minutes. Remove from the oven and turn the cake over onto a towel that's been dusted with confectioners' sugar. Lift off the pan and let the cake cool for 10 minutes. Peel off the wax paper from the cake. Carefully roll the cake with the towel, jelly roll fashion, and let the cake remain in this position on a rack for 20 to 30 minutes while it cools completely.

6. When the cake is cooled, unroll to fill. (Note: If the cake is even slightly warm, the whipped cream filling will weep.) Spoon the filling onto the inside of the cake, smoothing it to within 1 inch of all the edges.

7. Roll the cake up to form a log. Place it seam side down on a platter. Dust with confectioners' sugar and chill until serving time.

10 to 12 portions

**DESSERT PARTY
FOR 20**

Cranberry-Glazed Brie
· · ·
Candied Orange Peel
· · ·
Spiced Walnuts◆
· · ·
Chocolate-Almond
Pound Cake◆
· · ·
Lemon Cake Roll
· · ·
Tiramisu Cake
· · ·
Fruits in Midori◆
· · ·
Truffle Brownies
· · ·
Oatmeal Foggies

Vanilla Cream:
¹/₂ pint heavy cream
¹/₄ cup sugar
1 teaspoon vanilla

With an electric mixer, whip the cream, sugar, and vanilla until stiff peaks form. Refrigerate until needed.

CHOCOLATE CHIP-RICOTTA CHEESECAKE

This is a lighter version of the classic cheesecake. It boasts a cinnamon-scented, chocolate graham crust embodying a ricotta cheese filling that's dotted with chocolate chips and laced with Grand Marnier. The chocolate and orange have a wonderful affinity, adding an extra flavor dimension to the dessert.

Crust:
1¼ cups graham cracker crumbs
½ teaspoon cinnamon
1 tablespoon sugar
1 tablespoon unsweetened cocoa
⅓ cup butter, melted

1. Combine all of the crust ingredients and mix until evenly blended.

2. Pat the crumb mixture onto the bottom and 1½ inches up the sides of a 9-inch springform pan. Chill in the refrigerator while preparing the filling.

Ricotta Filling:
2 pounds ricotta cheese
4 large eggs
1 cup confectioners' sugar
¼ cup Grand Marnier
1 cup semi-sweet chocolate chips
cinnamon-sugar mixture for garnish

1. Preheat the oven to 350°F.

2. With an electric mixer, beat the ricotta and eggs until smooth. Add the confectioners' sugar, Grand Marnier, and chocolate chips and mix well.

3. Pour the batter into the crumb crust. Sprinkle with cinnamon-sugar.

4. Bake for 1 hour. Remove to a rack to cool completely. Chill for 2 to 3 hours, or as much as overnight before serving.

10 to 12 portions

ITALIAN FEST

Tomatoes and
Pine Nuts
. . .
Chicken Piccata
. . .
Spinach Romano
. . .
Pasta with
Black Olive Pesto
. . .
Chocolate Chip-
Ricotta Cheesecake

MAPLE-PECAN POUND CAKE

This light textured, buttermilk pound cake is encrusted with a maple-praline topping—a real delight for pecan fanciers! Many people are under the false impression that buttermilk is rich with butter and is fattening, as its name suggests. However, this couldn't be further from the truth. Buttermilk is actually made from low-fat or skim milk, making it a wonderfully, healthful food. It's an excellent ingredient in baking, as it yields a lighter texture and more cakelike crumb.

Praline Topping:
$^3/_4$ cup pure maple syrup
$^1/_4$ cup butter
$^1/_4$ cup packed light brown sugar
$1^1/_2$ cups chopped pecans

1 cup butter
$^3/_4$ cup granulated sugar
4 eggs
1 tablespoon vanilla
$2^1/_2$ cups all-purpose flour
1 teaspoon baking soda
$^1/_4$ teaspoon salt
1 cup buttermilk

1. Preheat the oven to 350°F. Generously grease a 10-inch bundt pan.

2. Prepare the topping. In a small saucepan, heat the maple syrup, $^1/_4$ cup butter, and brown sugar over low, stirring until the butter melts. Bring to a boil, then remove from the heat, and let cool for 10 minutes. Pour into the prepared pan and sprinkle with the pecans.

3. With an electric mixer, cream the butter and sugar until fluffy. Add the eggs and vanilla and mix well.

4. Sift together the flour, baking soda, and salt. Add the dry ingredients alternately with the buttermilk to the batter. Spoon the batter over the pecan mixture, covering completely.

5. Bake for 45 minutes or until a toothpick inserted in the center comes out clean. Immediately invert the cake onto a rack set over a sheet of waxed paper. Working quickly with a knife, scrape up any loose topping from the waxed paper, and spread over the top of the cake. Let cool completely.

12 portions

WORLD'S BEST SOUR CREAM COFFEECAKE

The classic coffeecake is further embellished with orange peel, chocolate chips, and walnuts. It's great for Sunday morning brunch with steaming mugs of coffee.

1 cup sour cream
1 teaspoon baking soda
1 cup butter
1½ cups sugar
3 eggs
1 tablespoon vanilla
1 tablespoon dried grated orange peel
2 cups all-purpose flour
2 teaspoons baking powder
¼ teaspoon salt
⅔ cup semi-sweet chocolate chips
⅔ cup coarsely chopped walnuts, toasted
cinnamon-sugar for garnish

1. Combine the sour cream and baking soda and let sit at room temperature for 30 minutes.

2. Preheat the oven to 350°F. Grease a 9-inch tube pan.

3. In a large bowl, cream the butter and sugar until fluffy. Add the eggs, vanilla, and orange peel and beat well.

4. Sift together the flour, baking powder, and salt. Add the dry ingredients alternately with the sour cream to the batter.

5. Mix in the chocolate chips and nuts. Spoon into the prepared pan. Sprinkle the top generously with cinnamon-sugar.

6. Bake for 50 minutes or until a toothpick inserted in the center comes out clean. Remove to a rack and serve warm, or let cool and serve at room temperature.

12 or more servings

BRUNCH

Iced Strawberry Soup
· · ·
Lobster and
Tortellini Salad
· · ·
Mixed Green Salad✦
· · ·
French and
Sourdough Breads
· · ·
World's Best Sour
Cream Coffeecake

TIRAMISU CAKE

This divine dessert is a cross between a white cake and a cheesecake, expanded with the flavors of the classic tiramisu. The rum-infused cake is rippled with a coffee-flavored mascarpone cheese that's utterly delicious.

*½ cup butter
1 cup sugar
2 eggs
¼ cup light rum
2 cups all-purpose flour
2 teaspoons baking powder
½ teaspoon salt
½ cup milk
Coffee Mascarpone (recipe follows)
1½ teaspoons instant coffee powder, crushed for garnish*

1. Preheat the oven to 350°F. Grease a 9-inch springform pan.

2. In the bowl of an electric mixer, cream the butter and sugar. Add the eggs and rum and beat well.

3. Sift together the flour, baking powder, and salt. Add the dry ingredients alternately with the milk to the batter. Turn the batter into the prepared pan.

4. Spoon the coffee mascarpone batter onto the cake; swirl with a knife to achieve a rippling of the batters.

5. Bake for 35 to 40 minutes, or until a toothpick inserted in the center comes out clean. Remove from the oven to a rack to cool completely. When cool, sprinkle the top with the crushed coffee powder and serve.

8 to 10 portions

*Coffee Mascarpone:
8 ounces mascarpone cheese
1 egg
2 tablespoons sugar
1 tablespoon instant coffee powder*

In the bowl of an electric mixer, beat all of the ingredients until smooth.

ASIAN PEAR TART

Asian pears are heavenly! They're a cross between a pear and an apple—shaped like an apple with a bosc pear skin, crunchy texture of an apple, and the buttery, juicy taste of a pear. This tart is truly French in nature, with its flaky pastry crust, sliced pear filling, and apricot glaze. It's best when made and served on the same day.

Pastry Crust:
1/2 cup butter, at room temperature
1 cup all-purpose flour
1/4 cup confectioners' sugar
1/2 teaspoon almond extract

1. Preheat the oven to 350°F.

2. Mix all of the crust ingredients until the dough comes together and forms a ball. Pat the dough into a 9-inch deep-dish pie pan.

3. Bake for 20 minutes until golden. Remove to a rack to cool completely before filling.

Fruit Filling:
3 Asian pears, peeled, cored, and sliced into 1/4-inch thick pieces
1/2 cup apricot preserves

1. Arrange the sliced fruit in concentric circles in the baked pie crust.

2. Melt the apricot preserves in a small saucepan. Brush the preserves over the fruit.

3. Bake for 45 minutes. Serve hot, warm, or at room temperature.

6 to 8 portions

DEEP-DISH BLUEBERRY-NECTARINE PIE

This open-faced pie captures the best of summer's bounty—plump, juicy berries and succulent nectarines—for a blast of fruity flavor. For real decadence, serve the pie with scoops of vanilla ice cream or frozen yogurt. You may substitute a pint of blueberries for the nectarines to make an all berry pie.

Pastry Crust:
1¼ cups all-purpose flour
¼ cup sugar
1 teaspoon vanilla
½ cup butter, cut into eighths

1. Put all of the ingredients in the bowl of a food processor.
2. Pulse until the texture of coarse meal. Remove the dough to a 9-inch deep-dish pie pan and pat into place.

Fruit Filling:
1 pint blueberries
3 large nectarines, pitted and cut into ½-inch chunks
1 teaspoon vanilla
½ cup sugar
3 tablespoons all-purpose flour
2 tablespoons cornstarch

1. Preheat the oven to 350°F.
2. In a large bowl, combine the berries, nectarines, and vanilla.
3. In a separate small bowl, combine the sugar, flour, and cornstarch. Add the dry ingredients to the fruit and stir until evenly mixed.
4. Turn the fruit filling into the pastry crust. Bake for 45 minutes. Serve warm or cool to room temperature.

6 to 8 portions

FRUIT TART

A sweet pastry crust houses a vanilla-mascarpone cream that's adorned with an array of fresh fruits. Picture pretty, this dessert is sure to garner praise. Use firm, ripe fruit to achieve the best results.

Crust:
1/2 cup butter
1/4 cup sugar
1 cup all-purpose flour
1 teaspoon vanilla

1. Preheat the oven to 425°F.

2. Cream the butter and sugar. Add the flour and vanilla and stir until the dough comes together. Using the heel of your hand, press the dough into a 9-inch tart pan. Prick the dough with a fork.

3. Bake for 10 to 12 minutes until golden. Cool completely before filling. (This may be prepared 1 day ahead.)

Filling:
8 ounces mascarpone cheese
1/3 cup confectioners' sugar
1 teaspoon vanilla

1. Cream the filling ingredients until smooth.

2. Spread the filling on the cooled shell. Refrigerate for 1 hour until firm.

Fruit Topping:
3 kiwis, peeled and thinly sliced
2 to 3 nectarines, pitted and thinly sliced into wedges
1 cup strawberries or 1/2 cup raspberries
3 tablespoons red currant jelly

1. Mound the berries in the center of the tart. Arrange the nectarine slices in a ring around the berries. Place the kiwi slices at the outside edge.

2. In a small saucepan over low heat, stir the currant jelly until melted. Brush the glaze over the fruit topping. Refrigerate until serving time.

6 to 8 portions

CASUAL SUPPER

Orange-Beet Soup◆
· · ·
Monkfish with
Plum Glaze
· · ·
Basic Couscous
· · ·
Dilled Carrots and
Zucchini Rounds
· · ·
Fruit Tart

CHOCOLATE-STRAWBERRY TART

This tart is a vision to behold, pairing two great American favorites, semi-sweet chocolate and succulent strawberries. A thick layer of almond-encrusted chocolate is spread in a flaky, sweet pastry shell. Ripe, plump berries are set in the warm chocolate and glazed with strawberry preserves.

Pastry Crust:
1/2 cup butter
1/4 cup confectioners' sugar
1 cup all-purpose flour

1. Preheat the oven to 400°F. Grease a 9-inch deep-dish pie pan.

2. Put all of the ingredients in the bowl of a food processor. Pulse until the dough comes together and forms a ball. Remove the dough to the pie pan and press it into place. Prick the bottom with a fork.

3. Bake for 10 to 12 minutes until lightly golden. Let cool before filling. (This may be made two weeks in advance and frozen; defrost before proceeding.)

Filling:
1 cup semi-sweet chocolate chips
2 tablespoons butter
2 tablespoons Creme de Cacao
1/2 cup sliced almonds, chopped
1 1/2 pints ripe strawberries, hulled
1/2 cup strawberry preserves

1. In a small saucepan, heat the chocolate and butter over low until the chocolate melts. It will form a thick paste. Remove from the heat and quickly stir in the Creme de Cacao and sliced almonds, whisking until smooth.

2. Spread the chocolate mixture on the pastry base.

3. While the chocolate is still warm, set the berries, point end up, in concentric circles in the chocolate. Refrigerate until set.

4. Melt the strawberry preserves. Paint the berries with the glaze and chill until set. Remove from the refrigerator 30 minutes before serving.

6 to 8 portions

PEANUT BUTTER-MASCARPONE PIE

Peanut butter lovers take heed! The light and delicate peanut butter and mascarpone filling is enriched with whipped cream and encased in a toasted pecan crumb crust. It's guaranteed to knock off your socks!

Pecan Crust:
1 cup finely chopped pecans
1/2 cup graham cracker crumbs
1/3 cup sugar
4 tablespoons butter, at room temperature
1/2 teaspoon cinnamon

1. Preheat the oven to 350°F. Grease a 9-inch deep-dish pie pan.

2. In a bowl, combine the crust ingredients, stirring until evenly mixed. Pat into the prepared pie pan.

3. Bake for 10 minutes. Let cool completely before filling.

Peanut Butter-Mascarpone Filling:
1 cup creamy peanut butter
1 cup confectioners' sugar
8 ounces mascarpone cheese
1 1/2 teaspoons vanilla
1 cup heavy cream, whipped
1/4 cup coarsely chopped, toasted pecans

1. With an electric mixer, beat the peanut butter, confectioners' sugar, mascarpone cheese, and vanilla until fluffy. Fold in the whipped cream.

2. Turn the filling into the cooled crust. Sprinkle with the chopped pecans. Refrigerate until set, at least 2 hours or as much as overnight. Store any unused pie in the refrigerator.

8 to 10 portions

PECAN PIE

Pecan pie is an old favorite from the deep South. This "new wave" version struts a rum-infused custard rich with brown sugar and pecan meats. Although this pie needs no further embellishment, you may choose to serve it with dollops of whipped cream.

THANKSGIVING DINNER

Cream of
Onion Soup
. . .
Spinach and Smoked
Oysters with
Cranberry Vinaigrette
. . .
Pumpkin Bread◆
. . .
Roast Turkey◆
. . .
Apple, Pear, and
Sausage Stuffing◆
. . .
Cranberry-Orange
Chutney
. . .
Turnips Anna
. . .
Pecan Pie

Pie Crust:
2 cups sifted all-purpose flour
2 tablespoons granulated sugar
1/2 teaspoon salt
1/4 teaspoon baking powder
1/2 cup butter

1. Sift together the flour, sugar, salt, and baking powder into a bowl. With a fork or pastry blender, work the butter into the dry ingredients until the texture of cornmeal.

2. Line a 9-inch deep-dish pie pan with the dough, patting it firmly into place.

Pecan Filling:
2 cups coarsely chopped pecans
4 tablespoons butter, melted and cooled
1/4 cup light cream
3 eggs, beaten
3/4 cup firmly packed dark brown sugar
1/2 cup dark corn syrup
2 tablespoons dark rum

1. Preheat the oven to 350°F.

2. Place the pecans in the pie crust.

3. In a bowl, mix together the butter, cream, eggs, brown sugar, corn syrup, and rum. Pour the custard over the pecans.

4. Bake for 45 minutes until set.

6 to 8 portions

INDEX